CONTEMPORARY SOCIAL RESEARCH SERIES
General Editor: MARTIN BULMER

19

*Methods of Criminological
Research*

CONTEMPORARY SOCIAL RESEARCH SERIES

Methods of Criminological Research

Victor Jupp

London
UNWIN HYMAN
Boston   Sydney   Wellington

Published by the Academic Division of
Unwin Hyman Ltd
15/17 Broadwick Street, London W1V 1FP, UK

Unwin Hyman Inc.,
8 Winchester Place, Winchester, Mass. 01890, USA

Allen & Unwin (Australia) Ltd,
8 Napier Street, North Sydney, NSW 2060, Australia

Allen & Unwin (New Zealand) Ltd in association with the
Port Nicholson Press Ltd, Compusales Building, 75 Ghuznee Street,
Wellington 1, New Zealand

First published in 1989

British Library Cataloguing in Publication Data

Jupp, Victor
    Methods of criminological research.
    (Contemporary social research series).
1. Criminology. Research. Comparative methods
I. Title   II. Series
364′.072

ISBN 0-04-445065-6
       0-04-445066-4 Pbk

Library of Congress Cataloging-in-Publication Data

Jupp, Victor
    Methods of criminological research.
Bibliography: p.
Includes index.
1. Crime and criminals—Research. 2. Criminal justice, Administration of—
Research. I. Title.
HV6024.5.J87 1989   364′.072   88-36279
ISBN 0-04-445065-6 (alk. paper)
ISBN 0-04-445066-4 (pbk.: alk. paper)

Typeset in 10 on 11 point Times by Fotographics (Bedford) Ltd
and printed in Great Britain by Billing and Son Ltd, London and Worcester

For Adam and Mark

Contents

Preface

A number of ideas influenced this book, particularly ideas which have developed during several years of teaching methods of social research to social science undergraduates and postgraduates. It is important that students learn about the technicalities of research design, data collection and analysis. However, such technicalities are too often treated as if they are hermetically sealed from other crucial aspects of social science. In particular, 'methods' have become separated from the problems they address, from the theoretical frameworks which open up particular aspects of these problems for investigation, and for the institutional and political contexts within which social research is conducted. Such separations invariably ensure that a consideration of matters of method become meaningless to students. In my experience, part of the problem lies with those who teach social science theories. In the main they have steadfastly refused to consider the relationships between theory and method or to recognize that social science has progressed not by theory alone but via the fruitful and innovative connections which have been made between theorizing and empirical inquiry. Equally, those of us who have taught students about matters of method have often failed to make the connections ourselves with the result that courses in social science research methods have been greeted with glazed looks on the faces of our students and with disbelief that such matters of methods are presented as if they are divorced from other courses of study and, perhaps more importantly, divorced from the realities of everyday life.

This book represents an attempt to look at matters of method in the context of specific social science problems – those relating to the study of crime and of the criminal justice system – and by taking account of, first, connections which are made with theories of particular kinds and, secondly, the influences and constraints of institutional and political contexts. In emphasizing the constellations of politics, problems, theories and methods it has been necessary to reduce the amount of space which could be devoted to the specifics of particular criminological theories, particular disciplinary contributions and particular methods of empirical inquiry. This has been done in the safe knowledge that there are specialized textbooks available which deal with these matters. Crime and criminology are appropriate contexts within which to examine methods of social inquiry because of the plurality of theoretical contributions which abound and because of the variety of institutional contexts within which research is conducted. What is more, issues of crime and of how it should be controlled are not only matters of profound political significance but also matters which are addressed by the state's own research output.

The basic themes presented here were formulated in skeletal form in the Open University's course *Crime, Justice and Society* (D310), particularly Block 5, *Research Studies in Criminology*, and I am grateful to the university for permission to reproduce some of that earlier material in this book. I am also grateful to the core members of the course team who, at one time or another provided comments on drafts of the course material which influenced their subsequent reformulation and elaboration here. At that time they were Rudi Dallos, Mike Fitzgerald, Stuart Hall, Frank Heathcote, Greg McLennan, John Muncie, and Roger Sapsford. In addition, Ian Taylor, course assessor, offered numerous detailed and valued comments. Particular thanks are due to Roger Sapsford for his subsequent comments on Chapters 1 and 2 of this book and also to David Graham for his comments on Chapter 3. Martin Bulmer gave encouragement throughout the project. Philip Judd provided valuable assistance in locating sources and Jean Findlay wrestled with the figures and tables while they were in production. Hilary Jupp prepared the manuscript but, most important of all, constantly reminded me that I was writing primarily for my students and not for my peers. Notwithstanding these contributions, and as is conventionally the case, the responsibility for the contents of the book lies with myself.

Victor Jupp

1

Theories, Methods, Politics and Problems

Introduction

The influence of positivism

Modern criminology has its roots in the mid-nineteenth century and particularly in the challenge to classical thinking represented by positivism. Early classical thinking emphasized free will and therefore portrayed crime as the outcome of voluntary actions based upon rational calculation. It was suggested that individuals committed crimes when they saw the benefits of law-breaking as far outweighing the costs or potential costs. Positivism succeeded in portraying an altogether different conception of crime and also in providing a different basis for its explanation. For example, crime was seen as something into which the individual was propelled by factors largely beyond his or her control and not as an activity into which he or she could freely enter after careful and rational balancing of costs and benefits. Thus positivism involved forms of explanation based upon determinism and the search for causes. Crime and criminality were dependent variables to be explained, and the search was for explanatory or independent variables upon which crime and criminality could be said to be dependent.

There is a further, but related, way in which classicism and positivism differed. With its emphasis upon rational calculation, classical thinking placed the focus upon the means by which the operation of the criminal justice system could increase the costs of criminal activity in relation to the benefits to the criminal. The main thrust of positivism was different. By focusing on deterministic explanations of crime and criminality, early positivists were less concerned with systems of justice and more with locating the 'propelling forces' to crime, particularly those assumed to lie within the individual. This is typified in the writings of the Italian biological positivists such as Cesare Lombroso. Lombroso's concern was to establish, in a systematic and scientific manner, those characteristics of individuals – particularly innate characteristics – which might be deemed to be the causes of criminality. Criminals, he argued, are born like that. His conclusions were reached by the application of theoretical ideas about predispositions towards crime in certain types of individuals, and also by the use of particular methods of research to collect findings which sought to relate criminal behaviour to such predispositions. By comparing the skulls of criminal and non-criminal men he claimed to have evidence with which to assert that criminals shared certain facial and other physical features, including receding forehead, large jaw, handle-shaped ears, dark skin and thick curly hair (Lombroso, 1911). Such physical features and associated criminal propensities were not only innate but represented features which non-criminal groups had outgrown. The criminal was seen as part of a sub-species of humanity.

From today's standpoint such conclusions seem bizarre and are usually treated with a certain degree of amusement. Nevertheless, forms of positivist methodology have been influential, albeit with different foci and different levels of analysis, and since these early beginnings of positivism there have been successive surges in the changing, and widening of, criminological explanations. For example what may be termed psychological positivism also has a concern with individual propensities to crime but has focused on aspects of personality and how they interact with learning (for example, Eysenck, 1964) whereas other work has placed greater emphasis upon socialization and upbringing (for example, West, 1967, 1969, 1982; West and Farrington, 1973, 1977). The contribution of sociological positivism has been to attempt to shift the focus from a concern with explanations in terms of individual attributes or experiences to an interest in social structure and, for instance, with the way in which crime can be explained in terms of social disorganization and anomie (see, for example, Merton, 1964).

Psychological and sociological strands of positivism have each had a major influence on social science in general and the study of crime in particular. They have played an important role in the development of criminology and still retain prominence in what has been termed conventional or mainstream criminology (Cohen, 1981). Historically, positivist forms of analysis and of explanation have sought to plant 'science', scientific thinking and systematic empirical investigation firmly at the heart of the study of crime. The emphasis upon empirical investigation has meant that positivism has been a major influence on the development of methods of social research, particularly those methods which collect and use 'hard', quantitative data. (The term positivism is used here in a very general sense and without reference to the different nuances which can be attached to its meaning. For a detailed discussion of these see Halfpenny, 1982; Bryman, 1988.)

The positivist position has also had secondary influences in terms of the theoretical critiques which have been mounted against it, ritiques which have themselves subsequently influenced criminological research: for example, in the late 1960s and early 1970s a number of specific theoretical approaches to the study of crime collected together under the general banner heading of 'new deviancy'. The influence of these various expressions of new deviancy has been to minimize the importance of deterministic causal explanations of crime in favour of an interest in the role of social meanings and interactions in the social construction of crime. A radical and critical approach to the study of crime subsequently developed out of the new deviancy school. This radical or critical strand within criminology shares with new deviancy the dislike of causal thinking but at the same time contributes a greater concern with social control, the role of the state in crime control and the historical development of social structure. In doing this it has also contributed an interest in the role of empirical criminological investigation in such crime control. What is more, feminist theory and research – which include elements of a radical approach – have sought to rewrite the criminological agenda to give greater emphasis to the reconceptualization of the nature of crime in terms of the structural position of women in society and also to the experiences of women as victims of crime. The various theoretical critiques of positivist explanations have been mirrored by debates about the appropriateness of particular methods of social research (especially those which collect 'hard' quantitative data); by the development of methods geared to the subjective and humanistic aspects of crime; by critical analyses of the political uses of criminological research; and by formulation of methods appropriate to feminist research. (In relation to the latter see, for example, Roberts, 1981; Bowles and Duelli Klein, 1983.)

In short, the development of criminology has not been characterized by theoretical or methodological unity. There have been variations in the degree of emphasis which has been given to positivist explanations in causal terms and also in the degree of emphasis which has been given to different units and level of analysis. The latter has seen shifts from a concern with individual crime and criminality to an interest in social structures within which crime is committed and including the historical development of such structures. However, whatever the corners that have been turned, criminology has developed by interactions between theory and the data generated by methods of investigation; by a self-reflective consideration of the respective contributions of theory and method; and via issues, debates and disputes about the way in which they should relate to each other. What is more, in more recent decades there has been critical discussion of the role of criminological investigation and its potential contribution as a mechanism of social control.

The value of considering 'methods'

Here we are not explicitly concerned with a discussion of what is, or should be, the appropriate territory of the criminological enterprise nor are we explicitly concerned with the range of broad theoretical approaches and specific theoretical positions which populate this territory. Rather, the aim is to focus on some of the main methods by which criminological research is carried out. However, in this endeavour it would be folly to ignore the central problems of criminology and the theories which are brought to bear on them. On the one hand, the methods that come to be used have implications for the way in which problems are conceptualized and for the type of explanations employed. On the other, the problems and theories of criminology have implications for the kinds of methods that are used. Some methods of research are more useful and appropriate to the investigation of certain aspects of crime than others. For example, detailed insights into the way in which crime is experienced are unlikely to be captured by the short and highly structured format required for self-completion mail questionnaires. What is more different theoretical positions seem to have preference as to method because of the types of data which can be collected, the level or unit of analysis which is used and the degree of primacy which is to be given to the search for causes.

Bearing this in mind, what is the value of a consideration of method? How one addresses a question such as this depends upon how widely or narrowly method is interpreted. Matters of method can be interpreted rather narrowly as being about the types of data collected by criminological researchers, about the methods by which they collect them and about the ways in which such data are analysed. The technicalities of such matters often remain buried in the main text of criminological writings or are treated cursorily in a brief methodological appendix. Either way they are invariably viewed by all except those with a specialist interest, as matters to be passed over in the rush to get to the central assertions and conclusions. After all in his classic exposition on the sociological imagination C. Wright Mills enthusiastically and persuasively implored us to avoid the 'fetishism of method and technique' (Mills, 1970, p. 246). This edict however, was not intended to warn us against all method but to warn against an obsession with the matters of method to the exclusion of all others. Indeed, a consideration of social science research methods and the data they collect is important at a number of levels.

In the first place, at a technical level, it facilitates an appreciation of the ways in which empirical investigation is, and can be, carried out. But secondly, and more importantly, it provides a platform from which to generate clues as to the credence which can be placed upon criminological findings and the conclusions which can be erected upon them. For example, official statistics on crime are collected and processed by the Home Office and are published each year in *Criminal Statistics*. Such statistics provide one means by which researchers can seek to measure the extent of crime in society. What is more, they can also provide the basis for explanations of crime by relating crime levels to the features of social areas, such as types of housing tenure (see, for example, Baldwin and Bottoms, 1976) or to other trends in society such as changes in levels of unemployment (see, for example, Tarling, 1982). However, such statistics should not be taken for granted. An understanding of the nature of official statistics on crime and of the way in which they are collected and processed leads to questions about whether or not they can be treated as objective indicators of the level of society's criminality. Part of the reason for this is that many criminal acts are unknown to the police. What is more, even when known, many criminal acts are not officially recorded. Also, as Kitsuse and Cicourel (1963) and others have argued, crime statistics could be viewed more appropriately as indicators of those organizational processes at work in the criminal justice system which result in the recording of some criminal acts and the non-recording of others. In short, questioning the ways in which data are collected, processed and analysed provides a base for evaluating findings of criminological research. In asking such questions we are asking about the validity of particular research designs and the data they generate and use. We can call this *method validity*. An assessment of method validity is not an end in itself but a contribution to the overall evaluation of how well social research methods can, and do, capture the social world as it is, or as people think it is.

Methodological validity

Closely related to the above is a third and much more fundamental justification for inspection of the methods of criminological research, one that goes much further than asking whether a particular method of collecting or using data is the most appropriate to the task at hand. This involves a consideration of the theoretical and methodological assumptions implicit in the use of particular methods and designs. All such assumptions are inextricably bound up with issues about the way in which theory and method connect. Two issues have already been identified as being important in the development of criminology and these can be made more explicit here. One of these concerns questions about what should be the appropriate focus and *unit of analysis* in any explanation of crime – the individual, the social group or the social structure. Whatever the level or unit of analysis chosen there are implications for the type of data which should be collected, for how it can and should be collected, and for the extent to which we can validly jump from data collected at one level (say, from individuals) to the making of assertions about another level (say, collectivities of individuals).

A second issue concerns the degree of credence which should be placed upon explanations founded upon *determinism* and *causal thinking*, irrespective of the unit of analysis employed. This is related to the fundamental debate about the appropriateness of the positivist paradigm to the social sciences in general and to criminological research in particular. The positivist paradigm brings with it key assumptions about the nature of social reality and about the way in which it can be investigated. For example, it is assumed that social phenomena such as crime can be treated as objective facts which can be apprehended, equally objectively, by the researcher. What is more, this is linked to the (often taken for granted) assertion that 'crime-as-objective-fact' can be quantified by the application of the basic principles of measurement. One typical use of quantification has been in relation to questions about the extent of crime and its social and historical distribution. On the surface, such questions would seem capable of easy resolution by reference to officially recorded crime statistics but, as has already been pointed out, such official statistics record the number of crimes reported to the police but exclude crimes about which the police know nothing or about which the police wish to know nothing. Such statistics might even be better seen as the outcomes of policing practices rather than indices of the extent of crime (see, for example, Box, 1981; Bottomley and Pease, 1986). More fundamentally, the use of official statistics to measure the extent of crime is based upon official definitions of criminal acts and completely skirts the question of what, in the first place, should be treated as crime. For example, it can be argued that criminological research should extend itself beyond legal definitions of crime to encompass the violations of basic human rights implicit in racism and sexism. (For a discussion of differing conceptions of what is crime, including a human-rights viewpoint, see Bottomley 1979.) It is because of major question marks against the quantification of aspects of crime, and particularly the often unthinking and indiscriminate application of numbers and their subsequent manipulation, that many eschew quantitative strategies in favour of so-called 'qualitative' strategies and so-called 'qualitative' data. Both the inbuilt quantitative assumptions of positivism and the challenge which have been made to them have had important implications for the range of methods which has been used to conduct criminological research.

Quantification is often closely related to the goal of developing and testing theories of the social world with wide applicability and strong explanatory power. Typically, this goal is founded upon viewpoint which sees research as a means by which hypotheses and models of the social world can be tested. Hypotheses are formulated (say, asserting that there is a relation between levels of crime in communities and various indicators of deprivation in these communities), and data are collected, perhaps from official statistics, to see how well such hypotheses 'fit' the quantified empirical reality. For example, in Chapter 3 we refer to studies summarized by Tarling (1982) which seek to establish statistical relationships between levels of unemployment and levels of crime with which to make inferences about causal connections between these phenomena. The methodological significance of such attempts to provide statistically verified models of the social world lies not just in the range of data and methods which are used but also in the way in which theory and method are seen to relate to each other. Method is typically seen as a handmaiden of theory, that is, as something to assist in the verification of theory.

An alternative strategy is to treat theoretical generalizations as the product of empirical investigation, or at the very least as the outcome of a flexible and continuous interchange between theory and data. This is often, but not always, linked to a belief that 'qualitative' data and not quantitative data provide more valid representations of the social world. It is also typically associated with the assertion that social science theories should be grounded in the everyday theories of the people they are studying. Within such a strategy of inquiry the researcher starts by getting immersed in the social world of those whose actions and ideas he or she wants to understand and explain. It is on the basis of such first-hand experience and as a result of data collection and analysis that generalizations about actions, ideas and experiences can be formulated. This is characterized in what Glaser and Strauss (1967) refer to as the *discovery-based approach*. Basically, this approach eschews any notion of an obligatory and unilinear transition from problem through theory to method. Rather, it advocates moving backwards and forwards between three broad phases of inquiry within each of which there is a constant exchange between problem, theory and method. In Chapter 3 the contrasts between discovery-based, qualitative research and the more formal protocols of quantitative research are illustrated by reference to ethnographic studies of school and youth culture. For example, in his study of kids in Sunderland Corrigan (1979) immersed himself in first-hand collection of data by the use of observational methods and detailed informal interviews in the schoolground and on the streets. One of his central conclusions is that the actions of the kids are only understandable in terms of the kids' perceptions of differential and unequal power relations between themselves and teachers and police officers. 'Messing about' at school and 'doing nothing' on the streets are means by which the kids can seek to subvert the power of others. For Corrigan, this conclusion has validity because it emerged spontaneously and naturally from the data and because it was founded upon the perceptions of the subjects themselves rather than imposed from above in the form of some preordained and rigid hypothesis. This grounded and flexible form of analysis implies a more interactive relationship between theory and method than is found in the stringent strategies of hypothesis testing.

The distinctions between positivist and non-positivist research and also between quantitative and qualitative data are easily exaggerated. So too are the positivism–quantitative and non-positivism–qualitative connections (see, in particular, Bryman, 1988). Nevertheless, such distinctions and connections do provide ways of mapping the range of criminological research studies and of bringing to the surface the methodological assumptions implicit in such studies.

To sum up, modern criminology has been characterized by the development and application of theories in search of explanations of crime and criminality and also by the systematic use of empirical investigation in relation to such theories. This book is primarily about methods of criminological research. Considerations of method are important for a number of reasons. First, at a very technical and practical level they allow us to gain some understanding of the way in which criminological research is, and can be, carried out. Second, they provide a basis for an evaluation of method validity. This refers to an assessment of the strengths and drawbacks of particular techniques of data collection and analysis, with particular reference to the way in which they can uncover different aspects and dimensions of crime. Third, and more fundamentally, such considerations involve us in questions about what may be termed *methodological validity*, especially questions which encourage us to address the implicit methodological assumptions in specific methods of data collection and analysis and to consider the extent to which such assumptions are tenable. Some of these are concerned with what is and should be the appropriate unit and level of analysis. Others are closely bound up with positivist analyses in criminology and with critiques of such analyses. These latter include debates about the type of data which can and should be collected and particularly about whether the nature of social reality is such that it can be quantified; debates about the weight which should be given to explanations cast in causal terms; and debates about the way in which theory and method should connect in terms of the formal testing of hypotheses as opposed to the discovery and formulation of theoretical generalizations. Such issues illustrate one central theme of this book, namely that the data collected by social researchers (and the methods used to collect them) cannot, and should not, be examined in isolation from the criminological problems under investigation and, more importantly, from the central theoretical ideas which are brought to bear on these problems.

The criminological enterprise

A fundamental premise of what is to follow is that the criminological enterprise exhibits plurality, variety and sometimes eclecticism in a number of interrelated ways and that a consideration of methods of criminological research needs to be examined within the context of this plurality. We shall use the term criminological enterprise out of recognition of this plurality and also to portray a sense of 'activity', that is, activity in an arena of teaching, research and policy-making in relation to issues of crime and criminal justice. This is not the place to get involved in debates about what is, or is not, the domain of criminology, nor to engage in minor territorial disputes between criminology, sociology of deviance, sociology of law, socio-legal studies or criminal justice studies. The use of the term 'criminological enterprise' not only skirts these but, more importantly, gives greater emphasis to the diffuse range of problems tackled in a variety of institutional contexts by a wide range of theories and methods coming from a number of disciplinary bases as opposed to the notion of a single unified discipline called criminology.

Problems

First of all, the plurality can be witnessed in the range of problems which criminologists have addressed. We have already referred to analyses which give primary focus to the individual. Four broad strands can be mentioned. One of these is concerned with biological differences between individuals and with the way in which human behaviour, in this case criminal behaviour, is genetically determined. The work of Lombroso, mentioned earlier, is typical of this strand. However, the more recent sociobiological theories, based on the claims that human behaviour should be viewed as the outcome of a process of biological evolution and that certain forms of behaviour – such as criminal behaviour – exist because of their survival function, also have a biological base (see, for example, Wilson, 1975). A second strand has a psychological base and focuses on personality differences between individuals and the way in which these might be linked to criminal behaviour. For example, Eysenck (1960, 1964), claims to have identified a typology of personality types and also to have evidence for the assertion that certain types of personality are less amenable to conditioning and learning and therefore are more likely to result in criminal and other anti-social behaviour. A third strand is less concerned with innate characteristics and more with the primary socializing groups, particularly the family, and with the way in which early socialization contributes to subsequent criminal behaviour. Some of these approaches focus on child-rearing practices (Glueck and Glueck, 1950, 1962), others focus on learning and conditioning and also on the possibility of 'unlearning' criminal behaviour by techniques of behaviour modification (see, for example, Feldman, 1976), and still others focus on stages of moral development and the way in which these might be productive of behaviour, such as criminal behaviour (see, for example, Kohlberg, 1969, 1975). A fourth line of research pays little, if any, attention to individual characteristics or early learning experiences which might be thought to cause criminality or which, in a much gentler sense, are viewed as predisposing factors. Instead it emphasizes freedom of action and the ability of individuals to interpret and construct social reality. Such a viewpoint owes much to the work of George Kelly and to his personal-construct theory and gives little credence to explanations cast in causal and deterministic terms. (For a summary and elaboration of this general position see Dallos and Sapsford, 1981.) The above theories come from different disciplinary bases and differ from each other in significant ways. Nevertheless, what is of interest to all of them is the individual, and they all address one central problem within the criminological enterprise that is *why do individuals commit crime?*.

By way of contrast, one of the main contributions of the sociological tradition is to focus on the social preconditions of crime. The general theoretical thrust owes a great deal to the work of the French sociologist Emile Durkheim and particularly to his concerns with the bases of social solidarity, with forms of social disorganization and with the central concept of anomie (Durkheim, 1952, 1964a). Durkheim left a legacy which subsequently influenced three broad analytical strands; first, analyses of structural factors making certain kinds of criminal actions more likely in some social groupings; second, sociological explanations of the social, cultural and spatial distribution of crime in societies; and third, examinations of the way in which criminal values and actions are transmitted within cultural groups. For example, Robert Merton (1938, 1957, 1964) reinterpreted Durkheim's concept of anomie as referring not to a state of normlessness but to one resulting from strains in the social structure which pressurize individuals to pursue goals which, because of their social situation, cannot be achieved by legitimate means. Instead they turn to illegitimate means such as crime. Durkheim's work also had a great influence on the Chicago school of urban sociology which was concerned less with the structural sources of social disorganiza tion and more with its ecological distribution. The Chicagoans were keen to draw spatial maps of social disorganization. For example, Clifford Shaw and his associates used official statistics to delineate areas of the city of Chicago which were characterized by high crime rates. Such areas he termed 'delinquency areas' (Shaw *et al.*, 1929). The Chicago school itself had a profound effect on subsequent sociological analyses of crime pointing the way forward into studies of sub-cultures of crime (see, for example, Cohen, 1955; Cloward and Ohlin, 1961; Matza, 1961) and also into the way in which criminal values are transmitted within sub-cultures (see, for example, Sutherland and Cressey, 1947). What all of these strands share is a concern with the sociological dimensions to crime. What they have contributed to the criminological enterprise are questions about the *social structural causes of crime, the ecological distribution of crime and the sub-cultural expressions of crime*.

Such questions, and particularly those concerning the ecological distribution of crime, are closely intertwined with questions about the extent of crime and of crime of certain types. Indeed, many of the sociologists we have already mentioned were crucially involved in the use of official statistics to measure the extent of crime and other deviant acts. For example, Durkheim's classic work on suicide is grounded in such statistics (Durkheim, 1952), Merton's work on anomie and crime starts from the assumption that official statistics provide the best, although imperfect, indices of society's crime level (Merton, 1938, 1957), and the Chicagoans used statistics to delineate the natural areas of their city. Since that time there have been major theoretical and methodological disputes as to whether official statistics can legitimately be used to measure the 'objective facts' of crime (see, for example, Kitsuse and Cicourel, 1963). There has also been the development and refinement of particular tools of data collection, such as victim surveys, which aim to obtain some estimate of the disparity between officially recorded crime and the true extent of crime (see, for example, Hough and Mayhew, 1983). The contributions of early writers such as Durkheim and Merton, the subsequent debates about the use of official statistics and the development of victim surveys have placed the question, '*what is the extent of crime?*' at the centre of the criminological enterprise.

This enterprise, however, has stretched its horizons beyond a primary focus on crime, whether this be cast in psychological or sociological terms, to encompass and embrace an interest in the criminal justice system. This can be broken down into specific concerns with the institutions of the criminal justice system (for example, police, courts, prisons), their internal functioning and their relations with one another; with the personnel who work within such institutions (for example, police officers, judges, magistrates, prison officers), their policies and practices; and with the social process of justice, taking account of the policies and practices of personnel and the functioning of specific institutions and of the system of justice as a whole. Interest in aspects of the criminal justice system can come from widely different strands within criminology. We can look at two examples.

One of these relates to what has been termed 'administrative criminology' (Young, 1986). Young locates administrative criminology in the Home Office Research and Planning Unit where, he argues, it has displaced what Cohen (1981) called mainstream criminology as the dominant paradigm. Mainstream criminology was described as being predominantly positivist in orientation and concerned, therefore, with the causes of crime. Administrative criminology, on the other hand, represents something of a swing back to classical thinking, as described in the previous section. Within this, crime is seen as a voluntaristic activity and as the outcome of a rational balancing of costs and benefits by individuals. Its interest in the criminal justice system lies in its concern with influencing the potential costs of criminal activity by limiting the opportunities for committing crime, increasing the risks of detection and increasing the punishment tariffs. Young comments:

> Its empiricist approach often disguises the fact that it has abandoned the search for causal generalizations and instead adopted a neo-classicist problematic centring around the principles of effective control. Social democratic criminology with its search for the aetiology of crime within the realms of social justice has been replaced by an administrative criminology interested in technology and control. (Young, 1986, p. 12)

A major part of this control comes from the institutions of criminal justice, particularly the police, and a major thrust of the research initiatives of the Home Office Research and Planning Unit has been geared towards improving the efficient functioning of such institutions (see, for example, Clarke and Cornish, 1983).

A second example comes from a different theoretical line and sees the institutions of criminal justice, and particularly the practices of its personnel, as of fundamental importance to questions about the generation of crime at both the level of the individual and at the level of society. Essentially, this is one of the contributions of the new deviancy strand within the criminological enterprise. This strand forcefully argues that explanations of crime and of criminal actions should be cast in terms of the processes by which individuals are labelled as 'criminal' by personnel within the criminal justice system rather than based upon notions of causality (individual predispositions or social preconditions). Indeed, labelling theory, as developed and refined by Becker and others, was an important influence on the new deviancy school (see, for example, Becker, 1963, 1974). The issues raised by this approach involve questions about the ways in which law is enforced and guilt determined and also about the subsequent consequences for those who are, or are not, labelled as criminal.

Administrative criminology and new deviancy have similarities in their emphasis upon the voluntaristic bases of human action. Beyond that, however, there are fundamental differences. For example, the institutional base of administrative criminology is essentially the Home Office, whereas for new deviancy it is primarily academia. More fundamentally, the former is primarily interested in the effectiveness of the policies of the criminal justice system in the control of crime, whereas the latter focuses on the role of the practices of criminal justice personnel in the generation of crime. In their differing ways, however, they contribute questions about *the operation of the criminal justice system* to the criminological agenda.

The institutions of criminal justice and the personnel who populate them do not operate in a vacuum. They are a fundamental part of society, its structure and the way in which social order is maintained. Therefore, to separate crime and systems of criminal justice from the wider social structure and the interests and conflicts which are a part of it would involve missing crucial dimensions of the generation of crime and of the operation of the criminal justice system in relation to such crime. Essentially, this is the contribution of the radical tradition which gained impetus in the 1970s from the development of a 'new' and 'critical' criminology (Taylor, Walton and Young, 1973, 1975). There are many sub-themes within the radical tradition (for an elaboration of these see Carlen, 1980; Hall and Scraton, 1981; Downes and Rock, 1982). In general terms, however, this strand within the criminological enterprise argues for a reformulation of the central issues of criminology in terms of social structure and its historical development, with particular reference to economic and class relations. It seeks explanations of crime, not in causal terms, but in terms of the economic and class relations in society at any given point in history; it seeks to understand the functioning of the criminal justice system in terms of the role of the state in maintaining social order, and the relationship of the state to economic and class interests; and, perhaps most fundamentally, it seeks to address questions about the nature of crime and about what, at any given time, is treated as criminal, and why. In short, the radical tradition contributes questions about *the relationship between crime and criminal justice*, on the one hand, and *the state, social structure and historical transitions* on the other.

In recent years the radical tradition has been opened up in other ways. In addition to seeking explanations in terms of economic and social relations in society, there has been a growing interest in examining crime and the operation of the criminal justice system within the context of racial divisions and gender divisions in society. One strong contribution of research emanating from both of these areas has been to draw attention to racial minorities and women as victims of crime. Such research has been one of the reasons for the development from within the radical tradition of 'left realism' (Lea and Young, 1984; Young, 1986). This owes much to the writings of Jock Young who in the 1970s was very much at the forefront of the radical 'new' and 'critical' criminology. Young's argument is that the radical tradition as it was expressed during that period – what he terms the 'left idealist' position – has failed to fulfil its promise for a number of reasons, and particularly because it has failed to recognize crime – especially working-class crime – as a problem of any significance (Young, 1986, p. 17). He argues instead for a radical victimology which has at its centre a realistic and empirically informed picture of the extent of crime (particularly crime within the working class), and of the extent to which sections of society (especially racial minorities and women) have a fear of anticipated crime.

> The central tenet of left realism is to reflect the reality of crime, that is in its origins, its nature and its impact. This involves a rejection of tendencies to romanticise crime or pathologise it, to analyse solely from the point of view of the administration of crime or to exaggerate it. And our understanding of methodology, our interpretation of the statistics, our notions of aetiology follow from this. Most importantly, it is realism which informs our notion of practice: in answering what can be done about the problems of crime and crime control. (Young, 1986, p. 21)

The realist position retains theoretical ideas and political ideals of the Left but differs from so-called idealism in its willingness to have a close engagement with matters of policy and also in the centrality which it gives to first-hand data collection to uncover the reality of crime. This includes the use of social surveys which have often been the butt of criticism from the Left for being too positivistic. Victim surveys, such as the Merseyside Crime Survey (Kinsey, 1984, 1985) and the Islington Crime Survey (Jones, MacLean and Young, 1986) have been used to gain some estimate of the true extent of crime, and of crime of particular types. This is done by interviewing samples of individuals, rather than relying solely on official statistics. The uncovering of unreported crime by such empirical work goes hand in hand with the specification of policy. This includes policing policy to reduce the amount of crime, to target crimes such as rape, woman-battering and racial attacks (which are most unreported), and to protect groups most vulnerable to such crime, thereby reducing the fear of crime.

This left realism and the use of surveys has developed in parallel with victim surveys conducted by the Home Office Research and Planning Unit, particularly the British Crime Survey (Hough and Mayhew, 1983). The latter is also concerned with measuring the extent of crime. However, unlike the 'realist' surveys, the British Crime Survey does not have specific theoretical or political underpinnings nor is it geared to specific forms of policy. Rather, it is a large data base with policy uses and policy implications.

The details of such surveys and the differing theoretical, political and institutional positions they embrace and represent will be covered in greater detail in Chapter 3. Here it is sufficient to note that although there have been previous victim surveys (see, for example, Sparks, Genn and Dodd, 1977) both the 'realist' surveys and the Home Office surveys place questions about victims of crime at the centre of the criminological enterprise. These not only include questions about *the extent of crime*, which we discussed earlier, but further questions about *the extent of unreported crime* (and how this varies according to type of offence), about *the fear of crime* and about victims' *experiences of crime*.

To sum up, what we have termed the criminological enterprise is characterized by a diversity of problems and questions. We have specifically drawn attention to questions about individual criminal behaviour and about the extent and distribution of crime in society; about the functioning of the institutions of criminal justice, and about the policies and practices of their personnel; about the historical and structural locations of crime and criminal justice; and about the extent of unreported crime and victims' experiences of crime. Such problems, issues and questions come from different strands within the criminological enterprise and they do not represent a collective agenda on which all would agree. Nevertheless, for our purposes they serve to draw loose boundary ropes around an area within which we can examine the methods by which research is conducted. Each problem and question opens up a particular aspect of crime as worthy for inquiry and as such often demands particular forms of data collected in particular ways. The diversity of problems within criminology is a major factor in accounting for the diversity of data and methods of research used.

Theories
Throughout the preceding discussion of the central problems of criminology there has been implicit, and sometimes explicit,

reference to theory. Theory is not the only influence on what is, or is not, on the criminological agenda: political issues also play a crucial role. Nevertheless, it is difficult to separate problems from theories. What is seen as problematic and how problems are conceptualized are closely related to theory and to the range of theoretical approaches which have come to populate the criminological enterprise. Indeed, the plurality and diversity of problems is in part mirrored by a plurality and diversity of theories. We shall look at the main theoretical approaches in greater detail in Chapter 2. Here it is sufficient to note a number of features of such approaches and of their plurality.

First, a number of disciplines have, at one time or another, made contributions to analyses of crime and of the criminal justice system. These include contributions from medicine, law, statistics, psychiatry, history, psychology, sociology and from the strong British tradition in social administration and social policy.

Second, such disciplines often develop as a result of internal tensions, disputes and conflicts as to what is theoretically important. In some instances, such tensions, debates and disputes have been imported into the study of crime. For example, the classic dispute within psychology between 'nature' (the criminal-as-born) and 'nurture' (the criminal-as-made) is reflected within the criminological enterprise. Similarly, theoretical tensions within sociology between theories grounded in consensual-functionalism (crime as a departure from value consensus) and those grounded in conflict (crime as an outcome of conflict of class or other interests) can also be witnessed.

Third, theoretical approaches which are concerned with the central problems of their discipline, but not solely or explicitly with matters of crime and criminal justice, have made subsequent contributions to the criminological enterprise. For example, Hans Eysenck's work, particularly his early work, was primarily concerned with the relationship between physiological mechanisms and personality and with the task of developing a typology of dimensions of personality (Eysenck, 1960). A questionnaire was developed to measure two dimensions of the personality: the neuroticism–stability dimension and extraversion–intraversion dimension. This questionnaire was intended as a means of diagnosing patients in mental hospitals and it was only after this that his ideas were applied to crime with the assertion that men convicted of crimes are more likely to be higher on extraversion and neuroticism than the remainder of the population (Eysenck, 1964). Also, as we have already noted, the sociologist Emile Durkheim has had a major impact on theorists subsequently interested in the connections between social disorganization and crime. However, Durkheim did not carry out any major investigation of crime and his theoretical views on crime were subsumed within his general theory of social organization and social solidarity. Similarly, the writings of Karl Marx have had a profound influence on sociological theory. He had very little to say about crime and what he did have to say was not central to his theoretical ideas. Nevertheless, Marxist theory has played an important part in the development of the radical paradigm within the criminological enterprise, particularly via the formulation of the 'new criminology' (Taylor, Walton and Young, 1973).

A fourth, but related, point is that some of the contributions to criminology have focused explicitly on crime and criminal actions but only as a medium through which to examine problems which are fundamental to social science disciplines. For example, *The Rules of Disorder* by Marsh, Rosser and Harré (1978) is a study of football supporters who frequented the Manor Road ground of Oxford United in the 1970s. The work is theoretically eclectic, drawing upon ideas from ethology, social psychology and sociology and its main theme concerns the problem of order and the way in which it is achieved and maintained. The main assertion is that, far from seeing themselves as disorderly, the supporters impute meanings to their actions which the authors suggest are rule-governed. In essence, the book is explicitly contributing to a central strand of social psychological theory and is not intentionally criminological; but it has subsequently been thrust into criminological debates, particularly in relation to soccer violence (see, for example, Taylor, 1982; Williams, Dunning and Murphy, 1984, 1987).

Finally, we can note the range of broad theoretical approaches which populate the criminological enterprise. One of these is founded upon a concern with *individual predispositions* to and *individual propensities* for crime. It focuses upon individual differences and individual criminality and draws its strength from biological determinism and from psychological determinism. A second approach is concerned with the *social determinants* of crime and of its social and spatial distribution. Crime is seen as socially determined ('hard' determinism) or socially induced ('soft' determinism) and aspects of social structure and the degree of social disorganization are given greater prominence in explanation than individual predispositions and propensities. This approach is characterized by sociological determinism. A third approach can be described as *micro-sociological*. It eschews explanations in positivist and causal terms and seeks, instead, to examine the way in which crime is socially constructed in the interactions between individuals and agents of the criminal justice system. Analyses centre on the ways in which actions are interpreted, defined and labelled as criminal. Typically, this approach is associated with what we have previously referred to as the new deviancy school. Finally, we can delineate explanations cast in terms of *social structure and history* and intersections between them. In essence, this is the radical or critical tradition within criminology which shares with micro-sociology a dislike of explanations in causal terms but differs from it in so far as it involves social structure and history as integral parts of the explanation of crime and criminal justice.

Methods

The introduction to this chapter indicated two ways in which such theoretical approaches differ from each other: first, in terms of the unit or level of analysis they employ, and second, in terms of the degree of commitment they have to causal thinking. As we have seen, these differences have important implications for the central problems of criminology, and for the way in which they are conceptualized and addressed. Furthermore, such differences also have implications for the range of methods used to carry out criminological research. Different methods vary in their appropriateness to uncovering the aspects of crime and criminal justice which are signalled by different theoretical approaches. For example, some methods – such as interviews – are more appropriate to the collection of data from and about individuals than others. The other side of the coin, however, is that such interviews are not particularly useful for directly focusing on interactions and social processes. The relationship between theories of crime and methods of conducting criminological research is the theme of the next chapter. Here it is sufficient to note that the diversity of problems and theories in the criminological enterprise is accompanied by an equally diverse range of methods of research.

The range of methods we shall consider reflects the influence of psychology and sociology in theories of crime and also the respective contributions of 'quantitative' and 'qualitative' approaches within those disciplines. The range spans *social surveys*, with their emphasis upon sampling, data schedules, interviewing and statistical (usually correlational) analysis; *experiments*, and the search for causes by the introduction of variables (or experimental 'treatments') to two or more previously matched groups; *interviews*, with particular reference to flexible, informal and detailed methods of collecting data about individuals' current experiences or past life histories; *observation*, particularly the use of participant and covert observation to examine social interactions at first hand; and *official statistics*, to measure the extent of crime, and to examine its social and geographical distribution. Such official data are sometimes also used to examine aspects of the functioning of the institutions of criminal justice (see, for example, Bottomley and Pease, 1986).

institutional contexts

So far we have looked at a variety of problems, theories and methods and indicated the importance of examining ways in which they relate to each other. It would be unwise, however, to look at such interrelationships as if they existed in a vacuum because what we have termed the criminological enterprise spans a number of institutional contexts. There are two aspects to this, each of which raises important political dimensions. First, many of the '*objects*' of criminological inquiry are either voluntarily or involuntarily within the institutions of the criminal justice system. This has importance for the politics of research practice. Second, *practitioners* of criminological inquiry are employed within different contexts, including the Home Office and the institutions of criminal justice which are its responsibility. This has implications for political use of criminological inquiry, and particularly the relationship of such inquiry to policy-making.

First of all, we can look at some aspects of the politics of research practice. The problems of gaining access to social groups and social situations have long been recognized by social scientists. By their very nature, many of the institutions of criminal justice are truly closed, particularly to those not doing officially sponsored research. This has implications for the practical aspects of the way in which investigations may be conducted but also, perhaps more crucially, for what in the first place can be researched and what subsequently can be published. The most closed institutions are prisons, not simply because of physical barriers but also as a result of the constraints of officialdom. We can illustrate this by reference to Cohen and Taylor's study of 'lifers' in Durham Prison's E Wing in the 1970s (Cohen and Taylor, 1972) in which they focused on the strategies by which prisoners coped with long-term imprisonment. Cohen and Taylor were ostensibly there to teach long-serving prisoners but, as they put it, 'slid' into what subsequently became described by the authorities as research. In prison research, gaining the confidence and support of gatekeepers, at whatever level, is crucial. Cohen and Taylor's experience was that Home Office officials, and not local prison governors, were the main gatekeepers to placate. Although initial stages of the investigation were completed, access to the prisoners became problematic and the inquiry was subsequently closed. (The history of this project will be discussed more fully in Chapter 4.) Following their own experiences, Cohen and Taylor summarize some of the problems which prison researchers are likely to encounter:

> Criminals who find themselves in institutions like prisons become in a real sense the 'property' of the Home Office: when a prisoner

enters through the gates, the prison officer in charge signs a pape certifying that he has 'received the body of the prisoner'. . . . Th researcher finds himself in a complex web of social and politic restrictions. Each of the standard textbook problems – acces sponsorship, financing, setting up relationships to obtain dat what can be published – pose unique difficulties when the agenc in control of the subject is an official one like the Home Offic (Cohen and Taylor, 1977, p. 85)

Apart from the constraints imposed upon research by physical an official barriers, there can be barriers of a more informal nature eve where official access has been granted. These have been encou tered, for example, in conducting fieldwork amongst police officer In the late 1970s Maurice Punch carried out an investigation everyday policing strategies in central Amsterdam, which followed up with a study of police corruption (Punch, 1979, 1985 His comments on his experiences illustrate the problems of gainir access to data:

The police is often held to be the most secluded part of the crimin justice system. Like other agencies of social control and like som client serving bureaucracies, the police organization erec barriers against prying outsiders and endeavours to present favourable image of itself to the extent of justifying and ev falsifying accounts for public consumption. These structur features of isolation and secrecy, coupled with the intrins dangers of police work, help to form an occupational culture whic is solidaristic, and wary of non-initiates. The researcher's ta becomes, then, how to outwit the institutional obstacle course gain entry and how to penetrate the minefield of social defenc to reach the inner reality of police work. (Punch, 1979, p. 4)

These problems of gaining access and of collecting data connect wi much more fundamental questions about what can be researched particular contexts, particularly where the gatekeepers are not ju low-level bureaucrats trying to be difficult but also governme departments such as the Home Office which have a vested intere in the running of the institutions which are the object of inquiry.

Mention of the Home Office leads us into a consideration of t institutional contexts within which research practitioners a located. The Home Office Research Unit (HORU) set up in 19 under the Home Secretary's statutory authority to conduct inquiri into crime and criminal justice policy is the main governme research institute. It has close links with, and is a major sponsor the Institute of Criminology at Cambridge. The unit has always h strong commitment to policy-related research. In 1981 it was retitled the Home Office Research and Planning Unit (HORPU) and reorganized to create an even stronger orientation towards policy-making and planning. The changes brought about by the reorganization of the unit were designed to introduce a closer liaison between researchers and administrators within the Home Office. For example, researchers are involved in the regular preparation of briefing papers for administrators and are called upon to join policy discussions (Home Office Research and Planning Unit, 1987). In addition, the small teams are required to develop a programme of both in-house and external research. In the main, the latter is commissioned by the unit from universities, polytechnics and research institutes although consideration is given to research proposals which emanate from outside the Home Office. However, whether in-house or external, commissioned or otherwise, the guiding principle is that research should be policy-related. This is ensured by what is termed the customer–contractor principle within which 'any project included in the programme must have a firmly identified customer" within the Home Office. This ensures that the programme remains in touch with and assists in meeting administrative and management needs' (Home Office Research and Planning Unit, 1987, p. 3).

According to Cohen (1981) the Home Office has been the institutional base of mainstream criminological research which has been characterized by four main features: *pragmatism* (an emphasis upon empirical inquiry to collect the 'facts'); *positivism* (a commitment to identifying the causes of crime, particularly causes which are believed to be located within individual, family and social backgrounds); *interdisciplinary work* (the belief that there are many causes of crime and therefore that several disciplines have contributions to make); *correctionalism* (an acceptance of the value of the correctional system and of the goal of making it more effective). However, Young (1986) suggests that in more recent years there has been a movement away from mainstream criminology in official circles to what he terms 'administrative criminology'. He argues that this has come about for two reasons: first, the failure of positivist research to provide explanations for the extent and distribution of crime; second, the failure of correctionalism to control and to rehabilitate. The new administrative criminology represents a return to classical thinking which sees crime in voluntaristic not deterministic terms. This playing down of causes switches the research focus away from policies geared to the reform of social circumstances to those policies concerned with reducing the opportunities of crime (crime prevention policies), increasing the possibility of being detected (police effectiveness policies), and increasing the certainty of punishment (sentencing policies).

This change of emphasis is reflected in the number of projects in the HORPU's research programmes concerned with crime prevention initiatives, with policies and practices of policing and with ways of improving police effectiveness. It is also reflected in the titles of major books emerging out of the unit's research activities. These include Clarke and Mayhew's *Designing out Crime* (1980), Clarke and Cornish's *Crime Control in Britain* (1983), Heal and Laycock's *Situational Crime Prevention: From Theory into Practice* (1986) and Hope and Shaw's *Communities and Crime Reduction* (1988).

Either way, 'mainstream' or 'administrative', the criminological enterprise within the Home Office has had two key strands. First there has been a strong investment in empirical research, usually quantitative research based on social surveys, official statistics or reforms-as-experiments. Second, such research has been firmly tied to the formulation or evaluation of policy. What is seen as problematic is what is problematic for official policy.

The criminological enterprise outside the official and quasi-official institutional bases is much more diverse and difficult to embrace adequately. In the main it encompasses research and teaching in universities and polytechnics and in research institutes attached to them. It was outside governmental research agencies that the contra-mainstream criminology movement developed in the 1960s. This crystallized around the National Deviancy Conference formed in 1968, which was the main forum for the development of new deviancy theories and the subsequent radical and critical versions founded upon Marxism. In the formative years new deviancy theories grounded themselves in micro-sociological explanations of the way in which deviance is generated in interactions between individuals and law enforcement agents, with particular reference to the process of labelling. It stood square against mainstream criminology by virtue of its focus on the 'agent of control' (rather than upon criminals), its insistence on non-quantitative enthnographic methods as opposed to surveys and official statistics, and its rejection of positivist explanations. The recognition that these earlier new deviancy theories did not satisfactorily incorporate matters of social structure and power led to the development within the conference of what earlier we have described as the radical and critical school within criminology initially signalled by the publication of Taylor, Walton and Young' *The New Criminology* in 1973 and their subsequent volume *Critical Criminology* two years later. The radical paradigm contains many interconnecting strands but they all centre around the problem of social order, the maintenance of such order by the state's agencies of control, and the way in which these agencies represent economic and class interests. (For a summary and discussion of the radical paradigm and its development since the mid-1970s, see Hall and Scraton, 1981.) The paradigm is theoretically and methodologically reflexive in addressing 'official' theories, policies and research as objects of inquiry in their own right. This involves examining and questioning what, in the first instance, is defined as problematic and examining the role of official criminological research as part of the defining process.

To sum up, the criminological enterprise takes place in a number of institutional contexts. Two aspects can be noted. First, the *'objects'* of criminological inquiry are often located behind the maze of formal and informal barriers which is the criminal justice system. This has implications for research practice, including problems of gaining access and of studying things as they normally are. The severity of such problems for any given researcher, and the way in which they can be addressed, are often dependent on the institutional context within which he or she is working. This relates to the second aspect, namely, that the *practitioners* of criminological inquiry are themselves in different institutional contexts. The significance of this derives from the role of state institutions, particularly the Home Office, in criminological inquiry. Such official criminological inquiry is itself part of the system of criminal justice and therefore can be viewed as an 'object' of inquiry in its own right. It is simplistic to suggest a sharp divide between the Home Office and academia just as it is to put forward simple equations such as 'Home Office equals policy-related research', 'academia equals radical paradigm'. It is probably accurate to suggest that the radical paradigm has failed to penetrate official criminology, let alone have any impact on it. In terms of the type of work which is carried out, the Home Office is typified by atheoretical, empirical research in which the problems of criminology are the problems of policy. Beyond this official territory the criminological enterprise is characterized by a much wider range of problems, theoretical approaches and methods. This range includes policy-related research, some of which is officially funded, but it also includes radical paradigms which adopt a fundamentally critical stance to such research.

Conclusion

What we have termed the criminological enterprise is characterized by plurality, diversity and variety. This is partly the outcome of the range of problems which is addressed, the variety of theoretical approaches contributed by disciplines, the range of methods by which criminological research is conducted, and the differing institutional contexts within which it is undertaken. Further, it is also partly the outcome of the complexity of interconnections which criminologists have made between different types of problems, theories, institutional contexts and methods. To undertake a consideration of methods of criminological research outside this plurality would be to treat 'methods' as if they were objective tools immune from matters of theory, from questions of what is problematic and from the constraints of institutions.

The relationships between types of theories and types of methods are complex. In Chapter 2, 'Methods of criminological research', we encounter a range of research strategies and methods by which data are collected and analysed, and seek to chart some connections between types of method and types of criminological theory.

A range of problems central to the criminological enterprise has been described, for example, how much crime is there; why do individuals commit crimes; how can we account for the social distribution of crime; how do the systems for the prevention, control and punishment of crime function and with what effect? Which aspects of these problems are exposed to investigation depends in large part on the theoretical approaches brought to bear on them but also on the institutional context within which the problem is being defined and conceptualized. In Chapter 3, 'Measuring and explaining crime' we focus on some of the problems of the criminological enterprise by examining issues concerned with the use of official data to measure the extent of crime, and also with seeking explanations of crime using quantitative and qualitative research.

Finally, we have emphasized that the interchange between problem, theory and method does not exist in a vacuum. Criminological research is conducted against political backgrounds and in institutional contexts. What is more, the central questions of criminological research – what is or is not crime; how much is there; how can it be explained; how should it be controlled? – are also the central concerns of politics. An appreciation of political backgrounds and institutional contexts of research is important to an understanding of who gets studied, what gets studied, and with what effect. In Chapter 4 we shall consider such issues in the context of 'Studying the criminal justice system'.

2

Methods of criminological research

Introduction

A major theme of Chapter 1 has been that criminology progresses both by the development of coherent and comprehensive theories about crime and its causes and also by the systematic collection and analysis of observations about the social world in relation to such theories. Such observations are usually referred to as 'data'. A wide variety of data are used to contribute to the criminological enterprise, data which are the products of the range of methods of research we shall consider in subsequent sections of this chapter. Typically, they are generated by forms of data collection (for example, structured interviews) and examined by forms of data analysis (for example, correlation analysis), both of which are housed within some broad research design or strategy (for example, social survey design). The variety of data are, in part, a reflection of the diversity of problems addressed and the plethora of aspects of such problems which are exposed for investigation by different theoretical approaches. Any given instance of criminological research represents a particular constellation between problem, theory and method and the data which are used are outcomes of that constellation.

We shall look at types of data not just to reinforce once again – but in a different way – the plurality and diversity within the criminological enterprise, but, more fundamentally, to consider some of the assumptions about the nature of crime and criminality which are implicit in different types of data. These include assumptions about whether crime can be legitimately measured; assumptions about the appropriate unit and level of analysis – individual, social group or society; and assumptions about the primacy which should be given to antecedents and causality in any such analysis. Distinctions between types of data are not hard and fast. However, making such distinctions helps to portray the range of data available and to uncover implicit assumptions, particularly as they relate to types of theory and types of method in criminological research.

Types of data

Quantitative and qualitative data
First, we can distinguish data which are *quantitative* and data which are *qualitative* (sometimes also referred to as non-quantitative). Whether or not the use of the term 'qualitative data' is indicative of superiority *vis-à-vis* quantitative data is one of the fundamental issues implicit in the distinction. Quantitative research in criminology is founded on the assumption that the objects of inquiry – whether these be the characteristics of individuals or features of whole societies – can be defined and delineated unambiguously. What is more, this is linked to assertions that particular features of these objects can be categorized 'objectively' by the researcher and can be measured by the application of numbers to such categories and also to the number of cases within each of the categories.

The emphasis which is placed upon measurement in quantitative criminology is closely associated with a strong investment in statistical analysis and particularly the use of 'statistics of association' which provide an indication of the extent to which variables co-vary. A typical example is the *correlation coefficient*, the size of which measures the strength of relationship between two specified variables. Correlation analysis will be considered in greater detail in Chapter 3, particularly in connection with studies concerned with establishing statistical relationships between levels of unemployment and levels of crime. Here it is sufficient to note that the value of a correlation coefficient can vary in size from 0 to +1 or −1. A score of +1 indicates that there is a perfect and positive relationship between two variables (for example, that high levels of unemployment are related to high levels of crime and low levels of unemployment are related to low levels of crime). A score of −1 indicates that there is a perfect inverse relationship between two variables (for example, that low levels of unemployment are associated with high levels of crime and vice versa). A score of 0 indicates that there is no relationship between the variables. In practice, the value of most correlation coefficients is likely to lie somewhere between the two extremes; the closer the coefficient is to ±1 (say, ±0.8) the stronger the relationship between the two variables; the closer the coefficient is to 0 (say, ±0.2) the weaker the relationship.

Correlation analysis can be used with data collected about different units of analysis. For example, data presented by Tarling (1982) about the relationship between unemployment and crime relates to England and Wales, whereas Baldwin and Bottoms' (1976) study of crime in Sheffield correlates crime rates with census data for small *areas* (enumeration districts) in the city. The Cambridge ongitudinal study of delinquency, on the other hand, seeks to relate riminality among *individuals* with personality, attitudinal and background features of those same individuals (West, 1982). Typically, correlation analysis is not restricted to the examination of relationships between just two variables. It is common to posit and test a composite model which specifies the collective and respective contributions of a number of explanatory variables at one and the same time, rather than examine a number of separate two-variable hypotheses. This is done by the use of techniques of *multivariate analysis* (including the calculation of multiple correlations) which permit the examination of the strength of association of several variables at one and the same time. So, for example, Baldwin and Bottoms used multivariate analysis to examine the relationships between crime rates for areas and thirty other variables for those same areas, of which housing tenure was found to be the most important. With regard to the relationship between unemployment and crime, Carr-Hill and Stern (1979) found significant and strong correlations between these two variables at the level of police areas. However, when they developed a multivariate model by introducing other variables such as social-class composition of areas, rateable value and age distribution, they found that the original statistical relationship between crime and unemployment virtually disappeared. This illustrates the complex way in which variables interrelate and the dangers of restricting analysis to two-variable hypotheses.

Quantitative criminological research, then, views aspects of crime and criminal justice as objective phenomena. They are treated as being measurable and therefore amenable to statistical analysis as in the formulation and testing of explanatory and predictive models of crime causation. Aspects of the social world, it is assumed, can be simplified and represented by such models. By its character this approach is most typically, but not exclusively, associated with the positivist paradigm within the criminological enterprise. As was pointed out in the preceding chapter, the positivist paradigm has found expression in different disciplines, such as psychology and sociology, which have contributed to criminology. Whatever the distinctions between the brands of positivism they each place objective' and quantitative data at the centre of their analyses. What is more, they also place emphasis upon explanations set in causal terms. This search for causality is often expressed via the calculation of correlation coefficients which are the means by which hypotheses are tested and causal models developed. However, although such coefficients provide statistical estimates of the strength of association between specified variables they do not by themselves demonstrate causality. Other supporting evidence is required but not necessarily

always available. So, for example, a correlation between unemploy
ment and crime cannot by itself demonstrate that changes in the leve
of unemployment produce changes in the level of crime. What i
required in addition is evidence that no other variables account fo
the changes in crime levels and also evidence that changes i
unemployment levels preceded those in the crime levels. It is als
essential to have some theoretical rationale which, by recourse t
existing theory, explains why we believe the explanatory variable ha
the outcome it has. We shall return to a discussion of th
methodological problems of seeking explanations of crime by the us
of correlations in Chapter 3.

One obvious difference between quantitative data and nor
quantitative data is that the former makes use of numbers and c
statistical analysis whereas the latter does not. However, th
contrasts are much more fundamental than that in so far as data whic
are non-quantitative or qualitative embody different assumption
about the nature of social reality (and therefore of crime) an
different assumptions about the way in which it can, and should, b
studied. In particular, qualitative data are used to capture the soci
meanings, definitions and constructions which underpin action
This is done in ways which are neither feasible nor desirable via th
use of 'hard' quantitative data. In criminological terms, qualitativ
data 'humanise the deviant' (Fitzgerald and Muncie, 1981). Schwart
and Jacobs summarize the differences between qualitative an
quantitative data as follows.

Sociologists produce data by translating their observations an
inquiries into written notation systems. The difference betwee
qualitative and quantitative sociology can be stated quite simpl
in terms of the notation systems used to describe the worlc
Quantitative sociologists assign numbers to qualitative observa
tions. In this sense, they produce data by counting and 'measurin
things. The things measured can be individual persons, group
whole societies, speech acts, and so on. Qualitative sociologist
on the other hand, report observations in the natural language ;
large. They seldom make counts or assign numbers to thes
observations. In this sense, qualitative sociologists report on th
social world much as the daily newspaper does. *This simpl*
difference in commitment to notation systems corresponds to va
differences in values, goals, and procedures for doing sociologic
research. (Schwartz and Jacobs, 1979, p. 4; italics added)

The procedures by which qualitative data are collected are variou
and, unlike the methods of quantitative research, have no fixe
protocols. They include, for example, the use of forms of observatior

articularly participant observation, detailed interviews such as life-story interviews and the analysis of various documentary sources ich as organizational records, diaries and letters. We can look at xamples of how such sources and types of data have been used to cus on aspects of the criminological enterprise. For example, the hicago sociologists laid down a tradition of studying deviant sub-ultures using participant observation and life histories which was ibsequently developed in America by Whyte (1943) in his classic nalysis of 'street corner society' and which has influenced many udies of criminal sub-cultures including examinations of male and male teenage gangs (Campbell, 1981; Corrigan, 1979; Patrick,)73; Parker, 1974). In addition, qualitative data have been brought) bear on studies of occupational cultures within the criminal justice /stem, for example the 'canteen culture' of police officers (Holdaway,)83; Punch, 1979), and also on the formal and informal ways a which justice is administered (Baldwin and McConville, 1977). or example, in *Inside the British Police*, Holdaway (1983) focuses n police actions and in doing so notes the importance of 'clear-up gures' to police officers as a readily identifiable measure of work. a such research, statistics on crime are not seen as the raw material or subsequent analysis but as phenomena which themselves require xplanation in terms of the everyday actions of police officers. The ata are in the form of written descriptions of meanings, actions and iteractions and these are typically grounded in the verbal descrip-ons of the participants themselves. For example, Holdaway uses ome quotations to support the assertion that officers use the practice f 'verballing' as a means of ensuring certain people end up in official atistics on crime.

I verbal people, and I think that it is justified. If we are given laws which can't be put into practice, then we have to try and make them work, and this means verballing. Look at 'offensive weapons'. You are almost obliged to give the prisoner a verbal to get a conviction on that charge . . . I take the oath, but it might as well be swearing on any old bit of paper. It doesn't mean anything to me. I don't have to say that I believe in it . . . I think I am fair to people. (Holdaway, 1983, p. 112)

Methodologically, qualitative data are most closely associated ith theoretical approaches which play down or which actively reject ositivist assumptions. Within such approaches the social world is een as something which is continuously under social construction ia social interactions by the participants themselves rather than as ome external, objective and all-constraining reality, aspects of hich can be measured and subjected to statistical manipulation.

The emphasis is not upon determinism and causality but upon the way in which social meanings, definitions and labels are generated and applied within social interactions and social processes. In terms of the development of criminological theory, such a viewpoint is symbolized by micro-sociological approaches which gained force in the late 1960s and early 1970s and which drew their strength from symbolic interactionism within social psychology and the Weberian social action approach within sociology. These approaches coalesced around the belief that in order to understand the way in which the social reality of crime and the criminal justice system is constructed it is important to gain access to the 'actors' viewpoint'. It is only by grasping the way in which individuals define situations, events and others' actions, and also the way in which such definitions frame and influence their own subsequent actions, that we can gain some understanding of how social reality is constructed. The validity of such data and analyses lies in the extent to which it is true to these actors' viewpoints. This is in stark contrast to the use of correlational and other analyses to develop statistical models of crime or any other social phenomena.

Individual and social data

Basically, this is the contrast between, on the one hand, observations collected about individual characteristics and individual acts of crime and, on the other, observations about the social and ecological distribution of crime and about social structure and social processes at work within it. In the preceding chapter we discussed some of the central problems of the criminological enterprise and we looked at the ways in which theories of particular kinds open up aspects of these problems as worthy of further investigation. Some of these theories raise issues or seek explanations in terms of the behaviour, experience, traits and attitudes of individuals. These involve research *on* people and are often posited on the assumption that the key factors in the explanations are to be found *in* people. Some of the explanations are in terms of individuals' physiological characteristics – what has been termed biological determinism – and other are in terms of individuals' psychological characteristics – psychological determinism. Either way, such theories demand individual data, that is, data collected about individuals and from individuals, often by the use of interviews, psychometric tests or experimental methods.

Research of this type can be distinguished from that which suggests that social processes, social structure, and the way in which this structure historically evolves, are just as important, if not more so, in any explanation of crime. In the main, this type of research emanates from the sociological tradition within criminology. The tradition has many strands to it. One of these is what we have previously termed sociological positivism, with its emphasis upon the social structural determinants of criminal behaviour. Other strands include micro-sociological approaches which focus on social meanings, definitions, interactions and the social construction of crime and radical criminology with its emphasis upon interrelationships between political and economic structures and historical processes. In their different ways these theories play down individualistic explanations, based on individual data, seeking instead to posit explanations on the factors at work within interactions, social structures and historical processes. Such explanations require social data. This is a broad catagory encompassing findings about small-scale interactions (social interactional data), observations about the characteristics of social groups (social groups data) or about features of social structure (social structural data). Social data can be derived from a number of sources including the use of large-scale social surveys to examine, for example, the social characteristics and conditions of particular social groups in society and how these relate to levels of crime in such groups; the use of observational methods to focus upon, say, interactions between individuals and police officers; the secondary analysis of official statistics on crime to consider the social and ecological distribution of particular types of crime; and the conduct of social history research to trace historical patterns in crime or to examine developments and continuities in patterns of, say, policing.

One major significance of the distinction made here concerns the ways in which theory and data can relate to each other in terms of what is seen as the appropriate level of analysis. There are problems inherent in moving between different levels of analysis and particularly in the use of data collected at one level to make theoretical statements about another level. For example, sociological theorizing typically operates at the level of the 'social' – social group, institution or social structure. Such units of analysis are enlisted to explain crime and its patterns. However, data cannot be collected directly from such units. Rather, sociologists often resort to data collected from individuals as when they interview large samples of people or when they carry out life-history interviews with specific informants. Findings collected from and about individuals in sample surveys are often aggregated to make statements about the characteristics of the social groups from which they come. This can be questioned on a number of grounds. For example, as Durkheim (1964b) pointed out, individuals may only be capable of 'ideological analysis', that is, they may only be capable of describing the social world from their own particular viewpoint. Further, there is no inbuilt guarantee that the aggregation of findings about the

background characteristics of large numbers of individuals consti-
tutes an adequate description of the sociological features of the social
and cultural groups of which they are a part. The inappropriate use
of statistical data collected at one level to make theoretical assertions
at another level is what is known as 'the fallacy of the wrong level'
and will be considered in detail in the following chapter in a
discussion of the relationship between unemployment and crime.

Problems in moving between different levels of analysis are not
specific to quantitative data. For example, qualitative data collected
by life-history interviews, participant observation or other ethnographic techniques are often welded to macro-theories about the way
in which society is structured. Data collected in, and about, small-
scale interactions are presented as instances of the way in which wider
social processes express themselves in such interactions. There is,
however, tension in this relationship in so far as the data do not in
themselves provide sufficient support for assertions about such wider
processes. In the end, the adequacy for such assertions can only be
judged in terms of the theoretical rationale supporting them. This
issue will be discussed further in the following chapter in connection
with Corrigan's (1979) ethnography of kids in Sunderland which
seeks to explain their actions in terms of power and economic and
class relations in capitalist society.

Present and past data
In essence this refers to the time period about which the data is
collected. Past data can include the kind of data which are collected
in social history research as in Raphael Samuel's (1981) study of
crime in the 'Jago' at the turn of the century, and a typical example
of present data is that collected by the British Crime Survey to
measure the extent of contemporary crime. Past and present data
can be collected and used independently of each other. However,
there are ways in which they can be used in conjunction which have
significance for the way in which theory and data relate to each other.
For example, longitudinal studies of delinquency, such as the
Cambridge Study of Delinquency (West, 1969, 1982) have used
survey findings to make theoretical statements about the causes of
criminal behaviour. They collect present data about individuals'
current behaviours which are then related to past data about the same
individuals, collected at some earlier time. This is done as a basis for
theorizing about the causes of individual delinquency. Such leaps
from data to theory must, however, be accomplished with caution.
For example, the explanatory variables included in any theoretical
statement are inevitably limited to those past variables about which
the researcher chose to collect findings at some earlier time. Also,
correlations are not by themselves sufficient as bases for making

causal statements. Social surveys can establish statistical relationships between background variables and present actions but what is also required is direct evidence that background variables actually produced the delinquent behaviour. Such evidence is rarely, if ever, available.

Primary and secondary data

Primary data are those observations collected at first hand for the specific purpose of addressing the criminological issues in question. The way in which the research is designed, and the categories which are chosen to give a framework to the collection of observations and to their subsequent analysis, are predominantly in the hands of the social scientist. They are influenced by the issues he or she is addressing and the theoretical ideas brought to bear on such issues. Surveys, interviews, experiments and forms of observational methods are all ways of collecting primary data. Secondary data are those observations collected by other people or other agencies with other purposes in mind. The ways in which such observations are collected, categorized, organized and presented are very much in the hands of others and may not be influenced by the theoretical ideas in which the researcher is interested. Secondary qualitative data can be found in a wide range of documents which individuals and organizations produce for a whole host of reasons, and these can include diaries, letters, biographies, autobiographies, newspapers, memoranda, police crime reports, probation case notes, to mention but a few. These are typical of what Plummer (1983) calls 'documents of life'. Quantitative secondary data come in the form of official statistics collected by central government departments as a tool to assist in future decision-making. Indeed the subsequent analysis by social scientists of official statistics, such as Home Office statistics on crime, is typically known as 'secondary analysis' (see, for example, Hakim, 1982).

Official statistics on crime are means by which the extent of crime can be measured and its spatial, ecological and social distribution examined. The use of official data in these ways owes much to the Durkheimian tradition of using such statistics to measure 'social facts'. The application of this tradition within criminology, and elsewhere in the social sciences, has generated a classic methodological debate. This centres on the positivist use of official statistics and particularly the implicit assumption that such statistics can be treated as objective indices of the 'criminality' of a society or of subsections of it. Against this have been placed two theoretical viewpoints. One of these – the *institutionalist* position – argues that official statistics are indicators of the everyday practices and procedures of law enforcers and of the implications which these have for who does, and does not, end up as a criminal statistic and not objective measures of the level of crime in society. Such a viewpoint has sympathy with the interactionist and micro-sociological approaches within the criminological enterprise. The *radical position* goes some way along the road with the institutional viewpoint in so far as it also rejects the positivist assertion that official statistics represent objective indices of societal phenomena. However, it does not regard such data as the outcome of a myriad of separate law-enforcement actions. Rather, data are viewed as reflections of the way in which society is structured, particularly in terms of class relations, and of the influence of such structural features on crime generation and on the construction of crime statistics. This position is most closely associated with the radical or critical tradition within the criminological enterprise.

To sum up, we have made a number of distinctions to illustrate the types of data used to study crime and the criminal justice system. Such distinctions should not be seen as hard and fast but as collectively constituting a loose categorization which is useful for three reasons. First, it provides a mechanism by which we can pose questions about the nature of data which are used in any criminological research study and also about the implicit assumptions buried within such data. These include assumptions about whether crime can be treated as objective, measurable phenomena, about the usefulness of explanations cast in causal terms, and about the appropriateness of different levels of analysis. Secondly, such a categorization indicates the wide range of data which is used across the criminological enterprise, a range which in large part mirrors the plurality of problems which are addressed and theoretical perspectives which address them. It also indicates the potential for the use of different types of data within the same research study. Crime is a multi-faceted phenomenon. It is an act which is capable of being counted and it is also a way of life requiring detailed and sensitive description. The use of different types of data to uncover, explore and report these different facets is what Denzin has called 'data triangulation' (1970, p. 301). Thirdly, and finally, a consideration of the range of data used in the criminological enterprise points us in the direction of the sources of such data. In the following sections we consider some of these sources and also examine ways in which methods of criminological research connect with theory.

Social surveys

Three aspects of the development of social surveys are worthy of note. First, social surveys have been closely tied to the empirical sociological tradition in Britain. Although crude survey-like forms of data collection were used in the last century, the modern social survey tradition dates from the work of Charles Booth and Seebohm Rowntree who, at the turn of the century, began systematically to collect what they deemed to be objective 'facts' about poverty. Since that time surveys have been closely connected with social policy, social reform and the collection of findings in relation to these, and as Abrams (1968) has pointed out, this empirical survey-based tradition established its roots not only in universities but also in those government departments involved in the formulation of social policy. Much social survey research in Britain has been applied and policy-related (see Bulmer, 1982). For example, since its inception in 1958, the research section of the Home Office has commissioned and conducted its own surveys in relation to issues of criminal justice policy. Second, the development of social surveys has received impetus from parallel developments in statistical theory. Indeed, many of the early surveyors were statisticians. The use of probability theory in survey analysis and the formulation and refinement of techniques of statistical modelling have served to place social surveys at the centre of the quantitative approach within social science research. Third, this close association with quantification, and also with the search for causes via the use of correlational and other statistical analyses, is paralleled in a loose association between surveys and positivism.

Social surveys have been used to examine many features and problems within the criminological enterprise. For example, surveys played a central role in the Cambridge Studies of Delinquency in the search for correlates of such delinquency (West, 1967, 1969, 1982). Further, surveys have been employed to assess public attitudes towards crime and policing, as in the Policy Studies Institute's examination of the attitudes of Londoners to the policing strategies and practices of the Metropolitan Police (Smith and Gray, 1983); to survey occupational groups within the criminal justice system, as in Cain's (1973) comparison of the policeman's role in urban and rural areas and Jones's (1979) consideration of the organizational constraints on police behaviour; and to gain some estimate of the 'dark figure' of crime by the use of victim surveys such as the British Crime Survey (Hough and Mayhew, 1983, 1985) and the Islington Crime Survey (Jones, MacLean and Young, 1986).

Sampling techniques

We can briefly consider central features of the social survey design. First of all, surveys are usually based upon samples. Instead of directly studying whole populations, surveys typically collect evidence from a small sample of people selected from the population. The word 'population' is used in the statistical rather than geographical sense and can refer to any group to which we want our results to apply. The intention is to infer that the findings and conclusions drawn from the sample are likely to be equally true of the population as a whole. This is done by drawing upon a branch of statistical theory known as probability theory. Let us assume that we are not at all happy with official statistics as measures of the true extent of crime and of crime of different types. As an alternative we might decide to ask individuals if they have recently been the victim of a criminal act. It would be difficult, if not impossible, to ask all individuals in the country so we would be well advised to base our conclusions on a small sample of, say, a thousand individuals.

The 'true' figure relating to the number of people who have been victims of crime in the population as a whole is known as the *parameter*. Although this is the figure we want to acquire, it remains 'unknown' to us because we are not surveying the whole population. Therefore we must rely upon statistical inferences about what this figure might be. The results we collect from our sample survey about the number of victims are called *statistics*. They are known to us once

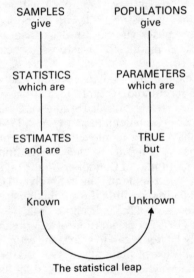

SAMPLES give

POPULATIONS give

STATISTICS which are

PARAMETERS which are

ESTIMATES and are

TRUE but

Known

Unknown

The statistical leap

Figure 2.1 *The statistical leap*

we complete our analysis, but the difficulty we face is that we do not know whether our known statistic is the same as the true parameter for the population as a whole, or indeed whether it is remotely close to it. All is not lost, however, because probability theory provides a way of making a statistical leap from one to the other. It provides a means by which we can estimate, with a certain level of probability of being correct, the extent to which the statistic about the percentage of the sample who have been victims of crime is close to the true figure for the population. What is more, assume that we want to examine the hypothesis that being a victim of crime is related to ethnic background. This could be assessed by calculating a correlation coefficient between these two variables within our sample. Probability theory can help us here too, because it provides a means by which we can assess – again with a certain level of probability of being correct – whether a relationship found in our sample is likely to exist in the population as a whole.

The ways in which samples are drawn from such populations are various and involve technicalities which are well beyond the aims of this book. However, two broad strategies can be indicated. The first of these is known as *random* or *probability* sampling, in which individuals to be included in the sample are chosen at random and each individual in the population has an equal and non-zero chance of becoming a sample member. The selection is often from a sampling frame, which is a numbered list of all members in the population and is often accomplished using tables of random numbers which are numbers generated at random. With large samples drawn from large populations, computer programs are available to make random selections. Non-random sampling – the second broad strategy – is sometimes also known as *purposive* sampling. This is because individuals are selected deliberately and with some particular purpose in mind. The major form of non-random sampling is called quota sampling in which the population is split into sub-classes according to attributes or variables, which are seen as being theoretically relevant to the investigation (for example, ethnicity, age or social class). In order to ensure that a sample includes representatives from different ethnic, social class and age groups, it is necessary to set quotas of numbers of individuals in each of the sub-classes to be selected for the sample. Interviewers are given instructions to interview individuals who fit between the boundaries of the quota controls. If the instructions are followed faithfully the sample should include specified sub-samples of the population in terms of ethnic background, social class and age. Such samples are not strictly random because they have not been constituted as a result of random selection from complete and accurate sampling frames. Rather, once the quotas are set, interviewers usually select sample members on the basis of approaching individuals who happen to be on the streets at the same time as themselves. Nevertheless, quota samples can be representative of the population as a whole and can provide precise and accurate estimates of population parameters.

Data collection
Whether random or non-random, surveys typically employ a schedule for the collection of data from individuals chosen to be in the sample. The schedule is a composite of questions, some of which invite quite lengthy, open-ended responses and others which merely require a tick in an appropriate box. The questions can collect data about different aspects of the individual, sometimes in the same schedule. For example, some questions are framed to collect findings about *background* variables such as social class, age, occupation, education, gender, ethnic origin. Others may be geared to the measurement of social *attitudes*, for example, anti-establishment attitudes, by the presentation of a battery of questions or items. The responses are scored with the total score taken to indicate an individual's position on the attitude scale. A third type of question collects data about individuals' *actions* and *behaviours*, for example, their involvement in criminal activities of various kinds and their association with others who are involved in such activities. Where data on all three aspects are collected on the same schedule, and within the same survey, there is the capacity for the development of statistical models which portray relationships between particular kinds of backgrounds, particular attitudinal dispositions and particular criminal actions and behaviours. Whatever the type of data collected, the social survey data schedule imposes much more structure on responses from individuals than the more informal and unstructured *aides mémoire* associated with the ethnographic and life history interviews we shall consider later in this chapter.

The data schedule is administered in a number of ways. In some cases interviewers are used to ask each sample member the questions on the schedule, in which case the schedule is known as an interviewer-administered questionnaire. In other cases, sample members are asked to complete the schedule themselves, in which case it is typically known as a self-completion or mail questionnaire.

Data analysis
The findings collected by questionnaire are subjected to statistical analysis, usually by computer. In some cases, the analysis is geared to counting how many people have a particular attribute or attitude. Such surveys are sometimes known as *descriptive* surveys. Victim surveys, such as the Home Office's British Crime Survey, which are concerned with estimating the extent of crime, are typical of this category. They count how many people in the sample have been the victim of a crime in a given period of time and then make estimates for the population as a whole (Hough and Mayhew, 1983). In other cases, the analysis is concerned with examining whether, within the sample as a whole, there is a relationship between answers to one set

questions and answers to another set. Because such relationships
e usually examined statistically using correlation coefficients or
lated measures, these kinds of survey are sometimes known as
rrelational surveys. What is more, because such relationships are
ten used, sometimes incorrectly, as evidence of why phenomena
e distributed the way they are or why individuals behave the way
ey do, they are also sometimes known as *explanatory* surveys.

Earlier we considered the ways in which surveys sample indi-
duals or other units. There is another aspect to the way in which
rveys draw samples, namely by sampling through time. We can
stinguish three types of sample: cross-sectional designs, time series
r trend) designs and longitudinal designs. Each of these can be
mbined with the various forms of random sampling or with quota
mpling.

ross-sectional designs

ith *cross-sectional* designs a sample of individuals is selected and
terviewed at a particular point in time about their present attitudes
behaviours and, in some studies, about what has happened to them
the past. There is, then, the capacity to collect both past and
esent data, perhaps to find relationships within and between these,
t with cross-sectional designs the validity of past data is inevitably
pendent upon the memories of respondents. In Figure 2.2, a cross-
ctional survey could be represented by a random or quota sample
individuals taken at *one* of the points A, B or C. It is, in effect, a
gle and particular slice through time.

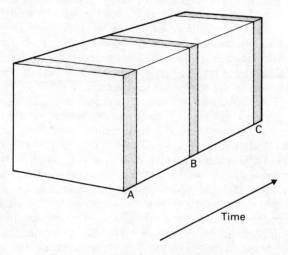

Figure 2.2 *Sampling through time*

We can illustrate this type of design by reference to a survey of th attitude of Londoners to crime and to policing which was commis sioned by the Metropolitan Police and conducted by the Polic Studies Institute (Smith and Gray, 1983). Its commission followe concern about relations between police and the communit particularly ethnic minority groups in London, and the final repo concluded by being critical of the way in which police related sections of the community, particularly ethnic minorities. Th overall research programme has a number of strands to it. One these was a cross-sectional survey of residents of London to colle data about the extent and nature of past contacts with police with view to relating these reported experiences to data collected from tl same individuals about present attitudes towards the police and kno ledge of police activities. The other components of the overall strateg were a participant observational study of young black people, a surv of police officers using a self-completion questionnaire, and a numb of small-scale studies of police organization and police work.

The survey component involved a random sample of 2,420 peop designed to be representative of all those aged 15 and over in tl Metropolitan Police District. This was made up of two sub-sample one of which was a general sample (1,411 people) of the populatic and the other a special sample (1,009) of people of Asian and We Indian origin. The general sample was compiled by random selecting addresses in eighty polling districts chosen as bei representative of London. At each selected address a set procedures was followed to pick one person randomly to be part the sample. It was essential to the research aims that a sufficient large group of young people was included for interview and therefo the procedures for selection were devised in such a way as to mainta the principle of randomness while boosting the number of you people in the sample in relation to their proportion in the populatio It was also important to include sufficient numbers of Asians a West Indians in the study and this was the function of the spec sample. This was based upon enumeration districts (small geographic units of approximately 150 households) which were known have proportionately high concentrations of Asians and W Indians. Within each of these districts a sampling frame of Asia and West Indians was constructed by contacting all households a from this sampling frame a final random sample was selected in su a way as to boost the numbers of young people included as membe At the analysis stage the two samples were merged so that samp members could be sorted into 'ethnic' and 'other' groups, irrespect of the sample from which they originated, so that comparisons co be made between these two groups in relation to the data collect by the questionnaire.

This survey of Londoners is typically random, representative and oss-sectional. It takes a sample of Londoners at a particular point time (August and October 1981) with a view to measuring their titudes towards policing. Although data are collected about past ontacts with police, the survey is ahistorical. Much contemporary ebate about relations between police and community has been ouched in social structural and historical terms and has been ontributed by the radical and historical traditions within the iminological enterprise (see, for example, Scraton, 1987). Cross-ectional surveys can offer only an 'instamatic' snapshot to such analyses. What is more, such surveys do not typically involve an storical analysis of evolving relations between the police – as an stitution of control – and various sections of the community lthough, of course, an examination of this kind may provide a ackcloth for such surveys).

me series designs

ke cross-sectional surveys, *time series* (or *trend*) designs do not give imacy to explanations in structural or historical terms. They do, owever, have inbuilt mechanisms for the collection of data at fferent points in time which facilitates some limited historical omparisons within the survey. In terms of Figure 2.2, the same, or nilar, items of information are collected at points A, B *and* C. The dividuals chosen to be sample members at each of the different ints are not the same although the procedures of selection are. ne samples, therefore, are equivalent and permit researchers to ok for trends in society over time. The British Crime Survey lough and Mayhew, 1983) is an example of a trend design which mples the extent of crime at different points of time. The first rvey was carried out in 1982, the second in 1984 and there are ans to sample at subsequent intervals. At each point in time sample embers are asked whether they have recently been the victim of crime; they are asked to specify the type of crime; and they are ked to indicate whether the crime was reported to the police. ne extent of crime is traditionally measured using officially corded statistics. The value of the British Crime Survey *vis-à-vis* ficial crime statistics is that it permits some conclusions to be ached about the amount of unreported crime. It also facilitates me examination of changes in trends in the extent of crime but is not intended as a means of providing explanations of changes such trends. In essence, it is a descriptive study which aims to easure crime at particular points in time with no pretensions to explanatory power. A much more sophisticated analysis ating to changes in crime levels to other trends in society would necessary for this.

Longitudinal designs

By studying the same groups at different points in time, *longitudina* surveys seek to provide a stronger basis for providing explanations Such explanations are usually in terms of relating individuals behaviours (for example, crime), to initial characteristics of those same individuals (for example, personality), to maturationa features (for example, family socialization) or to intervening event (for example, unemployment). This is facilitated by collecting dat from the same individuals at different, and often key, points in thei life span. In terms of Figure 2.2, an initial sample is selected at point A and the researchers return to the *same* sample members at points I and C. It is because of this procedure of following a group o individuals through the various stages of their development tha longitudinal surveys are sometimes also referred to as cohort studies

One of the most celebrated cohort studies was the National Chil Development Study, which selected a national sample of childre born in one week in 1947 and followed them through until they wer in their late 20s (Douglas, 1964; Douglas, Ross and Simpson, 1968) Within British criminology the longitudinal or cohort study i typified by the Cambridge Study of Delinquent Developmen carried out by West and his associates. The aims and broad strategie of the research were very much influenced by the previous work c the Gluecks in America which had indicated the important influenc of early family socialization and family circumstances on who did and did not, subsequently become delinquent. In 1950 the Glueck had matched 500 'delinquent' boys with 500 'non-delinquent' boy on a number of variables such as ethnic background, intelligence age and the type of neighbourhood in which they lived, and the retrospectively collected data from parents, schools and socia workers about the boys' upbringing and family circumstance (Glueck and Glueck, 1950). The Cambridge study intended to follo these broad aims although by the admission of its director it 'bega as a basic, fact-finding venture without strong theoretical preconcep tions and without much clear notion of where it might lead' (Wes 1982, p. 4). Nevertheless, from the outset a number of broa explanatory variables were identified, influenced by the previo work of the Gluecks.

> We wanted to assess the relative importance of social pressure (such as low income), individual style of upbringing (manifest parental attitude and discipline), personal attributes (such intelligence, physique and aggressiveness) and extraneous even (such as the mischance of being found out). As a by-product, w hoped to identify criteria, present at the early age of 9 or 10, th could be used to predict which individuals would be likely

become delinquent. The Gluecks had claimed that this was possible, but no similar prospective data were available on the predictability of delinquency in an English setting. (West, 1982, p. 3)

Although it followed the basic research aims of the Gluecks, the Cambridge study departed from its American predecessor by adopting a prospective (or longitudinal) rather than retrospective (or cross-sectional) research design. In effect, this involves examining which individuals, out of an initial sample, subsequently become convicted of delinquent acts as opposed to retrospectively studying the backgrounds of those who have already been convicted of delinquent offences. The reason for this is as follows.

Research with established delinquents can be misleading. Once it is known that one is dealing with a delinquent, recollections and interpretations of this upbringing and previous behaviour may be biased towards a preconceived stereotype. Moreover, deviant attitudes may be the result rather than the cause of being convicted for an offence. In spite of the length of time involved we decided to embark on a prospective study, collecting and assessing the sample while they were still below the legal age for finding of guilt by a juvenile court. Those who subsequently became official delinquents could then be compared with their non-delinquent peers, using unbiased assessments made before it was known to which any group belonged. (West, 1982, p. 3)

In effect, this is a longitudinal study, the details of which are as follows. In 1961 a sample of 411 working-class boys, aged 8, was selected from the registers of six state primary schools in an area of London. The area was chosen because it had a reasonably high delinquency rate but also because it was close to the researchers' London office. Girls were not included in the sample, and only twelve boys came from ethnic minority groups. 'In other words, it was an unremarkable and traditional white, British, urban, working class sample. The findings are likely, therefore, to hold true of many similar places in southern England, but they tell us nothing about delinquency in the middle classes or about delinquency among girls or among immigrant groups' (West, 1982, p. 8). The sample members were contacted at the ages of 8–9, 10–11, 14–15, 16–17, 18–19, 21 and 24. (In 1989 they were in their mid-30s.) Finally, at the ages of 23 and 24 sub-sections of the sample were purposively selected and interviewed. These included persistent recidivists, former recidivists who had not been convicted of an offence for five years and, for the purposes of comparison, a random sample of non-delinquents.

In the early years of the boys' development, data were collected from the boys themselves and also from parents. Interviews with the latter were much less structured than the interviews with the sons and were conducted by social workers. Data relating to subsequent delinquency were based upon which of the boys were officially convicted of criminal offences and also upon self-report interviews with the boys in which they were asked about their law-breaking behaviour, irrespective of whether they were officially recorded as having committed criminal acts. The basic analytical strategy of the research programme was to compare the 'delinquent' (officially recorded and self-reported) group – which constituted about one-third of the total sample – and the 'non-delinquent' group with regard to the potential explanatory variables about which data were collected in the early stages of the research. A wide range of findings and assertions emanated from the study as well as a multiplicity of research reports and three main books corresponding to different stages of the research (West, 1969; West and Farrington, 1973, 1977). A central aspect of these findings relates to the identification of five clusters of items which have some statistical relationship to subsequent delinquency. These clusters were summarized in terms of five key factors which, it is claimed, can be used as predictors of delinquency. They are:

1 Coming from a low income family
2 Coming from a large sized family
3 Having parents considered by social workers to have performed their childbearing practices unsatisfactorily
4 Having below average intelligence
5 Having a parent with a criminal record

Each of these factors is taken as having an independent effect on subsequent delinquency. However, analysis indicates a substantial overlap between these factors and some sections of the sample had more than one such factor. Where this occurred it increased the likelihood of subsequent delinquency.

Longitudinal surveys represent a relatively powerful tool in explanatory and predictive studies. As Douglas, a leading exponent of longitudinal surveys, points out, such designs have several advantages over cross-sectional designs. These include the following:

A cohort study allows the accumulation of a much larger number of variables, extending over a much wider area of knowledge than would be possible in a cross-sectional study. This is of course because the collection can spread over many interviews. Moreover, information may be obtained at the most appropriate time: for example, information on job entry may be obtained when it occurs even if this varies from one member of the sample to another. (Douglas, 1976, p. 18)

and

Longitudinal studies are free from one of the major obstacles to causal analysis, namely the reinterpretation of remembered information so that it conforms with conventional views of causation. It also provides the means to assess the direction of effect. (Douglas, 1976, p. 18)

This is not to say, however, that longitudinal surveys are without difficulties. For example, they are very costly and they produce their results very slowly. What is more, the sample can often be seriously depleted by drop-out over the years and there is the possibility of sample members being affected in some way, say in their responses to questions, by the fact that they are part of some on-going study. Further, it is likely that the strengths of such surveys in terms of demonstrating causality are overrated. Even though it is possible to demonstrate temporal sequence by showing that certain actions and behaviours (for example, delinquency) are subsequent to initial characteristics, maturational features and intervening events, longitudinal surveys still rely on statistical evidence of relationships between outcomes and what are taken to be the explanatory variables. Such statistical evidence does not by itself provide conclusive proof as to the causes of delinquency.

A more fundamental methodological critique comes from those who question the implicit positivism in longitudinal surveys and the predictive assumptions which are associated with such positivism. In commenting on the work of the Cambridge group – particularly from the methodological, theoretical and political viewpoint of the National Deviancy Conference – Cohen writes:

In methodology and conception their research went no further than the extraordinary jumble of eclectic positivism that had already rendered the work of the Gluecks such an anachronism. Sociologists could hardly be expected to be impressed with a study which states that although it is more concerned with individual characteristics, it is also interested in the 'demonstration' of the extent to which troublesome boys and other family problems are concentrated amongst the poorest. (Cohen, 1981, p. 229)

It is not just the positivist and predictive assumptions implicit in such surveys that attracts Cohen's criticism but their association with what he and others have termed 'mainstream' and 'conventional' criminology. It is the use of surveys, such as the Cambridge survey, to reach the conclusions that they do, and the 'managerial' and reform pre-suppositions in connection with the use of such findings, that leads critical criminology to challenge the conventional, positivist tradition.

To sum up, social surveys are important sources of primary data. Their contributions are in terms of studies of the correlates of crime (and of delinquency in particular); studies of victims and of the extent of crime; studies of attitudes towards crime and towards personnel and practices within the criminal justice system; and studies of the system itself. The design of surveys is a highly technical task and what, in Chapter 1, was referred to as method validity concerns the extent to which technical problems are overcome. Questions of methodological validity relate to criticisms about the positivist connections of surveys. These include objections about the notion of crime and criminality as an objective and immutable attribute of individuals and also objections about the notion of causality and determinism, particularly the reliance upon correlations to make causal inferences. Positivist and political criticisms of the use of surveys within the criminological enterprise are often combined in the criticisms which have been levelled at official Home Office conventional criminology (see, for example, Cohen, 1981). It is argued that, on the one hand, there is heavy reliance on determinism, particularly in terms of explanations of crime (and particularly working-class crime to the exclusion of crimes of other classes) and, on the other, reform and control functions implicit in the use of survey findings. Whilst having some credence, such criticisms do not amount to a case for the abandonment of surveys. Surveys have valuable contributions to make in terms of facilitating the collection of data from samples which can be generalized to wider populations. What is important is the researcher's awareness of, and sensitivity to, the potential pitfalls of surveys. For example, it is unwise to erect firm causal statements upon correlations between variables (the strength of which is often relatively weak in social science research). Nevertheless, the search for statistical relations can be a useful strategy of suggesting ways in which social life is patterned and structured, ways which can be examined further in subsequent research, perhaps using other methods. What is more, the survey can be a useful way of examining aspects of crime which other methods are unable to examine, or which they are not able to adequately tackle. For example, official statistics are notoriously bad at providing valid estimates of the true extent of crime. Surveys of victims have made valuable contributions in terms of providing some estimate of the 'dark figure' of crime, and therefore of the extent to which official statistics underestimate the true extent of crime.

Official statistics

Here we shall deal very briefly with official statistics since issues concerning the use of officially recorded crime statistics and also the ways in which they relate to theories of different kinds will be discussed more fully in the next chapter. For the moment it is sufficient to signpost such issues.

Official statistics are compiled on a wide range of topics including the amount of crime of differing types, the number of known offenders, aspects of court proceedings and the size and composition of the prison population (see Bottomley and Pease, 1986, for a useful guided tour around statistics on crime and punishment). The main source of official statistics on crime in England and Wales is the annual publication *Criminal Statistics*. An equivalent volume is available for Scotland. Two types of statistics are particularly important. The first concerns offences known to the police. These are known about either because they have been reported by victims or witnesses or because they have been discovered by the police themselves. Such statistics have been traditionally used to measure the extent of crime in society and as a basis for examining trends in crime patterns. They are also used as a basis for explanations of crime by seeking to correlate levels of crime statistically with levels of other phenomena, such as unemployment. This is the ecological, areal or epidemiological tradition of criminology. Second, there are statistics on offences which are cleared up by the police which are used as a measure of police effectiveness in dealing with the extent of crime. Offences which are cleared up include those which are 'taken into consideration', those for which a person is cautioned and those which are not proceeded against for whatever reason, as well as offences for which a person is subsequently charged and found guilty.

The extent to which we can rely on official statistics to measure the extent of crime or a basis for explanations represents one of the classic disputes in criminology (see Eglin, 1987). Basically, three methodological positions can be discerned, each of which represents a distinctive connection between official data and a particular theoretical position. First, the *realist* position is closely associated with the positivist use of data. The basic assumption is that crime represents an attribute of society and of groupings within society and that this attribute can be objectively measured by crime statistics. It is recognized that there are gaps and flaws in such statistics but these are not so great as to obviate their use. In any case, victim surveys (where members of the public are sampled and asked if they have recently been the victim of a crime) and self-report studies (where individuals are sampled and asked if they have recently been the perpetrator of a crime) are viewed as means by which gaps and flaws can be partially corrected. Second, the *institutionalist* position, whic is closely associated with micro-sociological theories, starts from th premise that crime statistics do not represent objective indices c society's criminality but are indicators of the organizational prc cesses and everyday interactions by which certain kinds of action and individuals come to be defined as criminal. The emphasis, then is on methods of research which focus on these processes an interactions and particularly upon subjective aspects such as socia meanings, definitions and stereotypes. Third, the *radical* positio draws much of its strength from radical or critical criminology. Whils not denying the importance of organizational processes and every day interactions, the radical position emphasizes that such processe and interactions are the product of wider social structural arrange ments, particularly those relating to class conflicts. Therefore official crime statistics are themselves products of these wide structural arrangements and should be treated as such.

Each of these positions represents a different viewpoint on th nature of criminal statistics and on the patterns which lie within them What is more, each suggests differing ways in which such statistic should be handled and asks differing questions of them.

Experiments

The experimental tradition in the social sciences represents th application of methods of scientific inquiry to the study of huma behaviour. It has traditionally been associated with the developmen of psychology and particularly with theories and empirical researc based on behaviourism, that is, the study of external behaviour an the psychological processes underlying it. Such experiments woul typically be laboratory-based but not exclusively so. However, th experimental method has not remained the exclusive domain o psychologists. It has, for example, played a central role in th evaluation of social policies – such as policies of crime contro prevention and treatment – via designs which are variously calle field experiments, reforms-as-experiments or evaluation research.

What, in the previous chapter, was described as the correlationa or explanatory survey is typically concerned with providing explana tions of crime on the basis of observed statistical relationships - calculated by correlations – found within the data. The same is als true of the more positivist analyses of official statistics, particularl those which seek to correlate crime levels of areas with othe characteristics of these areas. As noted earlier, to make statement about causality on the basis of such relationships is often quit dubious. Just because crime levels are statistically related to, say levels of unemployment, is not to say that it is changes in the level o employment that cause changes in crime levels although that is always a possibility. The cautionary slogan when reading survey findings on crime is always 'correlations do not by themselves show causality'. The experiment, however, attempts to demonstrate causality directly by building sufficient control into the design so that predicted outcomes can be observed at first hand. Because of its specific goal of searching for causes, the experiment is typically positivist in orientation and in so far as forms of the experimental method are used to evaluate reforms within the criminal justice system there are also strong connections with official, policy-oriented criminology.

Principles of experimentation

Like the social survey, the experiment has developed its own set of procedures, many of which are quite elaborate. Here we can note only its basic design features. The basic aim of the experimental method is to achieve strict control over all variables, except those which are deliberately manipulated, with a view to specifying the effects of such manipulation. The variables which are manipulated are known as independent variables and the subsequent effect is

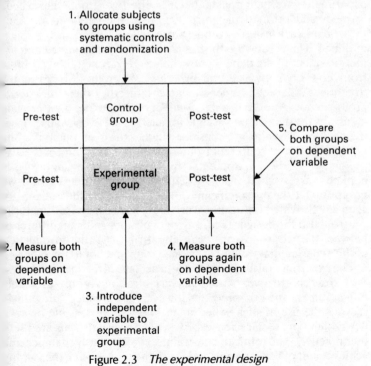

Figure 2.3   *The experimental design*

examined in relation to a specified dependent variable. The control of all variables other than those deliberately manipulated is tackled by attempting to ensure from the outset that two groups of individuals are as identical as possible. In the social sciences it is not easy to ensure that the groups are identical in all respects but methods have been devised to ensure some degree of similarity. For example, individuals are matched to form 'matched pairs' on factors which are seen as important alternative explanatory variables and therefore deserving of control (for example, age, gender, social class). This is one way of introducing what are termed *systematic controls*. The variables on which the groups are matched or controlled are chosen because of their known theoretical relevance to the topic being investigated. Once the pairs have been formed the individuals in each pair are randomly allocated to one of two groups, say, by the toss of a coin. This is a second form of control, known as *randomization*. Its value is that it is not possible to control for all relevant variables systematically, even if they were all known. By randomly allocating individuals from matched pairs to groups it is assumed that most other extraneous variables are more or less equally distributed between the two groups and therefore, for the purposes of the experiment, are held constant. Once the two groups have been formed, and prior to the introduction of the experiment, some measure of each group's average score on the dependent variable is obtained. This is known as the *pre-test* and it represents a preliminary measurement of the dependent variable. Next, one of the groups – from now on known as the *experimental* group – is given the 'treatment', that is, the independent variable; the other – the *control* group – is not. After, say, a six-month period the experimenter again measures the dependent variable for each of the two groups. This is the *post-test*. The aim is to consider whether the experimental group is now significantly different from the control group, and in the way predicted by the experimental hypothesis. Statistical tests are applied to assess whether any subsequent difference between the two groups is statistically significant rather than merely the outcome of chance. Provided all other variables have been satisfactorily controlled at the design stage, any statistically significant difference between the two groups can be causally attributed to the introduction of the experimental treatment to one group and not to the other.

The experimental ideal is not easy to achieve in the social sciences. Such strict control over extraneous variables is really only attainable in *laboratory-type experiments*. However, for practical and ethical reasons the use of such experiments is often not feasible or even desirable in the social sciences. Even where such designs are used the practical and ethical constraints can seriously hamper the achievement of the experimental ideal, thus influencing the validity of the conclusions drawn from such research. Nevertheless, some laboratory-type experiments have been used to study crime and the criminal justice system and these have largely stemmed from the psychological and social psychological influences within the social sciences. One celebrated example is a social psychological examination of interpersonal dynamics in a simulated prison (Haney, Banks and Zimbardo, 1973). Haney and his associates were primarily concerned with the dehumanizing effects of prison life upon prisoners and prison guards alike. Whilst noting the tendency to blame these effects upon the nature of the people who populate the system, both prisoners and guards, they argue that such a viewpoint directs attention away from the acute effects of the prison environment, particularly the social environment. The research design was geared to separating such environmental effects on behaviour from the characteristics of the prisoners and their guards.

The researchers built a simulated prison in a way which made it socially, psychologically and physically comparable to a real-life prison. A sample of twenty-one volunteers was chosen to take part in the experiment, the selection being on the grounds that the individuals did not deviate from the normal range of the population on a number of factors. Half of the volunteers were randomly allocated to the role of prisoner, the other half to the role of guard. The 'prisoners' were arrested and locked in the prison while the guards operated a three-shift system, each shift lasting eight hours. When not on duty they were allowed home. The experiment lasted one week during which the researchers sought to collect data on two aspects. First, they were interested in individual reactions to the situation in which each had been placed. Data about these reactions were collected by using questionnaires, mood inventories, personality tests and interviews. Second, they were interested in interactions between groups and within each group. These were examined by direct observation and video recordings. The researchers were interested in the extent to which being allocated to the role of guard or prisoner and being exposed to the prison environment resulted in emotional, attitudinal and behavioural changes. The results support the assertion that custody had an effect on individual states of both guards and prisoners and also on interactions between and within groups. But, further, it was noted that there were subsequent and important differences between guards and prisoners. For example, the guards directed aggressive and violent behaviour toward the prisoners who, in turn, became docile, depressed and submissive. Overall, the researchers witnessed 'a sample of normal, healthy American college students fractionate into a group of prison guards who seemed to derive pleasure from insulting, threatening, humiliating and de-humanising their peers – those who by chance selection had been assigned to the "prisoner" role' (Haney, Banks and Zimbardo, 1973, p. 96).

Reforms as experiments

Not all experiments take place in such controlled situations, although the same general principles of experimental design apply. A *field experiment* is one which takes place in a natural or 'field' setting in which the researcher is able to allocate subjects to treatment and control groups at random. This may be done, for example, to study the possible effects of some policy change and for this reason they are sometimes also known as *reforms as experiments* (Campbell 1969) or methods of *evaluation research* (Bulmer, 1986b). Field experiments are much more common in criminological research than laboratory experiments and tend to contribute to analyses of the functioning and efficacy of the criminal justice system rather than to explanations of crime and criminal behaviour.

In the main such experiments require 'captive' populations from which to select subjects and it is not surprising, therefore, that the Home Office has been a prime initiator of such experiments. Such research can be viewed as part of what in Chapter 1 was described as the 'correctionalist' tradition in mainstream, conventional British criminology. It can also be seen as part of the social policy and social reform tradition within British social science in general and British criminology in particular. Typically, this tradition has not been heavily laced with theory and certainly not with radical critical theory (that is, theory which has at its centre the critical analysis of the role and functioning of state institutions). It has concentrated on the collection of first-hand data in order to evaluate reforms within a system which it largely takes for granted.

A summary and discussion of some of the main experiments initiated under the Home Office's research programme can be found in Clarke and Cornish's *Crime Control in Britain* (1983), most of which are concerned with evaluating reforms in the treatment and control of offenders. By way of illustration we can look at one of these – IMPACT (Intensive Matched Probation and After-Care Treatment) (Home Office, 1974, 1976). Whereas Haney and his associates were concerned with the control of offenders by incarceration and with the dehumanizing effects on both prisoners and guards, IMPACT focused on the treatment of offenders by the systems and practices of probation in the community. Typical of such officially sponsored criminology, the central problem was defined in terms of what, in the 1970s, was seen as problematic for the system. In the 1980s the value of tough prison regimes was very much on the political agenda and in Chapter 4 we shall examine an experiment which was conducted to evaluate the effect of such regimes particularly the 'short, sharp shock' programme (Home Office, 1984). IMPACT, however, was designed to contribute to decision-making about 'softer' and community-based forms of treatment:

In recent years probation and after-care service has become responsible for an increasing number of offenders, many of whom have already been in borstal, and there is a possibility that in the future probation might be used more extensively as an alternative to an institutional sentence for some offenders. These developments pose questions about how the service can organise its resources to cope with such offenders and how effectively it can treat them. (Home Office, 1974, p. 17)

The research was supported by a broad social-psychological framework in which personality and social situation (and interactions between them) were seen as important determinants of criminal behaviour and each of which require particular forms of treatment. In this latter respect, the researchers distinguished between 'individual treatment' and 'situational treatment'.

'Individual treatment' can be used to describe anything which is said or done to the offender, within the context of the relationship between him and his probation officer, most often in the form of discussions in office interviews. 'Situational treatment' can be used to describe anything which is said or done, not directly to the offender, but in relation to people or circumstances in his social environment, with special reference to situations of family, work and leisure. It will be concerned with practical intervention in these situations, and seek to make active use of the offender's relationships with other people. (Home Office, 1974, p. 18)

This distinction forms the basis of the field experimental design. The design was as follows. Four probation and aftercare areas were chosen – parts of Sheffield, London, Dorset and Staffordshire – and each case in these areas was allocated randomly to an 'experimental' group or a 'control' group. Using social background data and personality data the researchers checked that the two groups were as well matched as possible. The experimental group received its 'treatment' on a low case load with emphasis upon situational intervention. The control cases received what was described as traditional, individual treatment on a case load of normal size. At the end of a period of time, the two groups were compared to see if they differed significantly in terms of a number of outcome variables, principally subsequent reconviction rates. The results of the experiment showed 'no significant differences in one year reconviction rates between experimental and the control cases, therefore producing no evidence to support a general application of more intensive treatment' (Home Office, 1976, p. 22). In short, it could not be asserted safely that intensive individual treatment had a causal effect upon subsequent criminal behaviour.

Internal and external validity

The designs used by Haney and his colleagues and also by the IMPACT team serve to illustrate the ways in which the basic features of the experimental method have been used in criminological research. However, they also pinpoint a number of issues which are central to any evaluation of the contribution of experiments to such research. It is often suggested that experiments – laboratory or otherwise – are high in terms of what Campbell and others referred to as *internal validity* (Campbell, 1969; Campbell and Stanley, 1963). By this is meant the ability, in any particular research study, to rule out alternative explanations and therefore provide strong evidence that a 'treatment' or independent variable really did produce the outcome that is asserted. The argument can be made on two counts. First, by applying the treatment to one group and not to the other, the researcher is able to observe at first hand whether a predicted outcome follows, and is caused by, the introduction of a preceding variable. Whereas cross-sectional surveys have to rely upon correlations between some current behaviour or condition and data collected about past variables in order to make tentative assertions about causality, experimenters have the facility to observe causal sequence directly. Second, strict control over the allocation of individuals to groups by techniques such as matching and randomization provides a means by which other variables can be ruled out in any explanation. The strength of the argument about internal validity rests upon the ability to fulfil both of these conditions. However, the reality is often that experiments carried out in criminology can only be rough approximations to the experimental ideal. This is particularly the case with field experiments such as IMPACT. Whereas there is little problem about the application of treatments to one group and not to the other, the ability to rule out all other competing explanations can be severely restricted. For example, there is a limit to the number of relevant variables which can be matched and an experiment which is carried out in the 'field' as opposed to strict laboratory conditions has little opportunity to rule out or indeed observe all the potential influences on subsequent criminal activity. Where this occurs there can be considerable ambiguity surrounding the interpretation of results. Well designed experiments can make valuable contributions to social science. However, the claim for high internal validity is always a relative one and needs to be examined in relation to the specific design details of particular experiments.

There are other difficulties with the experimental method, one of which is directly related to the introduction of strict experimental controls – particularly in laboratory-type situations – in order to achieve high internal validity. The more that theoretically relevant variables can be controlled, the higher the internal validity of any explanation of findings collected in a particular study. However, the greater the control, the more contrived and atypical of everyday life the experimental situation becomes. This has serious consequences for the extent to which explanations grounded in a specific experiment can be generalized beyond it and can be valid for other people in other situations. For example, one would need to consider whether one can generalize from Haney's simulated prison with its twenty or so 'inmates' to the prison system in general. This is the question of the *external validity* of findings. (Note that Bracht and Glass (1968) further elaborated Campbell and Stanley's concept of external validity by distinguishing between *population validity* – generalizing to wider populations – and *ecological validity* – generalizing to other contexts, settings and conditions.) The dilemma facing any researcher is that the more he or she attempts to establish the clarity of any explanations by experimental controls the greater the dangers of asserting that such explanations are externally valid. Internal validity and external validity are often in inverse relation to one another and the problem is one of achieving an appropriate compromise and balance between them.

Experiments and ethics

Other threats to validity – both internal and external – stem from the danger that the behaviours and other reactions of the experimental subjects are not the outcome of belonging to either the treatment or the control group but reactions to being part of an experiment and due to the knowledge that they are being studied, and for what purpose. Such threats to validity can be tackled by not telling subjects that they are participants in an experiment or, where this is not possible, by issuing a 'cover story' to mask the true purpose of the experiment. There are, however, serious objections on grounds of ethics to the use of individuals as subjects of an experiment without their knowledge and consent. Indeed, there is sound reason for arguing that the principle of 'informed consent' should extend to the use of cover stories, particularly where such stories disguise experimental procedures which have the potential to harm subjects. In Milgram's studies of obedience, for example, subjects were told that they were taking part in a study of the value of punishment to learning, and the procedures implied that subjects were inflicting severe electric shocks on other individuals sitting behind a partition (Milgram, 1973, 1974). In fact, they were participating in a study of the extent to which people will obey what they perceive as legitimate authority and they did not inflict any physical pain or damage on any of their fellow subjects. In demonstrating the almost unlimited boundaries of obedience, Milgram's experiments made a valuable contribution to our knowledge of this matter. However, in deceiving people into believing that they were inflicting severe damage upon other individuals, perhaps to the point of death, and then implanting the realization that they had the potential to kill even though – on debriefing – they were told they had not, Milgram himself inflicted considerable psychological stress and personal humiliation upon his subjects to a point which far outweighs the benefits of his research.

Milgram is not alone in placing individuals in stressful and humiliating situations. For example, by their own admission, Haney, Banks and Zimbardo subjected their 'prisoners' to insulting, threatening, humiliating and dehumanizing behaviours (1973, p. 96). Most experiments are not so extreme. Nevertheless, even where they are not, there are still ethical issues concerning the application of differential treatments and effects. This is the case where participants in the criminal justice system have no say in whether or not they are included in, or excluded from, an experiment, and have no say in whether or not they are in the group that gets the 'treatment'. For example, the cases in the IMPACT experiment were not given a choice as to whether they participated in the research programme and the kind of probation treatment they received was determined by random allocation. Much the same is true of the 'short sharp shock' experiment, to be discussed in Chapter 4, in which youths were allocated at random to tough or standard regimes of punishment. The strength of such arguments is given added weight when participants have no say over their use as research subjects and also are not even aware that they are subjects in the first place. This latter point relates not just to the ethical dimensions of experimental procedures but also to the political aspects of the Home Office's involvement in researching subjects who are, to all intents and purposes, 'captives' in the criminal justice system. Such aspects relate to what in the preceding chapter were described as the political and institutional constraints and influences on criminological research. We shall return to these in Chapter 4.

Observation

Observation encompasses a wide range of activities. It can embrace observation which is overt or covert, highly structured or highly unstructured, and of course there is a variety of approaches between these two extremes. Here we shall focus on participant observation which, in the main, is typified by covert and unstructured means of collecting data. Participant observation is closely associated with the ethnographic tradition in the social sciences, a tradition which has its roots in social anthropology but which has placed an important part in the examination of institutions, communities and sub-cultural groups in modern industrial society. A basic assumption of the ethnographic tradition has always been that any description and explanation of such institutions, communities and groups should proceed by seeking to apprehend the culture of their participants. Valid descriptions and explanations are sought by reference to the everyday meanings and definitions of individuals being studied rather than by imposing what may be alien and distorting concepts of academic social scientists. Data about culture, beliefs, values, meanings and definitions – as well as about the social interactions within which they are embedded – are collected by a variety of methods. Indeed, one of the hallmarks of the ethnographic tradition is that it has steadfastly refused to tie itself to any particular form of data collection. Typically, it eschews the following of fixed protocols as to the way in which data should be collected and analysed. The main sources of data include forms of observation, unstructured interviews, and documents of various kinds. Typically, however, participant observation stands at the centre of any ethnographic investigation.

Participant observation

Within what we have described as the criminological enterprise, participant observation was pioneered by the Chicago sociologists of the 1920s. It was often used in conjunction with life-history interviews (which will be outlined and discussed in the next section). The classic observational studies of the time were Anderson's ethnography of the hobo area of Chicago (Anderson, 1923), Thrasher's study of gangs (Thrasher, 1928) and Cressey's *The Taxi-Dance Hall* (Cressey, 1932). These were subsequently to provide the inspiration for Whyte's celebrated participant observational study of gangs in the Italian neighbourhood of Boston, *Street Corner Society* (1943). In Britain, the development of the new deviancy approach in the late 1960s and early 1970s encouraged a number of ethnographies of deviant sub-cultures such as Young's study of drug takers (Young, 1971). In a commentary on the period, Cohen summarizes the attraction of participant observation as follows:

Some of the original, and even more of the later members of the Deviancy Conference, were on the fringes of what Jock Young nicely called 'the Middle Underground'. Involved as participants, we couldn't resist the lure to be also observers – and make a decent living from it! The romantic, voyeur-like appeal of the subject matter was thus important; one doubts whether a similar group could have sprung up around, say, industrial sociology, educational sociology or community studies. (Cohen, 1981, p. 234)

Beyond the study of deviant and criminal sub-cultures, participant observation has also been used to penetrate the inside workings of the criminal justice system as in Holdaway's *Inside the British Police* (1983), Punch's study of Amsterdam police, *Policing the Inner City* (1979), and of police corruption, *Conduct Unbecoming* (Punch, 1985).

As a method, participant observation refers to the collection of findings by participating in the social world of those one is studying. This involves taking on some role in the social group, or on the fringes of it, and observing, reflecting upon, and interpreting the actions of individuals within the group. Characteristically, participant observers become immersed in the 'field' (see, for example, Burgess's *In the Field*, 1984). Therefore, in comparison with social surveys and experiments, it is often difficult to separate the data from the researcher and to separate the act of collecting data from the act of participating. What is more, participant observation places emphasis upon *naturalism* – that is, studying groups in their natural surroundings with the minimum of disturbance; upon the direct observation of interactions with particular emphasis on the social meanings which such interactions have for the participant; upon empathy in order to achieve understanding of such meanings; and upon descriptions and explanations formulated with direct reference to the everyday descriptions and explanations employed by the participants themselves. Unlike methods of research which are typically associated with the positivist tradition in criminology, participant observation plays down the exclusive collection of quantitative data, the control of variables, and the search for explanations cast in causal terms. Rather, participant observation progresses by a 'discovery-based approach' in which there is a development, refinement and perhaps even reformulation of research ideas in accordance with what is discovered as fieldwork continues. This is what is known as *progressive focusing*. An essential part of this process of refinement and reformulation of generalizations also involves *analytic induction* something akin to the more formal testing of hypotheses by surveys and experiments. It involves the systematic and deliberate search in the data for what appear to be disconfirming cases. By reformulation to take account of such cases, a greater 'fit' between theoretical generalizations and empirical data can be achieved. However, consistent with the 'discovery-based approach', this is continuous process rather than a once-and-for-all test of hypothesis.

In sum, then, participant observation – like other ethnographic methods – involves a constant interchange between theory and data, and while it is conceptually possible to distinguish between data collection, analysis and interpretation, in reality this is often not possible. Further, there are no strict procedures to be followed in the collection of data. However, a succession of *reflexive accounts* written by participant observers describing and reflecting upon their work has gradually yielded an informal set of guidelines to follow and a set of pitfalls to avoid. And because procedures by which data are collected, analysed and interpreted are specific to particular research contexts and particular researchers, such reflexive accounts provide a vital clue to the reliability and validity of findings. We can look, by way of example, at one such reflexive account – Simon Holdaway's reflections on his research into police work – to illustrate some of the practices and difficulties of participant observation.

Observing police culture
Two basic themes guided Holdaway's research. One of these concerned the everyday meanings and definitions which low-ranking police officers use to 'understand' their work, their role and the area and people they police. A second theme concerned the way in which such understandings frame, and perhaps even determine, the way in which officers carry out their police work. In essence, both aspects are concerned with the occupational culture of police officers. Holdaway chose to ground his research in the direct observation of day-to-day policing because the methodological commitments of ethnography to naturalism, empathy and to capturing everyday theorizing are most suited to an analysis of police culture. Most prospective participant observers encounter one problem very early in their research, the problem of gaining *access* to the social field. At one level, this was not a particularly difficult hurdle for Holdaway in so far as he was a serving police officer who had been seconded to university to study for a social science degree and who had recently returned to his duties in the force. However, at another level, he was not necessarily guaranteed access to the occupational culture of police work. As Holdaway points out:

> Research and my previous experience of police work demonstrated the power of the lower ranks, not least their resistance to external control of their work. Any effective research strategy would have to pierce their protective shield if it was to be successful. (Holdaway, 1983, p. 4)

Participant observation may well be used for strong theoretical and methodological reasons – to uncover social meanings and definitions – but an equally powerful rationale is to evade the informal and formal institutional constraints upon social research.

The decision to collect data by participant observation carries with it certain consequences for the researcher. For example, the personal and ethical problems generated by carrying out the dual role of observer and participant which have been recognized by many fieldworkers are echoed by Holdaway.

> Covert research and the ethical questions its raises create conditions of stress within which the sociologist has to live with himself. For example, tension resulted from working with officers who did not share my values and assumptions about policing. Such, it might be said, is the nature of a nasty world; but I had some direct responsibility for the manner in which these officers behaved. I occasionally retreated from conversations and incidents over which I have no control and which I found distasteful. At times I had to deal with an officer whose behaviour exceeded the bounds of what I considered reasonable conduct. These situations could easily get in the way of research and increased the pressure of my work. (Holdaway, 1983, p. 9)

Participant observers also refer to the condition of 'going native', a term which is suggestive of ethnography's early roots in social anthropology. This refers to the problem of over-involvement in the group being studied with the consequence that the researcher becomes more of a participant and less of an observer and also begins to take statements and actions for granted rather than as data to be examined, questioned and treated as 'anthropologically strange'. Punch, an academic sociologist who has also studied police culture, has observed, 'more and more I became involved in a participant role. I chased people, searched people, searched cars, searched houses, held people, and even shouted at people who abused my "colleagues" ' (Punch, 1979, p. 12); and also,

> However, the more I was accepted the more they expected me to act *as a colleague*. In my willingness to be accepted by the policemen I over-identified perhaps too readily and this doubtless endangered my research role. For the patrol group is a cohesive social unit and the policeman's world is full of seductive interest so that it is all too easy to 'go native'. (Punch, 1979, p. 16)

As a serving police officer, the risks of 'going native' were perhaps greater for Holdaway. Indeed, he refers to an almost constant drift into taking things too much for granted, a drift which was only counteracted by what he considered to be particularly distasteful events. He refers to an entry in his research diary:

I reacted badly to the conversation yesterday and want nothing to do with such sentiments. I remember saying to myself, 'Underneath, these policemen are ruthless and racist'. I seem to have slipped into the mould easily during the last couple of weeks and wonder if I should have been so easy with my feelings. The balance of participant observation is one which can so easily be submerged and forgotten. Now it has been brought before me in glaring lights, and all the old issues of ethics – when to speak out, how involved one should get, whose perspective one takes on – loom large. (Holdaway, 1983, p. 10)

This quotation illustrates both the personal character of participant observation and its wider ethical dimensions. Indeed, by the very nature of the method there is bound to be a close interaction between the two. The ethical dilemmas and the personal anguishes about them are exposed not just in the collection of data but also in its publication. There is a number of considerations to balance: first, individual subjects provide the raw material for any such publication and yet they have done so without their knowledge and without any say in the way in which it is portrayed; second, the academic community has a responsibility to research institutional interests and yet to do so may be to incur the wrath of such interests and to close the doors to future researchers. Holdaway aptly summarizes the dilemmas.

Covert researchers therefore take risks when they publish their work: they risk the charges that they are simply engaging in a polemical exposé of an easily accessible 'whipping boy' and that their data are unreliable; they risk the possibility of action for attempting to convey the truth about a powerful institution in British society; they risk the consequences of a calculated deception of trust. (Holdaway, 1983, p. 13)

Holdaway's reflexivity is typical of many such accounts which have been written by participant observers. It has been examined in some detail to give an indication of the flavour of participant observation. The style of participant observation lies in the practices, procedures and commitments of particular researchers in particular contexts and not, as with surveys and experiments, in the technical protocols which can be read in standard textbooks. The account also provides us with some insight into the crucial dilemmas implicit within this mode of research. One of the values of participant observation lies in the theoretical insights to be gained, insights which are made available by methodological commitments to naturalism, and explanation-by-understanding. Another of its values lies in its commitment to overcoming the institutional constraints on research by the development of covert methods of collecting data. It is ironic that adherence to such commitments generates parallel personal and ethical constraints upon the participant observer himself, constraints which emanate from the dual role of being on the one hand participant and observer, and on the other police officer and sergeant. In this respect, the ethics of participant observation can be different from those of experimental research. Nevertheless, as with experiments, the theoretical and other payoffs from participant observation must be set against the potential damage to subjects and researchers alike.

Observation and theory

Earlier we considered the relationship of participant observation to strategies of inquiry and emphasized that, as a methodological approach, as well as a form of data collection, it sought to ground itself in the detailed and careful collection of findings. This does not mean, however, that participant observers are theoretically blind when they enter the field nor that the products of participant observation are without any theoretical basis. The use of participant observation by the Chicago sociologists has already been mentioned. Their detailed studies were located within theories of urban ecology which had been influenced by the positivist-functionalist approach of Emile Durkheim. Theoretically, the city was viewed as a living organism made up of component parts each of which was undergoing development, change and transition in relation to one another. Such development, change and transition was examined by reference to a range of empirical sources. For example, official data were used to map zones or natural areas around the city whereas participant observation was used to collect detailed and appreciative observations about life within these areas. We have also made reference to the use of observational methods by the micro-sociological new deviancy approach which flourished in the late 1960s and early 1970s and which has left a considerable legacy within the criminological enterprise. New deviancy of that period represented a broad church which encompassed specific theoretical influences derived from symbolic interactionism and labelling theory. The central ideas and concepts of these theoretical approaches pointed participant observers to a consideration of why, in certain social situations, only certain kinds of act and certain kinds of individual come to be defined and labelled as deviant and not others. Such dimensions are within the reach of the participant observer who grounds himself in interactions between individuals and law enforcement officers.

However, the concentration on interactions in specific contexts plays down the importance of the historical and structural forces shaping such contexts and the interactions and meanings which develop within them. Such wider historical and structural processes are not directly accessible by participant observation. This is not to say, however, that such methods can have no place within historical and structural analysis. Participant observation can provide valuable insights into specific intersections between social interactions, history and social structure. This is very similar to C. Wright Mills' insistence on the 'sociological imagination' being about the intersections between biography, history and structure (Mills, 1970). It is the task of the sociological imagination, argues Mills, to examine the way in which individual biographies – in terms of both (say, criminal) external career and its internal meaning – shape, and are shaped by, interactions between historical and structural processes. Participant observational studies can give insights into meanings, definitions, actions and interactions in specific contexts. But it cannot *directly* show how such meanings, definitions, actions and interactions have been shaped by wider historical forces. That is the task of theory. We shall return to the problems of establishing meaningful connections between specific ethnographic studies and macro-theories concerned with historical and social structural forces in the third section of the following chapter.

Informal interviews

In social surveys it is not unusual to collect data via a large number of interviews, using a fairly structured questionnaire and from a sample which is representative of the population. Superficial data are collected from a lot of people. Structured questionnaires typically leave little room for the individual to express his or her own feelings and attitudes. It is very much a matter of squeezing oneself into one of a predetermined number of boxes which may or may not be appropriate. There are occasions, however, when the researcher wants to minimize the risk of imposing a false structure. In such instances detailed insightful interviews are conducted, in which individuals are encouraged to answer for themselves and in their own terms. Such interviews are conducted with a much smaller number of people, and they may or may not be representative of the general population. In some cases, interviews are conducted with a sample of one. Where individuals write down details of, and reflections on, their life without the guiding hand of a researcher the life histories are also what Plummer (1983) has called 'documents of life'.

Life histories
The ethnographic life-history interview is very typical of a means by which very detailed and insightful data are collected from one

individual. In the main, such data are 'qualitative', although the collection of statistical data (for example, number of criminal offences) is by no means precluded. The life-history tradition in the social sciences is closely associated with the Chicago school of the 1930s. The Chicagoans were typically eclectic in their collection and analysis of data, and life histories were used alongside official statistics and participant observation in their researches into the urban ecology of the city. Official data provided bases for the mapping of zones within the city, and participant observational methods and the collection of life histories provided means by which the deviant sub-cultures within the zones could be unearthed and understood. In this endeavour, life-history research characteristic- ally shared with participant observation the methodological com- mitments to ethnography outlined in the preceding section.

A typical example of a life history from the Chicago school is Shaw's *The Jack Roller* (Shaw, 1930). This is the story of Stanley, an adolescent boy, who Shaw met in prison, where he had been sent for 'jack rolling' (an activity similar to what we would now describe as the 'mugging' of drunks). It tells, in graphic detail, of Stanley's early upbringing (his mother died when he was young and he hated his stepmother so much that he frequently ran away from home) and his years in various institutions before living on the streets and eventually becoming a jack roller. The data took six years to collect and included a number of stages: first, details about Stanley's arrests were presented to him as signposts around which he could relate his story; second, the verbatim record of this story was presented to Stanley who was then asked to expand it by including greater detail. The life history is not presented by Shaw as an end product in itself but as a way of developing, illuminating and perhaps even subsequently testing hypotheses about criminal behaviour. Of life histories he says:

> They not only serve as a means of making preliminary explorations and orientations in relation to specific problems in the field of criminological research but afford a basis for the formulation of hypotheses with reference to the causal factors involved in the development of delinquent behaviour patterns. The validity of these hypotheses may in turn be tested by the comparative study of other case histories and by formal methods of statistical analyses. (Shaw, 1930, p. 19)

In fact the story of Stanley was only one of a series of case studies which led Shaw to transfer the focus of his investigations from the physical aspects of the environment to the relationships of known criminals with others and to the methods by which criminal attitudes and values were transmitted among them.

Many other life histories have followed in this ethnographic tradition. For example, one of the theoretical contributions to emanate from the Chicago school was Sutherland's *differential association theory*. In essence, this theory is organized around the propositions that criminal behaviour is learned and not inherited and that such learning takes place via interactions within close knit social groups. Learning involves acquiring definitions, motives, drives and techniques which are either favourable or unfavourable to violation of the law. A person becomes delinquent as a result of having learned an excess of definitions, motives and techniques contrary to the law, and such learning comes from association with groups within which such patterns are valued. In emphasizing the definitional aspects of crime, Sutherland's ideas were anticipatory of the subsequent concerns of labelling and other theories which were to have an influence on the new deviancy school within the criminological enterprise. Although the fullest outline of the theory of differential association appeared in 1947 (Sutherland and Cressey, 1947) Sutherland began to formulate his ideas earlier via his interviews with a professional thief (Sutherland, 1937). This reinforces once again the discovery-based approach of the ethnographic tradition and, in this particular case, the life-history approach within this tradition. Empirically, Sutherland's life-history approach influenced much subsequent research including a more recent example of detailed biographical interviews with a criminal, Klockars's *The Professional Fence* (Klockars, 1974). In the United Kingdom Tony Parker has collected a number of life histories including those of a violent working-class recidivist (Parker, 1963), a middle class criminal (Parker, 1967), five female criminals (Parker, 1965), and sex offenders (Parker, 1969), although not in the context of a wider social theory as was the case with the Chicagoans.

Social history research
Life histories have also been used to draw attention to previously neglected aspects of crime and criminal justice. We can mention two broad strands, social history research and feminist research. Recognition of the contributions of historical analyses to the criminological enterprise is fairly recent. This has largely corresponded with the challenge to the ascendency of the predominantly ahistorical positivist tradition from the *radical and critical strands within criminology*. These strands are concerned with the relationship between crime and criminal justice on the one hand and social structure and its historical transitions on the other. Historical materials can provide insights into this relationship (see, for example, Fitzgerald, McLennan and Sim, 1987; Hall and McLennan, 1987; Scraton, 1987). What is more, historical research can be

used to challenge contemporary theories about present-day crime. For example, Pearson's *Hooligan: A History of Respectable Fears* (1983) presents historical materials which seriously question assertions that, in comparison with twenty years ago, current crime levels are at a dangerously high level and require, therefore, to be addressed by tough law and order campaigns. The materials he presents not only support his claim that the seriousness and incidence of crime in past centuries is no different from today but also the existence of what may be termed a 'twenty-year rule', that is, the constant use throughout this century of the assertion by politicians and others that life was so much more tranquil and idyllic twenty years ago.

Much historical research inevitably relies upon documentary sources. However, the life-history interview, and oral history in general, has also been important to social history research. Such histories are used not just to tell a personal story but also to shed some light on social behaviour, social structure, the functioning of social institutions within that structure, and relationships between them. One such life history is that of Arthur Harding who describes community life in the East End of London at the turn of the century, particularly the operation of the criminal underworld in that community and relationships with the police (Samuel, 1981). Harding describes petty crime as a way of life for most people in the 'Jago' and as such questions the validity of the dominant explanation of the time that criminality was to be found among a small number of people who represented, as the biological positivists would have it, a biological throwback. Indeed, he says of the thieves who populated the coffee shop, 'of the whole gang only one became a real professional criminal conforming to the characteristics of Cesare Lombroso's ideal criminal' (Samuel, 1981, p. 113). What is more, his descriptions of police actions provide warnings about the validity of assertions about the harmony of relations between the police and working-class communities. The validity of Harding's descriptions and reflections must also not be accepted unquestioningly. Nevertheless, life histories such as his provide a means by which received theories can be questioned and revamped.

Feminist research

Much criminological research comprises studies by men about men. In recent years, however, there has been a growing interest in gender as an important dimension in social science and this has been reflected in criminological work. Going hand in hand with this there has been increasing concern with addressing issues specific to feminist research and feminist research methods (see, for example, Roberts, 1981). Feminist research methods coalesce around the

viewpoint that positivist, quantitative approaches are male domi-
nated and by their procedures and structure miss many of the issues
which are specific to women (see, for example, Mies, 1983). Two
aspects of this can be noted. One relates to how data should be
collected and from whom. The formal interview is viewed as a form
of exploitation stemming from the differential relationship between
researched and researcher (particularly if the former is female and
the latter male). Oakley (1981), for example, argues that formal,
survey-type questionnaires and interviewing are inappropriate in
feminist research because they objectify women. She argues instead
for semi-structured strategies which avoid an exploitative and
hierarchical relationship between interviewer and interviewee.

A second, and related, aspect concerns the way in which dominant
theories influence the way in which questions are framed, data are
collected, and categories for statistical analysis are developed. Such
questions, data, and categories are not inherently 'male'. Rather,
they can take the form that they do because they are posited on
existing theories and research derived from 'malestream' literature.
This leads to further support for the argument that feminist research
methods should be 'qualitative' and non-positivist. In this way, the
experiences of women can be exposed in their true form rather than
being distorted, degraded and even hidden by potentially arbitrary
and abstract categories used for data collection and analysis. Pat
Carlen's *Criminal Women* (1985), which is grounded in life stories of
four women, is illustrative of this viewpoint. She not only takes issue
with the traditional explanations of female crime, given in terms of
the failure of individual women to adjust to their supposedly natural
destinies, which followed Lombroso and Ferrero's *The Female
Offender* (1895), but also with any theory which is based upon
misleading distinctions between masculine and feminine criminality.
She argues that any theories, even if they be self-styled, radical, or
Marxist, must be as reductionist as the much-maligned biological-
positivist ones. She writes:

> the point remains that there can be no one theory of women's crime
> because there can be so such thing as the 'typical' criminal woman
> – either in theory or practice. The book is about four criminal
> women whose stories are important primarily because they deny
> the existence of the criminal woman. (Carlen, 1985, p. 10)

Semi-structured interviews

So far we have considered detailed interviews with single individuals,
and particularly the life-history interview. It would be wrong to
believe that detailed interviews cannot be used with much larger
samples. However, where they are, they tend to be more structured

than life-history interviews and typically use *aides mémoire* or check-lists of topics to be covered. For example, Baldwin and McConville's (1977) study of plea bargaining in the Birmingham Crown Court used semi-structured interviews with 121 defendants, all of whom initially intended to plead not guilty to an offence but who subsequently changed their plea just before the trial or soon after it had started.

Another example comes from Bennett and Wright's *Burglars on Burglary* (1984). The authors were concerned with uncovering burglars' perceptions and definitions of their own and others' action with particular reference to whether or not to commit a burglary. Data were collected from 128 convicted burglars and the semi-structured interview was used because 'it allows subjects to speak freely and at length using their own concepts and terminology. As the interviews can be tape-recorded and transcribed verbatim respondents' methods of describing and explaining their behaviour can be preserved' (Bennett and Wright, 1984, p. 7). The researchers found that the definitions and perceptions of burglars which determined their decisions as to whether or not to commit a burglary were not necessarily the same as the assumptions built into crime prevention programmes and practices about such decision-making. In this way, the research not only contributed to theory, particularly our understanding of the definitional and perceptual referrents of decision-making and criminal actions, but also had strong implications, and indeed recommendations, for crime-prevention policy. Qualitative research, and not just quantitative research, can contribute to policy-making although its credibility within the definitions and perceptions of policy-makers may not be as high. (For a discussion of the contributions of qualitative research to policy making, see Bulmer, 1986c.)

Psychological interviews

Up to now we have been primarily concerned with the sociological interview, whether the detailed, unstructured interview with a single individual or semi-structured interviews with a sample of a hundred or so. Conclusions from such interviews can be used to suggest policy making interventions of various kinds. Yet, by its very nature, the interview is particularly suitable to the examination of individual and psychological influences on actions and in some cases the interview may be linked to interventions of a different kind, that is, therapeutic interventions in the lives of individuals. Detailed, unstructured and one-to-one interviews are associated with what has been termed the 'new psychology' (see, for example, Dallos and Sapsford, 1981). Dallos and Sapsford describe this psychology as being characterized by a dislike of positivist and behaviourist explanations in favour of an emphasis upon understanding what meaning particular actions (say, crime) or particular contexts (say, prison) have for an individual.

> Most fundamental of all is the tenet that the proper subject matter of psychology is the *meaning* of actions and situations, not the causes of behaviour. We may live in a physical world, and to some extent our potential for action may be limited by physiology or environmental conditioning. However, what is seen as more important is the fact that we are thinking, probing and interpreting beings who live in a complex culture and are free, up to a point, to put our own construction on events and act accordingly. (Dallos and Sapsford, 1981, p. 433)

In this context, the detailed interview is used to elicit individual and personal meanings. In some cases such interviews employ repertory grid techniques as devised by George Kelly. Kelly devised these techniques in conjunction with his general thesis that every person is his or her own scientist, seeking to predict and control his own world (Kelly, 1955). This is done by using a set of personal constructs which are ways of perceiving and interpreting what is happening and what is likely to happen. Such perceptions and interpretations form the basis for subsequent actions. The grid technique is used by presenting individuals with words or objects which act as triggers for articulations of personal constructs.

Detailed psychological interviews, of which the use of repertory grid techniques is but one example, are typically used in certain applied areas of criminology, such as psychiatry, probation work and clinical psychology. Interviews are used to build a *case study*. In some instances the interviews are conducted by a researcher-cum-therapist who is not only collecting data for research purposes but also assisting in therapy and in attempting to bring about changes in the individual. What is more, this can be extended into a type of experimental method favoured in clinical psychology, which is known as the *single case research design*. Essentially, this is a hybrid between the case study and the experiment. Rather than attempting to make group comparisons the technique treats an individual as the focus of the experiment, with therapeutic interventions or treatments introduced and subsequently withdrawn in order to examine the efficacy of a treatment.

Interviews and theory

The examples used throughout this section have shown ways in which interviews have contributed to the analysis of what, in Chapter 1, were described as the central problems of the criminological enterprise. Implicit within the range of examples there are different connections between the use of interviews and criminologica theories of particular kinds (for example, urban ecology, new deviancy); and also different methodological roles for the use of interview data in relation to theory in general. We can make the latter more explicit by drawing upon a categorization, developed by Plummer (1983), of the connections between theory and the method of personal document research. In fact, this categorization could easily be applied to all the types of interview outlined here as well as to the use of observational methods discussed in the preceding section.

First, Plummer distinguishes 'theory as orientation' whereby the central concepts of any specific theory provide an agenda with which to enter the field. This agenda influences – but does not determine – what is seen as problematic, what data are collected in relation to that problem, how they are categorized and subsequently analysed. For example, Maurice Punch describes how central concepts of symbolic interactionism, such as 'negotiation', 'social construction' and 'social process', influenced his research on the police in Amsterdam:

Underlying my selection of data and my interpretation of material for this study is a theoretical perspective that also colours my view of control, deviance and organizational reality. Working within the symbolic interactionist paradigm my approach particularly builds upon and extends those who adopt an interactionist perspective on the police. People working within this paradigm emphasize the extent to which social life is fragile, negotiated and in a constant process of construction in interaction with others. (Punch, 1979, pp. 1–2)

Second, there is 'building theory from life histories', which is most closely associated with Glaser and Strauss's *The Discovery of Grounded Theory* (1967) and with what earlier was described as 'the discovery-based approach'. The development of theory as a result of its constant interaction with data can take place within a particular study or can be a long-term process, as in the systematic formulation of Sutherland's theory of differential association in 1947 which had its foundations in data collection and analysis for his much earlier *The Professional Thief by a Professional Thief* (1937). Third, Plummer distinguishes 'falsification and the negative case'. Here life histories or case studies are used to examine the 'fit' between theory and empirical data, often by the deliberate and systematic search for cases which self-evidently do not fit existing theory. Typically, such data do not lead to the rejection of any particular theoretical system but to its amendment to take into account the 'negative' cases. Fourth, there is the use of qualitative data as a means of 'illustrating theory'. Plummer refers to Rettig, Torres and Garrett's (1977) telling of the life of a Puerto Rican drug addict and criminal via the use of established criminological theories such as Merton's strain theory, Sutherland and Cressey's differential association theory, and the variants of labelling theory. Finally, and perhaps most interestingly, Plummer notes a significant theoretical and methodological development of the 1970s and 1980s within which documents and other such sources of data are treated not as means of studying the social world but as objects of inquiry in their own right. He describes this as treating 'life history as "text" '. This approach is most closely associated with the theoretical ideas of Foucault (whose main theoretical writings are *Discipline and Punish* (1977); *History of Sexuality*, Vol. 1 (1979); vol. 2 (1986). Basically, Foucault is interested in networks of power and control in society and the way in which these are determined by knowledge and by unofficial or official discourses. The latter could include, for example, Lord Scarman's report on the Brixton riots (Scarman, 1981) or Lord Popplewell's report on violence at soccer matches (Home Office, 1985) as defining and constructing what is 'good' and 'bad', 'right' and 'wrong'. For Foucault, discourses are not merely means of communication but its very substance. Hence the need to treat documents as objects of inquiry or 'text'. One such text is Foucault's history of Pierre Riviere, a man who murdered his mother, sister and brother in 1835. The following, quoted by Plummer, illustrates the way in which the history is viewed as a document which embodies and expresses power relations at a particular time:

> Documents like those in the Riviere case should provide material for a thorough examination of the way in which a particular kind of knowledge (for example, medicine, psychiatry, psychology) is formed and acts in relation to institutions and the roles prescribed within them (for example, the law with respect to the experts, the criminally insane and so on). They give us the key to the relations of power, domination and conflict within which discourses emerge and function and hence provide material for a potential analysis of discourse (even of scientific discourses) which may be both tactical and political and, therefore, strategic. (Foucault, 1978, pp. xi–xii)

Data and method

We can now bring together the preceding sections. A number of distinctions have been used to draw attention to the range of data used within criminological research. Such distinctions are not hard and fast and run the risk of portraying false dichotomies. For example, the dividing lines between qualitative and quantitative data and between primary and secondary data are ones that are often difficult to draw. Nevertheless, the distinctions provide a framework for recognizing the types of data used in any particular study and for examining and evaluating the assumptions built into such data. An evaluation of such assumptions is important to a consideration of the validity of data. Different types of data are used across the criminological enterprise as a whole and sometimes also within particular studies. The use of different types of data within one study to open up varying facets of crime and also to improve validity is known as *data triangulation* (Denzin, 1970).

A substantial part of this chapter has been concerned with data sources. There is not a precise, or even necessary, relationship between types of data and types of method. Labels such as 'social survey' or 'reforms as experiments' also run the risk of crudely compartmentalizing ways of collecting data. For example, methods often merge one into another. Within ethnography, life-history interviews can often be indistinguishable from forms of observation; and before–after surveys are very similar to experiments. Further, within any given method there can be variations in the types of data collected. For example, social surveys generate hard statistical data and also qualitative accounts via open-ended questions. Nevertheless, the preceding sections have noted broad connections between types of data and types of method. These are summarized in Figure 2.4.

Data and method triangulation

The triangulation of data within criminology is mirrored by the triangulation of method. This is what Denzin (1970), following Webb *et al.* (1966), refers to as 'methodological triangulation'. Denzin describes two forms of such triangulation; within-method and cross-method. Within-method concerns the use of differing strategies within a broad research method. It would include, for example, the use of structured questions in a survey to generate statistical data and open-ended questions to generate qualitative descriptions. Cross-method refers to the procedure of using dissimilar methods of research to examine the same phenomenon. It could include, for example, the use of official statistics, observational methods and life histories to examine deviant sub-cultures (as, for example, with the Chicago sociologists). The value of such cross-method triangulation is that it balances the strengths and the weaknesses of differing methods. What is more, as we have seen, methods have particular methodological assumptions and connections with types of theory.

Figure 2.4 Data–method connections

	(A)	(B)	(C)	(D)	(E)
Quantitative–qualitative	Primarily quantitative but supporting qualitative data are often derived from open-ended questions	Quantitative data	Primarily quantitative but sometimes qualitative accounts of subjects' reactions to 'treatments' are provided	Primarily qualitative but quantification is not ruled out, particularly with more structured forms of observation	Primarily qualitative but, as with observation, numbers are not excluded. These are likely to relate to 'objective' features, e.g. number of offences
	(F)	(G)	(H)	(I)	(J)
Individual–social	Surveys typically collect data from individuals but, in analysis, data are often aggregated to make assertions about social groups	Social data, although they represent compilations of data about individuals and individual acts	Experiments collect data from, and about, individuals but data are social in so far as experiments seek to make assertions about group differences as outcomes of treatments	Primary aim is collection of social data about interactions but sometimes with a view to making assertions about features of social structure	Interviews collect data from individuals. Data may be exclusively about individuals, but may also seek to make assertions about the social groups of which they are part
	(K)	(L)	(M)	(N)	(O)
Past–present	Descriptive surveys mainly collect present data. Explanatory surveys seek to correlate present data about individuals with past data about same individuals	Sometimes past data, sometimes present data	Experiments collect present data about groups, using post-tests, to be compared with past data collected in pre-tests, on a before–after basis	Primarily present data collected about contemporary interactions but some historical contextualization may be provided	May be present data or past data. Life history interviews are primarily concerned with past data
	(P)	(Q)	(R)	(S)	(T)
Primary–secondary	Primary, but there can be secondary analysis of survey findings	Secondary	Primary	Primary	Primary, but may make use of existing documents and other data sources

Figure 2.4 Data–method connections

The use of differing methods, therefore, maximizes the theoretical value of any research by revealing aspects of phenomena which the use of one method alone would miss.

We can illustrate the use of such triangulation within a specific study. In the discussion of the interview method, reference was made to Karl Klockars's *The Professional Fence* (1974). As with any study it is vital to assess the validity of such research. Two aspects of such validity can be noted: external validity and internal validity. External validity is concerned with the extent to which conclusions can be generalized to other people, in this case other professional fences, and also to other contexts and time periods. With regard to the internal validity of ethnographic accounts it is necessary to ensure that the account reported is an accurate representation of the fence's perceptions, meanings, definitions and actions. In a reflexive account, Klockars outlines his data-collection procedures. In the main, these included detailed life-history interviews but were complemented by corroborative interviews with the fence's friends and family, observation of his dealings with thieves, customers and others, and the use of personal documents.

> I managed to secure some documents which corroborated Vincent's testimony. These included newspaper articles, orphanage records, probation records and many miscellaneous documents which Vincent himself showed me. Among these personal documents were letters, photographs, bills, sales receipts, stock certificates, and licenses. I also saw merchandise and money. (Klockars, 1974, p. 224)

The use of such multiple methods provides an example of cross-method triangulation to increase the validity of Klockars' account. Such triangulation need not, however, be used simply within the confines of a particular study. The use of a range of methods across the criminological enterprise as a whole is also highly desirable. This is for two reasons. First, as was argued in Chapter 1, this enterprise exhibits plurality of problems, problems which are sufficiently wide ranging to require an equally wide-ranging selection of methods of collecting data. Second, social phenomena, like crime, have different aspects and dimensions to them. A criminal act is not only something which can become part of the official statistics on crime but also something which has meaning for both the perpetrator and the victim, and such meaning is deserving of data which does justice to its quality and its intensity in a way that statistics cannot. Theory plays an important role in drawing attention to the differing aspects of crime and the criminal justice system which are worthy of investigation. It is appropriate, therefore, to look at types of criminological theories and to reinforce some of the ways in which they relate to the types of methods of research which we have detailed in the preceding sections. The main connections between types of theory and types of method are summarized in Figure 2.5.

The theoretical connection

A consideration of methods of criminological research cannot be isolated from a consideration of theory. Here we introduce four broad theoretical approaches or tendencies which, in the main, emanate from the psychological and sociological contributions to criminology. It is, however, necessary to introduce a few cautionary words. First, the broad theoretical approaches hide within them differences between specific theories and specific theorists. However, in a book primarily concerned with methods of collecting data some licence is exercised in the presentation of theoretical positions. They are presented in such a way as to permit some charting of typical theory-method connections. Second, the broad theoretical sweeps are described in terms of features which have significance for this theory–method connection. In particular this relates to their commitment to measurement, to explanations cast in causal terms, and to explanations using particular levels of analysis. This inevitably involves playing down other differences between the broad approaches, for example, commitments to underpinning models of society. Some criminological theories are posited on a consensual-functionalist approach (crime as a departure from society's values) as opposed to a conflict model (crime as the outcome of class or other conflict). Such differences are not considered here. Third, the distinctions which are made between theoretical approaches are not necessarily watertight. This is because theories have a tendency to borrow one from another and also to merge. Developments within criminological theory, just like in any other area of social science, occur as existing ideas are developed and refined and others rejected or reverted. The categorization presented here is a simple version of what is a complex area. With such qualifications out of the way, we can turn to a consideration of different ideal typical theoretical approaches.

Theories based on individual predispositions to crime
Such theories stem largely from the biological and psychological influences in criminology. The primary determinant of crime is considered to lie within the individual and explanations of variations in criminality are cast in terms of differences between individuals. Within this broad sweep lies the classic debate, which is not specifically criminological, between 'nature' (the-criminal-as-born)

	Surveys	Official statistics	Experiments	Observation	Interviews
Individual differences	(A) Surveys used to correlate criminal actions of individuals with individual differences in terms of personality, attitudinal and socialization variables, often using longitudinal designs	(B) Official statistics are social data and are not used to seek explanations in terms of individual differences	(C) Experiments can be used to examine the way in which 'treatments' affect the subsequent behaviours of individuals of particular backgrounds and dispositions	(D) Observation focuses primarily on social interactions and the meanings embedded in them. This includes a concern with individuals but only as actors in interactions	(E) Interviews collect data from, and about, individuals. In some instances – as with the single case study – this is to examine individual backgrounds and dispositions
Sociological determinants	(F) Surveys used to measure levels of crime within particular sections of society with a view to seeking the social correlates of these levels	(G) Official statistics provide bases for examining the extent of crime, the social and ecological distribution of crime and the sociological determinants of these	(H) Experiments are not typically associated with the sociological tradition because controlled experiments are not feasible in macro-situations, even if ethical. Reforms as experiments sometimes used	(I) Participant observation is used, often in conjunction with quantitative methods to provide 'appreciative' understanding of social and cultural responses to wider social processes	(J) Life-history interviews used, often in tandem with participant observation to carry out 'appreciative' studies and by looking at individual careers, to 'humanize the deviant'
Micro-sociological	(K) Surveys based on questionnaires are	(L) Official statistics are not viewed as	(M) Experiments are not favoured because of	(N) Observational methods, especially	(O) Interviews are often used in conjunction

	Surveys	Official statistics	Experiments	Observation	Interviews
	rarely used because of their perceived inappropriateness to the collection of data about interactions and about social meanings	objective indices of crime levels but as social constructions. The focus is on statistics as the outcome of small-scale interactions and processes	the degree of control implicit in their design. This precludes the collection of 'naturalistic' data about interactions	participant observation, focus on small-scale interactions in particular contexts and as such generate naturalistic data as bases for micro-sociological propositions	with observational methods to collect qualitative data about the meaning individuals attach to actions and interactions
Structural-historical	(P) Surveys do not give access to structural or historical processes. They are, however, objects of interest in their own right as means by which the state legitimise policies of crime control	(Q) Official statistics are not viewed as objective indices of crime levels, nor as the outcome of small interactions. Rather, they are a reflection of fundamental economic and class relations in society	(R) Experiments do not give access to structural or historical processes. Reforms as experiments are of interest in their own right as means by which the state justifies reforms	(S) Observational methods provide data on the way in which historical and social structural processes are worked out in particular contexts	(T) Life-history interviews may provide some access to historical processes. Also, they facilitate an examination of individual biographies as lying at particular historical-structural intersections

Figure 2.5 Theory-method connections

and 'nurture' (the-criminal-as-made). The former views criminal propensities as innate and passed to individuals by heredity. Some aspects of this approach have already been considered in Chapter 1. For example, the early Italian biological positivists, such as Lombroso, portrayed individual criminality as the outcome of certain physiognomic features. Other theorists, such as Eysenck, focus upon inherited personality traits, certain constellations of which make an individual less amenable to socialization into non-criminal values and actions. On the 'nurture' side, the focus is more upon aspects of the individual's socialization which either directly cause him or her to commit criminal acts or which produce predispositions to criminal behaviour and perhaps also to other forms of anti-social behaviour. Typically, the focus is on the early and formative socialization within the family. An example of this is the early work of West and his associates at the Institute of Criminology, Cambridge, which we considered in the section on surveys. Longitudinal surveys were used to collect data about, amongst other things, the family background and socialization of boys, with which to correlate other data about subsequent deliquency. Such theories may focus on family socialization and also on the wider social environment. Whether 'nature' or 'nurture', the main interest is upon individual differences and upon the way in which either the individual's physiological and psychological makeup or the individual's socialization, or both, result in subsequent criminal actions on his or her part.

The nature of the explanation is typically deterministic and causal. Statistical correlations are sought between data about an individual's makeup or background and subsequent crime. Such correlations are used as a basis for making assertions about determinants of crime. Explanations such as these are made without reference to the meanings individuals attach to events and to their own or others' actions.

Theories based on sociological determinants

Such theories focus upon the social group, social interactions or society, rather than upon the individual. Here the influence of Durkheim is important. Durkheim's work was avowedly sociological in his endeavour to demonstrate that social phenomena (such as suicide or crime) could be explained at a social level rather than in terms of 'aggregate' psychology. Such phenomena were viewed by Durkheim as 'social facts', that is, as features of societies rather than of individuals. Social facts, he believed, should be studied by reference to indices of society (such as official statistics) rather than by collecting data from, and about, individuals. Since that time, the sociological tradition has charted a number of paths. For example,

Durkheim influenced the work of the Chicagoans and also of Robert Merton. Merton's strain theory saw deviancy as arising from the discrepancy between aspirations which were culturally induced and which could not be realistically achieved by legitimate means. In turn, the theoretical ideas of the Chicagoans and of Merton had, in their differing ways, an influence upon the sub-cultural theories of delinquency which flourished in America in the mid-century (see, for example, Cloward and Ohlin, 1961; Cohen, 1955; Matza, 1969).

Although there are differences between these theories, what they share in common is analysis at the level of the 'social' rather than at the level of the individual. All view crime as being socially induced. In the main, the forms of explanation are typically deterministic. Durkheim represented the archtypical sociological positivist. For him, society was an external constraining reality and 'social facts', such as crime, could only be explained in these terms. The subsequent developments, particularly sub-cultural and differential association theories, presented a much softer form of determinism. Within this, society and its structure are viewed as providing an overarching framework within which there is scope for individual free will and action. There is a greater focus on interaction and transmission of criminal values and more scope for methods of research such as observation and detailed interviews, which facilitate an understanding and an appreciation of these aspects.

Theories based on micro-sociology
The two broad theoretical strands we have considered share a deterministic approach to explanations of crime. They differ, however, in so far as one emphasizes individual predispositions to crime whereas the other focuses on explanations in terms of social forces and constraints. Micro-sociological approaches have different theoretical thrusts. In the first place they play down explanations in deterministic terms seeking instead to portray crime as something which is constructed in small-scale interactions in particular contexts. Secondly, they choose to focus upon the social meanings and definitions of individuals and upon the ways in which these are expressed in interactions between law-enforcement agents and those who subsequently are labelled as criminal. This is instead of analysis which is explicitly at the level of the individual or at the level of social structure.

The theories founded upon these broad assumptions make a number of contributions to the analysis of crime and the criminal justice system. First, they view individuals as being actively involved in constructing their own social world rather than as automatons acting out their destinies in a world which is already pre-constituted for them. The existence of social structure is not denied but is played down as an all-constraining reality and as the sole means of explaining crime. Second, social constructions are seen as the outcome of the way in which individuals define and give meaning to events, contexts and situations, and of the ways in which individuals and groups of individuals subsequently act on the basis of such meanings and definitions. Third, a central theme of any analysis is that there is no consensus on values and ideas in society. Therefore, there can be, and usually are, different and competing social constructions of the social world. Further, such social constructions are not static and are constantly being reworked and reinforced in interactions in specific contexts.

Crime, then, is not something with an objective quality but something which is socially constructed. What is more, the view that 'criminals' constitute a breed apart (either because of individual make-up or social circumstances) is viewed as being inappropriate. 'Criminals' do exist, but it is argued that they do so because of the meanings, definitions and constructions of those with power to apply criminal labels and not because of individual physiological or psychological predispositions or of social structural determinants. In this way, micro-sociological approaches have extended the criminal agenda to include questions about the practices and policies of those who work within the criminal justice system and those who enforce and apply the law.

The basic features of this broad approach can be found in symbolic interactionism, in the labelling approach of Lemert (1967) and Becker (1963, 1974) and what, on the foundation of the National Deviancy Symposium in 1968, subsequently became known as new deviancy theory. It also has its roots in some 'softer' deterministic approaches mentioned in the preceding section, which as well as emphasizing the primacy of social structure, also recognized the importance of examining meanings, interactions and the processes by which criminal values are transmitted.

Methodologically, micro-sociology seeks an explanation of the interactions which take place between individuals and law enforcement officers in specific contexts and as such eschews the idea of positivist and universal explanations. It chooses methods which give access to such interactions and the meanings and definitions embedded in them and also gives particular credence to the accounts which individuals provide of what they are doing and why. As such it shuns the hard quantitative data associated with official statistics, surveys and experiments in favour of the more appreciative data of observational and life-history styles.

Theories based on historical and structural intersections
The distinctiveness of this category can be explicated by reference to the preceding three broad theoretical tendencies. First, there is little,

if anything, in common with theories concerned with individual predispositions to crime. The idea that there is a separate and distinct class of people who are criminal, and that there membership of this class is determined by individual physiological or psychological makeup, is rejected. Analytically, individuals are only of interest in so far as their destinies are shaped by where they stand in the intersections between social structure and history and not in terms of individual backgrounds. Second, in its emphasis upon social structure this approach shares much in common with theories posited on sociological determinants. It is interested in the connection of crime to social disorganization and to sub-cultures, but particularly from the viewpoint of the way in which these are underpinned by economic and class relations in society. In this sense, it forcefully rejects the consensual-functionalist assumptions of theories based on sociological determinants in favour of a conflict model, and particularly a class conflict model. Within this formulation crime reflects, and is the outcome of, class relations and of the way in which they historically evolve. Such a historical dimension is explicitly in terms of social structure, and particularly the development of advanced industrial capitalist society, and not – as in other theories – in terms of the antecedents of individuals which are deemed to propel them into crime.

Historical-structural explanations, like those founded on micro-sociology, recognize the need to focus on the way in which the law is enforced as well as on those who subsequently become labelled as criminal. In this sense they share a wish that the criminological agenda includes questions about the criminal justice system as well as questions about those individuals who commit crimes. However, the historical-structural approach gives a central role to the concept of power in any analysis. Typically, this is in contrast to the appreciative studies of micro-sociology which either ignore matters of power or treat them as a background against which to examine interactions between individuals and law enforcement officers.

Power relations between the criminal and the law enforcer are traced back to fundamental economic and class relations in society. The importance of such relations is not restricted to the way in which law is enforced but also extends to an analysis of what, in the first place, is legally defined as criminal. In examining the role of power in law enactment and law enforcement, crime is located within wider questions of social control and of the role of the state in such control.

There are many variants of this broad theoretical strand. The most explicit formulation is the 'new criminology' approach of the mid-1970s which represented an attempt to produce a comprehensive and radical criminology. It grew out of the early new-deviancy approaches and incorporated many of its ideas. For example, it shared an interest in the social processes by which law is applied. However, it sought to introduce a radical edge by seeking to explain such processes in terms of intersections between social structure and history.

The radical approaches are heavily theoretical. They are also radical in so far as their theoretical formulations represent challenges to what in Chapter 1 was termed conventional criminology. They are, therefore, critical of the range of methods typically associated with conventional criminology and particularly of the slavish use in search of causality. However, such radical criminologies are not against empirical investigation *per se*. For example, value is placed upon methods which provide some access to historical and social structural processes and to intersections between them. These could include case studies, life-history interviews, and, particularly, social history research. Case studies based upon observational methods of life-history interviews can be used to focus upon such intersections (for example, a particular criminal sub-culture at a particular time). Also, life histories, documents and social history research in general provide means for examining historical patterns. Radical approaches are also interested in the more conventional data sources of surveys, experiments and official statistics, but, in the main, their interest lies in examining their use by the state's crime control apparatus.

To sum up, we have outlined four broad theoretical frameworks in the criminological enterprise. In many respects they represent alternative and competing positions. Each has developed by responding to the others and in many cases inverting their central tenets. At times, criminology has been a battlefield with these theoretical approaches representing heavily fortified and unassailable fortresses. However, there are other ways of relating to theory. Each theoretical approach can be seen as contributing questions to the criminological agenda – such as those summarized in Chapter 1 – the value of which can be assessed by empirical research and in terms of the insights each provides about crime and about the operation of the criminal justice system. The subject matter of criminology is not uni-dimensional and there is value in a plurality of theoretical approaches in terms of the multiplicity of facets it exposes for investigation – facets concerned with the causes of criminal behaviours, the societal distribution of crime, the social construction of crime in interactions, the experiences of crime by victims, and the connections of crime to social structural and historical processes, to mention but a few. What is more, the use of different theoretical approaches as sources of questions or propositions is not to be confined to the criminological enterprise as a whole. It also has the potential for the setting of a theoretical and research agenda within any given study.

Theoretical triangulation

Reference has already been made to triangulation of data and triangulation of method. The use of different theoretical approaches can be called triangulation of theory. Denzin (1970) applies the term theoretical triangulation' to the use of a range of theories in a particular study but there is no reason why, as here, they should not also be applied to their combined and complementary contributions to the enterprise as whole. As Denzin points out, the benefits of such triangulation are numerous. First, it provides an antidote against a researcher being blinkered by a particular theoretical approach. It encourages the formulation of a wide range of, possibly competing, propositions, the respective values of which can be subsequently examined. Second, triangulation ensures that the greatest use is made of any set of observations in so far as they are not merely used to test a proposition specific to one theory, but can be used to relate to as many propositions as possible. Third, triangulation encourages systematic and continuous interchange between theory and research in so far as it is very rare that any investigation unambiguously supports, confirms or disconfirms a set of propositions. In this sense theoretical triangulation is very consistent with a discovery-based approach to criminological research. Finally, triangulation encourages a viewpoint that there can be some meeting of theoretical fortresses. No one theoretical framework provides a total and universal explanation of crime and of crime of all types. For certain types of crime, such as rape and other sexual offences, there is a strong possibility that the explanations lie within individual dispositions, whereas for other crimes the answers are more likely to be found in terms of social structure. However, the individual dispositions to sexual crimes are likely to be channelled in particular directions in social structures which are organized around inequality between sexes. In short, this argues for the bringing together of concepts and propositions from a number of theoretical approaches which populate criminology.

Concluding comments

Earlier we noted the plurality of method in criminological research. This is, at least in part, the outcome of the range of theories which abound. Methods are not always the handmaiden of theory. There is, for example, a strong empiricist research tradition in British social science which, at least on the surface, appears atheoretical. Nevertheless, much criminological research shows a close and often mutual exchange between theory and method with theory suggesting lines of research action and data derived from methods indicating ways in which theoretical propositions need refinement or should perhaps even be abandoned.

There is no necessary connection between types of theory and types of method. To attempt to lay down precise protocols or to map clear patterns in relationships would be extremely hazardous if not singularly inappropriate. There is certainly no unilinear connection between specific theories and specific methods in criminological research. Nor, however, is it a free for all in which methods of research are thrown at criminological problems in some random and haphazard manner. The choice of methods in any given inquiry is very much a matter for individual researchers and justifications must be sought and examined in the publications of such inquiries. Taking the criminological enterprise as a whole, however, there are mutual attractions and liaisons between types of theory and types of method. Such attractions and liaisons stem from the assumptions implicit in the theoretical approaches and in the amenability of particular methods to these. As we have indicated throughout the chapter three key assumptions concern the respective commitments of particular theoretical approaches to measurement, to explanation posited in individual or social terms and to explanations cast in causal and deterministic terms.

Figure 2.5 shows the main connections which have been made between types of theory and types of method. Implicit in these differing connections are important methodological issues. In the following chapter we will look at three of these. One concerns the use of official statistics to measure the extent of crime and how this use relates to different theoretical approaches within criminology (cells G. L and Q). In essence, this is the issue of whether statistics can be treated as objective measures of crime or whether they reflect institutional policies and practices or class and economic relations in society. The second issue concerns the collection of social data at the level of the social or ecological area and the correlation of such data with levels of crime (cell G). An important question is whether correlations established at this level can be used to provide explanations of crime, especially explanations of criminal behaviours at the level of the individuals. This is what has been referred to as 'the fallacy of the wrong level'. Finally, we have referred to the use of ethnographic methods such as participant observation and life-history interviews to focus upon small-scale situations and contexts (cells N and O), and to the way in which ethnographic data can relate to theory cast in terms of social structure (cells S and T). This is, in effect, the issue of the switching of level of analysis in another way, namely from the small-scale to wider macro theory.

3

Measuring and explaining crime

Introduction

Proposition 1: the crime rate is rising and has reached record levels.
Proposition 2: unemployment is also rising and this is a major cause of the increase in crime.
Proposition 3: the increase in crime is greatest amongst the young.
Proposition 4: the increase in crime among the young is largely due to teachers' inability to instil moral standards and personal discipline in their pupils.
Proposition 5: the increase in crime among the young is also due to the inability of parents to provide adequate supervision of, and control over, their children.
Proposition 6: too many of our young are allowed aimlessly to hang around street corners and therefore inevitably get involved in crime.

These propositions are not derived from criminological research but were distilled from media reports and from everyday conversations on just one day in the summer of 1988. There was nothing special about that day. Much the same kind of propositions could have been derived on any other day. For the people who espouse them they have validity; they represent 'true' statements about the extent of crime and about the causes of crime. Propositions derived from criminological research differ from everyday propositions in so far as they are based upon the systematic application of theoretical concepts and frameworks to the understanding and explanation of crime and also by the systematic collection of data in relation to these concepts and frameworks. The relationship between methods and theories was one of the themes of the last chapter and, in general terms, a number of connections between types of theory and types of method were made. In this chapter we look at some of the ways in which specific theories and specific methods of data collection and analysis interrelate when criminologists address some of the everyday propositions listed above.

First, we shall consider how criminologists have set about addressing the question 'how much crime is there?'. The debates about the extent of crime are closely bound up with debates about how best to measure crime and particularly about the validity of crime statistics as measures of the 'true' level of crime. In turn, such debates derive from the connections which have been made between official statistics as forms of data and three theoretical perspectives: sociological positivism, micro-sociology and radical criminology. (In essence these connections are encapsulated in cells G, L and Q of Figure 2.5.)

Second, as well as being used as measures of the extent of crime, crime statistics have also formed the basis of causal explanations. Such explanations are typically founded upon statistical correlations between quantitative estimates of crime and quantitative estimates of other social phenomena, such as type of housing, level of deprivation, level of unemployment. Such work is within the *areal, ecological* and *epidemiological* traditions within the criminological enterprise (and can be found primarily in cell G of Figure 2.5). In the second part of this chapter we consider studies of the relationship between crime and unemployment to examine methodological problems inherent in attempts to make precise causal statements about the relationship between these two phenomena.

Third, popular and political concern often centres around the youth–crime couplet. Much criminological research uses so-called 'qualitative' research methods of observation and detailed informal interviews. This is especially the case with research which seeks to provide close and detailed descriptions and explanations of youth sub-cultures. Such qualitative research has close associations with micro-sociological frameworks (see cells N and O in Figure 2.5) and yet often also seeks to locate and explain small-scale interactions in terms of wider social structure (see cells S and T in Figure 2.5). The third section of this chapter focuses upon methodological issues implicit in this interchange between data collection in specific contexts and wider structural analysis, with particular reference to school and street culture.

The aim is not to provide confirmation, or otherwise, for the earlier propositions nor to give definitive answers to questions about the extent of crime, the causal connections between unemployment and crime, or the influence of schooling and parenting on delinquency. Rather, it is to spotlight and discuss the methodological problems inherent in addressing such questions. The confrontation of such methodological problems is what is meant by being systematic and is what distinguishes criminological work from everyday theorizing.

Measuring the extent of crime

Official statistics on crime

Contemporary government statistics on crime represent key sources of secondary data within criminology. The main publication is *Criminal Statistics (England and Wales)*, which gives crime and court-proceeding statistics for England and Wales. An equivalent document is available for Scotland. An additional volume, *Supplementary Statistics*, which is available to researchers on request from the Home Office, includes crime and court statistics for each of the police authority areas. From time to time the Home Office produces publications presenting statistics on specific topics. There are also the annual reports of chief constables of the various police forces which provide data on crime and policing for each of the police areas. (In Canada, statistics can be found in *Canadian Crime Statistics* and in the USA in *Uniform Crime Reports*, issued annually by the Federal Bureau of Investigation).

Criminal Statistics includes data on two aspects of crime and criminal activity which provide ways of measuring the extent of crime and the numbers of people committing criminal offences. First, statistics are provided on the number of *notifiable offences* recorded by the police. Such offences are those typically used by the media and others to make assertions about the social health of society and to make comparisons with the past. The offences recorded are those which can be tried only on indictment in a Crown Court, or those offences which may be tried in a magistrates' court but for which a defendant may elect to be tried by jury in a Crown Court. They include 'violence against a person', 'sexual offences', 'burglary', 'theft and handling stolen goods', 'fraud and forgery' and 'criminal damage'. Although these are usually taken to represent the so-called serious offences, within each category there can be variations in the seriousness of the offence committed and the length of sentence it can attract. The statistics on offences do not include the lower-level offences such as traffic offences which are dealt with exclusively by magistrates' courts and which are by far the majority.

Second, statistics are provided on *known offenders*. In essence, these are statistics about offences which are 'cleared up' by the police, that is, offences which have been proceeded against irrespective of the outcome. An offence is taken as 'cleared up' if a person is summonsed or charged, or if an offence has been admitted by an offender and taken into consideration (offences taken into consideration are often admitted by offenders convicted of, and serving sentence for, other offences). Offences are also treated as 'cleared up' if there is sufficient evidence to charge a person but for some reason the case is dropped, if the victim (for example, a young child) is unable or unwilling to give evidence, or if the offender is under the age of criminal responsibility.

In so far as they include only offences which are 'cleared up' such statistics are often used as the basis for making assertions about the effectiveness of the police in dealing with the extent of crime (as measured by statistics collected about the number of offences recorded by the police), although research on the work of detectives has often indicated that statistics on clear-up rates are not necessarily good indices of police effectiveness (see, for example, Clarke and Hough, 1984). The statistics include, for instance, large numbers of offences which are not cleared up by detective work but which are the outcome of admissions by offenders. There is also evidence that detectives can be creative in improving clear-up rates. In 1986, for example, Scotland Yard's Serious Crimes Squad was asked by the Police Complaints Authority to investigate allegations by a police officer that detectives in Kent deliberately falsified reports about unsolved cases to improve their clear-up rates. Criminals already in prison are not usually prosecuted for offences they subsequently admit unless there is a compelling reason. It was alleged that the system worked by encouraging criminals already in prison to confess to crimes they had not committed in return for favourable police reports which might help the convict's allocation to 'soft' prison regimes. It was also alleged that one effect of this informal system was to increase clear-up rates for burglaries in one police sub-division from 25 per cent to 70 per cent within a year (*Guardian*, 12 August 1986). Apart from their use as an indicator – albeit a crude one – of police effectiveness, statistics about offenders can also be used to examine changes in the type of offender committing certain kinds of offences. However, the range of background variables about which data are collected is very restricted, often limited to gender and age.

Reference has already been made to the importance of crime statistics, particularly statistics about recorded offences, in shaping public concern and debate. This is often facilitated by the use of such statistics by politicians and by the media to generate images about the level of crime and the state of the nation. Such images are pushed to the forefront on the annual publication of *Criminal Statistics* and the Home Office's summary publication *Statistical Bulletin*. For example, after the publication of the statistics for 1986 one serious newspaper had banner headlines RAPES LEAD RISE TO RECORD CRIME RATE to head a report that official statistics showed that recorded crime in England and Wales had risen by 7 per cent in that year to 3.8 million offences and that the biggest increase 24 per cent, was for rape (*Guardian*, 17 March 1987). (Tabloid newspapers were less restrained.) Such headlines not only shape public debate but also develop in certain categories of individuals fears of crime beyond the actual risk of such crimes being committed against them (see, for example, Hough and Mayhew, 1983, 1985). Just one year later *The Times* newspaper had headlines which painted a different picture, HURD STEPS UP FIGHT AGAINST DESPAIR AS CRIME RISE SLOWS. The headlines fronted a report that crime in England and Wales rose by only 1 per cent in 1987, that burglaries were down by 5 per cent, and that the Home Secretary, Douglas Hurd, had said that cynicism and despair about crime were out of date. Mr Hurd is reported as follows:

> The police and public working together have started to outwit the burglar, and that is a big achievement. The figures show that rising crime is not inevitable. It can and will be cut back through determined action by the growing partnership between active citizens and the police. Of which the 45,000 neighbourhood watch schemes are the most important example. (*The Times*, 16 March 1988)

Official statistics also provide one basis for decision-making by governments at a national level. For example, the doubling of recorded burglary offences between 1977 and 1987 gave an important impetus to the encouragement of neighbourhood-watch schemes and also to the formulation of crime-prevention policies on a national scale, particularly directed at what were perceived as vulnerable groups in society such as the aged. What is more, statistics collected at a force level provide a basis for decision-making about operational policing by chief constables. For instance, statistics about increases in certain types of recorded offences are used to justify the targeting of certain crimes for special attention. Also, poor clear-up rates for certain offences such as house burglary have led to the introduction of crime-screening programmes whereby those burglaries which have little chance of successful detection are screened out. All police resources are then concentrated on those burglaries where there is a much greater chance of detection, thereby increasing the possibility of a higher clear-up rate.

Government statistics on crime play an important role in criminological research. For example, statistics about recorded crimes are used as a means of measuring the extent of crime in society at any given point of time and also as the foundation for examining trends over time. This is usually done by calculating percentage increases and decreases between two points. This exercise is fraught with difficulties, particularly as the Home Office occasionally changes the rules for recording certain kinds of offences and there can be variations in the way in which police forces interpret and apply these rules. What is more, the conclusions which can be derived about changes in levels of crime are dependent upon the points of time between which percentage changes are calculated. Crime statistics are also used to seek explanations of crime, often by seeking statistical relationships between crime levels and other social phenomena, for example, levels of crime and levels of unemployment. This can be done at a societal level or for small areas, such as enumeration districts. What is more, crime and unemployment can be plotted over time (time series analysis) or examined for the same time period but for different areas (cross-sectional analysis). The areal, ecological and epidemiological use of crime statistics will be considered later.

Official statistics and positivism

Both the attempts to measure the extent of crime and also to provide explanations of variations in the rates of crime have been influenced by positivism. Sociological positivists, in particular, have not been slow to make use of official statistics despite some scepticism about their validity. Early preoccupation with measuring the extent of crime can be found in the work of the 'moral statisticians' of the early to mid-nineteenth century. For them, statistics could be collected and analysed to provide a barometer of the moral health of society. From our point of view, two important and lasting influences can be found in their work.

First, there was an early indication of the role of the state in measuring crime with a view to taking political action and to formulating social policies in relation to what were seen as social problems and in terms of what were believed to be their causes. This welding of crime statistics to policy formulation was to form an important part of the pragmatism and empiricism which has subsequently characterized much British social science including what, in Chapter 1, was described as conventional criminology. Wiles summarizes the influence of the early statisticians as follows

> No important sociological theory of crime is associated with English criminologists. Instead English criminology has been much more concerned with questions of policy and treatment. But the early interest in empirical information about crime did mean however, that the English criminal statistics developed relatively fully and quickly – much more so than in the United States, for example – so that by the mid-twentieth century there were a host of public reports by departments or agencies concerned with the administration of justice. (Wiles, 1971, p. 177)

Second, there was the growing influence of positivist thinking in the social sciences which gave great emphasis to the 'scientific' study of the problems of industrialization – including crime – via the analysis of statistics. Positivist thinking encouraged the belief that crime was an 'objective' social phenomenon which could be measured validly by the collection and analysis of such statistics, and also a phenomenon which could be explained causally in terms of other phenomena. In this way, the foundations were laid for a sociologically oriented positivist criminology which ran alongside, but which was completely different from, the individualist positivism of the Italian biologists such as Lombroso.

The link between official statistics and positivism was given fresh impetus towards the end of the nineteenth century by the writing of the French sociologist Emile Durkheim. However, in his work there was a much sharper theoretical, as opposed to social-reform, edge to the use of official statistics. Durkheim argued strongly for the use of official statistics as indices of 'social facts', the study of which he saw as the essential domain of sociology. The positivist assumption of treating aspects of social life as 'objective' measurable phenomena can be found in his famous edict to 'treat social facts as things' (Durkheim, 1964b). Such objective phenomena were viewed by Durkheim as attributes of society and not of individuals and therefore they could not be accessed and measured by methods such as formal or structured interviews which rely upon collecting data from individuals. Instead, such attributes could be measured only by the use of official statistics. This methodological approach was expressed in *Suicide* (Durkheim, 1952), in which he used official statistics to study and explain variations in the suicide rate. Durkheim did not himself extend his use of official statistics to the study of crime but the implications were easy to see and the broad methodological tradition he laid down was carried forward by others, particularly the Chicago sociologists of the 1920s and 1930s who used crime statistics to delineate 'natural areas' of crime, and also by those concerned with the ecological and epidemiological aspects of crime and criminal activity.

The positivist sociologists have not been totally accepting of crime statistics and have been well aware of some of the problems of their use. For example, Robert Merton (1956) commented on the unreliability of such statistics and particularly their inability to account for the 'dark figure' of unrecorded crime. However, within this viewpoint the gaps in official statistics are seen as mere technical problems to be overcome by supplementing official data with data derived from other sources such as victim surveys and self-report studies. The basic positivist assumptions about official crime statistics remain unshaken, although it is considered necessary to be realistic about the validity and reliability of such statistics. This viewpoint forms the basis of what will subsequently be described as the *positivist realist* position on official statistics. The preface 'positivist' is used here to distinguish this position from 'left realism' which, as will be indicated later, also advocates the use of victim surveys but which has closer political and theoretical associations with radical criminology.

There are, however, much more fundamental criticisms which have been levelled at the positivist use of statistics. These are less to do with technical problems of the data but derive instead from theoretical critiques of sociological positivism. One position is that too much weight is given to official statistics as objective indicators of attributes of society and not sufficient to the way in which crime statistics are socially constructed. Here the emphasis is upon crime statistics as the outcome of everyday interactions between deviance or potential deviance and law enforcement officers, with particular reference to the way in which such officers apply meanings, definitions and labels to the actions of others. The concern with the way in which crime statistics are socially constructed derives in large part from micro-sociological frameworks which argue for an *institutionalist* approach to the use of official statistics. The distinction between realist and institutionalist approaches was first made by Biderman and Reiss (1967) and was subsequently adopted by Bottomley (1979). We can add a third position, the *radical*, which emanates from the viewpoint that sociological positivism has implicit assumptions about structural functionalism and consensus and therefore does not give recognition to the possibility of official crime statistics as reflections of, and products of, structural conflicts in society, particularly class conflicts. In so far as this position is typified by a Marxist approach to crime and to criminal statistics, and to distinguish it from the recent emergence of 'left realism', it is also sometimes referred to as 'radical-idealism' or 'left-idealism' (for an elaboration of the differences between these positions, see Young, 1986).

There are different emphases within each of these broad positions and inevitably there are overlaps between them. Nevertheless, the categorization provides a means of uncovering different methodological positions and also different prescriptions as to how to address questions about the extent of crime in society.

The institutionalist approach
The 'institutionalist' approach is as follows. Official statistics are not viewed as rough statistical approximations to the 'true' level of crime, the technical gaps in which can be plugged by victim surveys, self-report studies or any other methodological device. Rather, such statistics are seen as products of the criminal justice system in general, and specifically as indicators of the activities of those who work within it. In this sense, official statistics are not more or less

accurate measures of crime upon which to base causal explanations, but representations of individual and institutional policies and practices. Rate-producing actions may be the result of formal policy-making edicts – for example, when a chief constable issues an order to his officers to 'crack down' on drink-driving at Christmas or the outcome of established but informal practices such as 'verballing' of suspected offenders (see, for example, Holdaway, 1983) or 'plea-bargaining' in courts (see Baldwin and McConville, 1977). Equally important are the everyday labels, definitions, social definitions and stereotypes which agents of the criminal justice system apply which result in some offences and some individuals becoming an official statistic and others not.

The institutional approach owes much to the ideas propounded by Kitsuse and Cicourel (1963) and to the expression of these ideas in Cicourel's study of the way in which young offenders are processed by the official machinery of the American criminal justice system (Cicourel, 1976). Such work symbolized the 1960s and 1970s' challenge to positivism which crystallized around interactionist theorizing and also ethnomethodology. Kitsuse and Cicourel's approach is expressed as follows:

> We suggest that the question of the theoretical significance of the official statistics can be re-phrased by shifting the focus of investigation from the processes by which *certain forms of behaviour* are socially and culturally generated to the processes by which *rates of deviant behaviour* are produced.

and

> Rates can be viewed as indices of organizational processes rather than as indices of the incidence of certain forms of behaviour. (Kitsuse and Cicourel, 1963, p. 135)

Associated with this switch of focus is a break with the conventional, positivist use of official data and with its emphasis upon positing and testing statements about the causes of criminal behaviour. Such conventional use

> obscures the view that official statistics reflect socially organized activities divorced from the sociological theories used retrospectively for explaining the same statistics. Members of the community, law enforcement personnel, attorneys, judges, all respond to various behavioural or imputed symbolic or reported acts and events by juveniles with commonsense or lay conceptions, abstract legal rules, bureaucratic procedures and policies. (Cicourel, 1976, p. 37)

The methodological implication of the institutional approach is that official statistics are not the sole object of interest. It is argued that the criminologist must also consider the policies and practices (formal and informal) which create and generate them. The picture portrayed in the statistics can be examined only in connection with a detailed analysis of such policies and practices (say, using informal interview and observational methods). In so far as such practices are expressed in interactions with potential offenders and involve the application of social meanings, definitions and labels by law enforcement personnel, the institutionalist position is typical of a broad micro-sociological theoretical paradigm which encompasses interactionist and labelling theories and which reaches its zenith in the work of ethnomethodologists (for a discussion of these, see Eglin, 1987). This paradigm is consistent with a critical stance in relation to official crime statistics and with the use of non-quantitative data collected by ethnographic methods including detailed interviews and participant observation.

There is a real danger of an institutionalist approach rejecting official statistics out of hand and retreating instead into a total and exclusive consideration of specific interactions between potential deviants and criminal justice personnel in specific contexts at specific times. A consideration of these aspects is important because statistics start their life on the ground in interactions between individuals and representatives of the criminal justice system. But such a close and exclusive focus runs the risk of falling into extremes of relativism whereby all that can be explained is that which happens between particular individuals in particular circumstances and *only* in terms of the dynamics of interactions between those particular individuals in those particular circumstances. There are, however, other individuals, groups and social processes to take account of. For example, criminal justice personnel do not enter interactions as totally free agents. Granted, they have a certain degree of discretion in the way in which they deal with offenders or potential offenders and they are not immune from the processes of assigning meanings, definitions and labels to which various strands of the institutionalist approach have quite correctly drawn attention. However, nor are they immune from the constraints which are placed upon their actions by formal organizational practices and policies or the informal norms of 'cop-culture'. Indeed, the meanings, definitions and labels of, say, law enforcement officers are as much influenced by such practices, policies and cultural norms as they are by the exchanges that take place with members of the public. What is more, offenders and law enforcement officers cannot be extracted analytically from the organizational structure of which they are a part. This structure comprises certain junctions at which decisions are taken by officers about the destiny of individuals, and it is within this structure that such individuals are processed in such a way that they do or do not end up as a criminal statistic. What is being suggested, then, is that the theoretical contributions of an institutionalist approach – particularly those which come from various forms of phenomenology and interactionism, and which encourage a detailed consideration of social interactions – need to be placed in the context of the organizational structure of the criminal justice system and the practices and policies which abound within it.

One way of doing this is to focus research on decision-making, and particularly 'decision-making as action'. Much decision-making theory is highly deterministic, viewing decision-making as the deterministic outcome of individual personality or of organizational structure. By emphasizing 'action' as an essential ingredient of decision-making we can give emphasis to the way in which interpretative procedures – for example, interpretations of others' actions in relation to interpretations of laws and organizational practices – play a part in such decision-making. Further, by adding that such decision-making should be examined at various 'decision gates', it is possible to develop a research agenda which stipulates a consideration of particular forms of action (decisions taken by enforcement officers and others) at particular junctions in the criminal justice system which have significances in terms of patterns and trends in official crime statistics. Despite the battering which official data have taken, particularly from the institutionalist critiques of the 1970s, Bottomley and Pease argue for some rehabilitation of official statistics in criminological research and some of the ideas they present can be used to put some flesh on the preceding discussion. Bottomley and Pease adopt a theoretical perspective which is concerned with the social construction of crime statistics and which therefore is similar to the less extreme forms of the institutionalist position. In doing this, they indicate three important decision gates with regard to police work (the pre-trial and trial stages of criminal justice are excluded, but the same strategy of analysis could easily apply).

The first of these relates to the recording of crimes reported to the police by victims or witnesses or of crimes discovered by the police themselves. The evidence from victim surveys clearly indicates that a great deal of crime is not reported to the police. Even where it is, not all crime is officially recorded by police officers. For example, Bottomley and Pease report research by Sparks, Genn and Dodd (1977) which estimates that only about one-third of offences reported to the police end up in statistics. Part of the reason for this gap between crime which is reported or discovered and crime which is recorded can be found in the discretion which individual police officers exercise in their everyday work. This discretion may be the outcome of subjective assessments as to, say, the seriousness of the act, the nature of the individual concerned or the likelihood of achieving a conviction. The way in which such discretion is exercised can be officer-specific but is also likely to be influenced by the custom and practice of the 'cop-culture' of which he or she is a part. There is also the possibility of divisional or force policy with regard to whether or not certain types of crimes, of certain degrees of seriousness, should be deliberately screened out of the recording process.

The second main 'gate' is at the stage at which crime is detected and cleared up. The average clear-up rate during the 1980s was about one-third of all crimes. For examples, in 1986 the overall clear-up rate was only 31.6 per cent of all crime, although there were variations between offences ranging from 20 per cent for criminal damage to 96 per cent for all reported attempted murders. The percentages for rape were 62 per cent and for assault 80 per cent (*Criminal Statistics*, 1987). Forms of police work play some part in accounting for what is, and is not, cleared up. For example, we have already referred to the informal practice whereby offenders ask or are encouraged to ask for offences to be taken into account, the extent of which appears to be quite extensive, particularly with regard to burglary (see, for example, Lambert, 1970; Bottomley and Coleman, 1981). In addition, from time to time specific police forces adopt policies which target certain crimes by increasing the number of officers who are engaged in day-to-day surveillance and also in the detection of recorded incidents. This can have important effects upon clear-up rates for particular offences at the time at which they are targeted. However, evidence from research indicates that information provided by the public and by victims appears to be much more influential. Burrows and Tarling (1982) have shown that the clear-up rate is not so dependent upon the police themselves or the number of resources and men available to them but upon the amount of help that is supplied by the public. For instance, the high clear-up rate for attempted murders, assaults and sexual offences is largely accounted for by the fact that offenders are often known to the victim who can provide the police with a sufficiently clear description to facilitate arrest. Bottomley and Pease summarize the research evidence as follows:

> The clear message that emerges from practically all recent empirical studies of police work in the detection of recorded crimes is that the police are rarely faced with the classic situation of detective fiction, that is the search for the unidentified perpetrators of known offences. The majority of crimes are cleared up either

as a result of direct information about the identity of the offender provided by the victim at the time when the crime was first reported to the police or because they are automatically solved in the very process of crime discovery or because they are admitted through questioning for another offence. (Bottomley and Pease, 1986, p. 46)

A third 'gate' concerns the decision as to whether to prosecute an offender. In certain cases it will be considered that there is not sufficient evidence to prosecute. However, where sufficient evidence does exist or where an offence is admitted the police have the option of diverting the offender away from court proceedings by deciding instead to issue a caution. Such cautioning involves a formal recorded warning as to the offence and as to action which will be taken in the future in the event of further offending. There are variations in the extent to which cautioning is used, particularly with regard to types of offence and types of offender. For example, the extent of cautioning is greatest amongst first-time young offenders, particularly those committing low-level offences. Variation in cautioning rates is partly dependent upon the number of such types of individuals committing such types of crimes becoming known to the police. It is also influenced by the policy of particular forces with regard to cautioning as well as by discretionary decision-making by senior officers in relation to specific individuals and specific offences.

To sum up, the institutionalist approach encourages a research agenda which focuses upon decision-making at a number of 'gates' within the organizational structure of the criminal justice system. Decision-making has specific outcomes with regard to specific individuals in specific contexts, but also has implications for the generation of crime statistics in terms of recorded offences and known offenders. Such decision-making should not be viewed in a deterministic way but as action which involves the application of social meanings, stereotypes, definitions and labels. What is more, it is not solely a matter of the idiosyncratic judgement of law enforcement officers but is influenced by, and needs to be located within, the policies and practices of police work and the nature of law itself. The research implications of such an agenda are that empirical investigation moves beyond the exclusive consideration of crime statistics as 'facts' and objects of inquiry. It can, for example, involve a range of methods of data collection such as *observation* of the way in which police officers respond to complaints from the public and of what subsequently happens to these complaints (see, for example, McCabe and Sutcliffe, 1978); the *analysis of crime reports* which have implications for whether or not reported crimes are 'screened out'; or *interviews* with offenders as to their dealings with their legal representatives (see, for example, Baldwin and McConville, 1977).

The radical approach

The institutionalist position was radical in challenging the positivist use of statistics and mirrored the general new-deviancy critique of positivism in criminology. However, the institutionalist position has itself been the subject of criticism, particularly by those who argue for a radical approach to official statistics. This radical approach is part of what, in the preceding chapter, was described as historical-structural approaches to the explanation of crime. Within this general category there are variations of theoretical perspectives, but this is not the place to dwell on the various nuances. However, in general terms, the different approaches agree on the need to give primacy to explanations cast at a social-structural level. Such explanations differ from the more conservative sociological explanations based upon structural functionalism in so far as particular emphasis is placed upon structural divisions and conflicts rather than consensus. In those versions influenced by Marxism such divisions and conflicts are believed to emerge out of differential relations to the means of production. An analysis of historical processes is also considered important in order to highlight the way in which structural forms emerge and develop. It is argued that the examination of crime, of law and of systems of justice can only take place in these terms. Crime, law and systems of justice are viewed as the outcomes, and therefore expressions of, particular structural arrangements at particular points in history. The same is true, it is said, of official statistics on crime.

A major contribution to the radical tradition in criminology came from the New Criminology Project (Taylor, Walton and Young, 1973) which represented a move towards a Marxist criminology. In doing this, however, it sought to synthesize preceding theoretical developments and research, particularly that based upon the micro-sociological social reaction theory. In other words, there was an attempt to incorporate elements of an institutionalist approach. However, it was argued that whilst a concern with everyday life and social interactions was important, this was not by itself sufficient since adequate attention was not being paid to differential power relations in such interactions, nor to the origins of such power relations in structural – particularly class – divisions and conflicts. In doing this, Taylor, Walton and Young sought to create a theoretical approach which would link interactionist theories and Marxist concerns with historical processes and structural arrangements (although no major empirical work emerged out of this development with the exceptions of Pearce, 1976, and Hall *et al.*, 1978).

Radical theory was not only developed to explain crime (that is, why certain categories of individuals commit crimes) but also crime control and criminalization (how and why certain categories of ndividuals are criminalized by laws and their enforcement). In the atter, the role of the state and its crime-control operators (including, ncidentally, its crime-research apparatus) is important in so far as he state is viewed as a mere agent of the propertied class. Within his framework, official data reflect patterns of crime and also patterns of criminalization as structurally induced. Statistics are not viewed as the composite of a wide range of everyday interactions and herefore without pattern but as the outcome of class relations in society at any given time. It is because official statistics are outcomes of class relations that working-class people are overrepresented in statistics (both in terms of the forces inducing criminal actions and also in terms of state criminalization) and that 'crimes of the powerful' (Pearce, 1976) are underrepresented (either because their actions are not criminalized or because they can avoid detection and prosecution).

A similar viewpoint, although not restricted to crime statistics, can be found in some of the writings of the Radical Statistics Group, writings which are influenced by Marxist ideas (Irvine, Miles and Evans, 1979). But first, it is useful to consider an earlier commentary by Hindess (1973) on the use of official statistics in general with implications for criminal statistics. Hindess agreed with institutional-sts in terms of the need to focus upon the social production of statistics. However, he argued that the extreme of the institutionalist position was in danger of positing a relativist position by suggesting hat statistics could only be examined in terms of the subjective experiences of law enforcement officers. The logical extension, he argued, was that there could never be rational knowledge because all empirical investigations would be viewed as the products of the subjective experiences and everyday assumptions of social researchers. Statistics needed no reference to subjective experiences of law enforcement officers. Instead, he argued, attention should be paid to what he termed the 'instruments of production' of official statistics of which there were two forms: *technical* instruments (those involving technical errors and gaps) and *conceptual* instruments those involving the system of concepts and categories by which cases are assigned to classes within the statistics). Particular emphasis should be placed upon the latter. In arguing against the relativism in the institutionalist position, Hindess revitalizes the structural aspects of crime statistics. However, for radical theorists this emphasis upon he structural fails to fulfil its potential. Two members of the Radical Statistics Group offer a form of analysis which goes beyond that of Hindess (Miles and Irvine, 1979). Rather than looking at official statistics as products of the mechanical application of technical and conceptual instruments they view them as particular outcomes of particular structural (that is, capitalist) arrangements and particular historical processes. For them, the categories and instruments which Hindess emphasized have wider structural and class-based origins and individuals and organizations which apply them are mere automatons in these structural and historical processes. In adopting this form of analysis Miles and Irvine are very close to the position of the new criminologists.

The criticisms which can be levelled at a radical approach to crime statistics mirror those which can be levelled at radical criminology in general. For example, although there is an attempt to integrate interactionist theories, there is always a danger that these become overwhelmed by their Marxist bedfellows such that all actions and interactions are explained exclusively and deterministically in terms of class relations. The value of examining the scope for independence of social actions based on social meanings and definitions is largely thrown away. The same argument could be applied to the analysis of crime statistics, namely that they are viewed solely as a reflection of class relations in society and any patterns which lie within them (or indeed, which do not lie within them) are explained by, and subsumed under, some grand macro-theory. In doing this, there is a danger that the need for a research agenda based around official crime statistics will also be explained away.

However, it would be wrong to ignore the contributions of the radical tradition, particularly if one can cut away the crude Marxism. Such contributions are in terms of what it can offer to criminological research agendas, especially those grounded in a consideration of official data. First, the concern with patterns of law enforcement and more generally with criminalization, point the way to a consideration of the underrepresentation of certain crimes in official statistics, particularly so-called 'crimes of the powerful' (Pearce 1976), and also to the overrepresentation of other groups in society. Second, the concern with social structure is quite rightly reinforced. In the preceding discussion of the institutionalist approach it was argued that small-scale interactions should be set in the context of organizational practices and policies, practices and policies which have significances for who does, and does not, end up as a crime statistic. Such practices and policies are influential factors in decision-making. Organizational practices and policies do not exist in a vacuum. They are not the crude outcome of structural arrangements but neither are they completely independent of them. A theoretical perspective which emphasizes social structure encourages a consideration of the interconnections between such arrangements and the way in which organizational practices and policies in the criminal justice system are formed and implemented. Finally, and not least, by dragging the state into centre stage the radical tradition provokes questions about the use to which official

tatistics are put. The organizations of the criminal justice system are
ot solely involved in the implementation of policies and practice in
nforcing the law which have consequences for official statistics.
They also use such statistics to formulate these policies and practices.
Unfortunately, the intense and indeterminate debates within crimi-
ology about the meanings which can be placed on official data has
distracted attention from the very strong possibility that such debates
ave been of little consequence to key decision-makers. Yet such
decision-makers continue to make use of statistics. What is needed
s a greater concern with the way in which official data are used – and
sometimes ignored – in organizational and political decision-making
bout the structure and functioning of the criminal justice system. (A
discussion of the way in which some of the conclusions derived from
official data were bypassed in the decision to extend 'short, sharp shock'
egimes to all detention centres can be found in the next chapter.)

The realist approach

The positivist-realist approach is discussed here, after the institution-
list and the radical approaches, even though it preceded them and
ven though they drew much of their strength from criticisms of
ealism. This is done in order to emphasize recent developments in
victim surveys, some of which have their basis in the realist position.
Realism is founded upon the positivist supposition that official
statistics represent objective indicators of the level of crime and the
number of offenders in society at any given point in time. Despite
this, it is recognized that there are certain technical problems with
official statistics – principally the inability to include the 'dark figure'
of crime – which reduce their validity but which, to a certain degree,
an be corrected. Bottomley summarizes realism as follows:

> It is primarily concerned with supplementing police statistics with
> statistics of unreported crimes to give a more 'realistic' picture of
> the amount of criminal behaviour in society. The underlying
> assumption is that there exists an external, objective 'crime reality'
> waiting to be discovered, and a belief that the development of 'self-
> report and victimisation' studies has already gone a long way
> towards uncovering the dark figure of crime and of criminality.
> (Bottomley, 1979, p. 23)

As Bottomley points out, self-report studies and victim surveys have
lose associations with the realist approach to official statistics.

Self-report studies

Self-report studies tend to be based upon small-scale samples of
individuals, usually adolescents, who are asked to provide information

about the extent to which they have committed crimes of various types in a period of time specified by the researcher. Two methods are used to collect the data: interviews and self-completion questionnaires. With regard to the latter, individuals are typically given a list of items, each of which represents a criminal action, and they are asked to tick those they have committed and to give an indication of the frequency with which they have committed them. With interviews, sample members are asked to admit to committing offences. The interviews may be open-ended or may involve prompts, as when individuals are asked to sort a pack of cards. A criminal offence is printed on each card. This sorting procedure is followed by detailed interviews about those offences they claim to have committed. Whilst interviews lack anonymity, they do permit probing about frequency and intent and allow checking of accuracy. In some instances polygraph interviews have been used to validate data (see Clarke and Tifft, 1966).

Self-report studies have been popular in America (see, for example, Clarke and Tifft, 1966; Empey and Erikson, 1966; Hirschi 1969; and Johnson, 1979) and Scandinavia (Antilla and Jaakola 1966; Elmhorn, 1965). In Britain, self-reports were used in McDonald's study of the relationship between social class and self reported delinquency (McDonald, 1969), in Belson's study of stealing by boys in areas of London (Belson, 1969, 1975) and as part of the Cambridge Studies of Delinquency project (West and Farrington, 1973). Self-report studies have been used to get some estimate of the extent to which official statistics about known offenders underestimate the true figure. However, they have also been used as the basis for developing explanations of criminality by seeking to relate self-reported delinquency to a number of back ground variables (see, for example, Hirschi, 1969; Johnson, 1979 McDonald, 1969, West and Farrington, 1973). In an interesting recent development of self-report studies convicted offenders are asked not about the extent of their criminal behaviour but about the way in which they go about committing crime. For example, Bennett and Wright (1984) interviewed burglars about the strategies they typically used to break into houses. These strategies were found not to match the assumptions about such strategies which form part of crime prevention programmes.

There are serious question marks against the exclusive reliance on self-report data to provide precise estimates of the shortfall in officially recorded statistics on known offenders. First of all there is the obvious point that with sensitive matters of crime there must be doubts as to whether subjects will tell the truth. Second, it is extremely likely that admissions to certain crimes are over represented and that admissions to other crimes are underrepresented.

For example, there may be a tendency to report fully on trivial offences about which the police are unlikely to do anything and an unwillingness, despite assurances about anonymity and confidentiality, to admit to serious offences. What is more, self-report studies have failed to utilize social theories to take account of subjects' perceptions of what is criminal and therefore worth reporting, and of the way in which these perceptions relate to sub-cultural norms and values. For example, violent acts at soccer matches can have serious consequences for the victims but can be seen as orderly and normal by the perpetrators (Marsh, Rosser and Harré, 1978). There is also the problem that self-report studies have not typically drawn their samples from areas for which there are comparable crime statistics from the police, nor have they asked about offences committed in time periods for which statistics are collected. This has made difficult the comparison with official data for the purpose of estimating the under-reporting of statistics on offenders.

Perhaps the best that can be said of self-report studies is that they provide one means of challenging popular hypotheses which emerge out of official data. For example, specific studies (such as Short and Nye, 1958) have produced data to question the viewpoint that crime is predominantly a working-class phenomenon. Also, after a survey of forty self-report studies, Box (1981) concludes that the hypothesis that there is more delinquency among the working class is not supported by such studies. That apart, given the technical flaws previously mentioned, it is unlikely that self-report studies can fill significant gaps in official statistics. Box comments that:

> the obsession with juvenile self-reported delinquency and the limited number of items in the one adult self-reported crime study have resulted in rendering invisible the massive contribution to crime by government and corporate officials: this is ironic, considering that one purpose of such studies was to make good the deficiencies of the official statistics. (Box, 1981, p. 87)

Victim surveys

Victim surveys have been much more influential as tools of criminological research, particularly in the 1980s. Their popularity has been given impetus by governmental policies relating to law enforcement and also by a quite separate but significant theoretical development. The former is closely related to the instigation of the Home Office's British Crime Survey and the latter is connected with left' or 'new realist' victim surveys. (For a review of both of these, see McGuire and Pointing, 1988.)

Basically, victim surveys involve the selection of a representative sample from the population. Questions are asked as to whether sample members have been the victim of a crime within a specified period of time and whether they reported such crimes to the police. The primary goal, therefore, is to gain some measure of the 'dark' figure of unreported crime, and of the 'grey' figure of crime reported to the police but for one reason or another not recorded as such.

An early pioneer of victim surveys was Von Hentig (1948) but it was not until the 1960s that they were given impetus by their use in the United States President's Crime Commission (see Ennis, 1967). A number of victim surveys was commissioned, the largest of which was a sample survey of 10,000 households across the country. In addition, a number of smaller surveys was carried out in Washington, Boston and Chicago. The surveys reported a high incidence of victimization in the population, much higher than was recorded in official statistics on crime. In the 1970s Sparks and his associates (1977) carried out a victim survey in three areas of inner London which also reported high levels of unrecorded victimization. For example, they found that nearly half of the sample had experienced actual or attempted crime in a twelve-month period and also reported an 11:1 ratio of victim-perceived to police-recorded crime (Sparks, Genn and Dodd, 1977).

The most significant development relating to victim surveys in Britain was the introduction of the British Crime Survey carried out by researchers within the Home Office. (In the USA the equivalent is the National Crime Survey conducted by the Bureau of the Census.) The first survey was completed in 1982 and related to crimes committed in the preceding year. Subsequent surveys have been carried out in 1984 (relating to 1983) and in 1988 (relating to 1987) This overall time series design facilitates an examination of crime trends over time. Separate analyses are available for England and Wales (Hough and Mayhew, 1983, 1985) and for Scotland (Chambers and Tombs, 1984). The rudiments of the design are as follows In England and Wales 11,000 and in Scotland 5,000 households were selected at random from the electoral register. One person aged 16 years or over was interviewed at each address. An initial screening questionnaire was used to ascertain whether the subject had been the victim of a crime, and if so, a more detailed questionnaire was administered for each of the crimes mentioned. There was also a follow-up schedule which collected data about background variables, about contacts with the police and about subjects' lifestyle and own offending behaviours. This follow-up schedule was also administered to a sub-sample of those who did not report victimization, to facilitate comparison between victims and non-victims on a number of variables. The first and second surveys have spawned a large number of research papers on a wide range of topics (a comprehensive list of which can be found in The Home Office

Research and Planning Unit's annual publication, *Research Programme*). However, the main analysis provides data on crimes, of different kinds, reported and not reported to the police. Also, adjustments are made to the number of crimes reported by sample members to facilitate comparisons with crime officially recorded in *Criminal Statistics*. One important finding to emerge from the surveys is that there is great fear of crime, particularly among women, the elderly and those living in inner-city areas, fear which is out of all proportion to the realities of crime as measured by the surveys. The main analysis also provides insights into the subjects' reasons for not reporting crimes. Perceived triviality of the offence is by far the most important reason but perceived uninterest on the part of the police and police impotence were also important. The Crime Survey is characteristic of what, in Chapter 1, was described as administrative criminology. It is atheoretical and closely allied to official policy-making. Its main conclusions have played an influential part in policies geared to crime prevention, reducing fear of crime and increasing police effectiveness in relation to different types of crime.

Left realism

Victim surveys are also associated with 'new' 'left realism'. This brand of realism is also concerned with the reality and fear of crime amongst certain vulnerable sections in society and with the effectiveness of the police in tackling such realities and fears. However, it emanates from a different strand within the criminological enterprise. We consider this 'realist' position here because of the importance which it attaches to victim surveys but it should be recognized that it is *significantly* different from the more traditional and conventional positivist-realist approach which is primarily concerned with attempting to fill gaps in the positivist use of official statistics. 'Left realism' has emerged from a general shift in radical criminology. Indeed, one of its leading exponents, Jock Young, was also central to the earlier new criminology project.

The theoretical differences between this new realism and, on the one hand, radical Marxist criminology and, on the other, conventional mainstream criminology are complex. The exposition of these theoretical differences can be found in a number of sources (see, for example, Kinsey, 1986; Kinsey, Lea and Young, 1986; Lea and Young, 1984; Young, 1986, 1987). The basic tenets can be summarized as follows. Crime is not a social construction. On the contrary, it is a reality for many people, particularly vulnerable groups such as women and ethnic minorities. What is more, much crime is committed by working-class people upon working-class people. To ignore the reality of crime, particularly working-class crime, or to attempt to explain it away in grand theories, is morally reprehensible. Instead, social scientists should draw attention to such realities, say by victim surveys, and ensure that accountable police policies and strategies are introduced to protect the rights of those threatened by crime. Within this broad position it is argued that victim surveys should be used in the struggle for more effective policing and crime control. In essence, policing strategies should be founded upon findings about the extent of crime and its distribution across sections of the community. Further, the police should be accountable to the wishes of the community as captured by such surveys.

Left realist surveys combine elements of victim surveys with those which collect data about attitudes towards policing (as in the Policy Studies Institute's survey of Londoners' attitudes to the police, which was described in the preceding chapter). They have been carried out in Merseyside (Kinsey, 1986) and in Islington (Jones, Maclean and Young, 1986). Both are more geographically focused than the British Crime Survey but report similar findings with regard to the extent of victimization and fear of crime. However, greater emphasis is placed upon victimization among vulnerable groups in society, particularly women and ethnic minorities. What is more, it is argued that the fear of crime within these groups *is* realistic and therefore cannot be tackled by government or police sponsored educational campaigns to alleviate fears. Rather, it should be tackled by the police addressing these realities and fears and prioritizing their policies accordingly. (For a review of left realist victim surveys, see Young, 1988.)

There have been many criticisms of the swing to left realism. For example, it has been suggested that the focus on victims and the calls for greater and more responsive policing in relation to them distract attention away from the more repressive aspects of policing (see, for example, Scraton, 1985). Also, there is a certain irony that the social survey is a central pillar of new left realism. In another context and at another time surveys could easily have been cast aside as tools of state-sponsored, positivist criminology. Some have suggested that in the rush to champion certain ideals the sensitivity with which survey data should be treated has been ignored (see, for example, Brogden, Jefferson and Walklate, 1988). Nevertheless, whatever the worth of these criticisms, the value of drawing attention to the amount of crime committed against certain vulnerable sections of society cannot be ignored.

Victim surveys vary in their design. Nevertheless, there are certain general comments which can be made. Obviously, they are subject to the range of problems which are encountered in all surveys and the data must therefore be handled with care. Nevertheless, victim surveys do not have the number and depth of methodological flaws associated with self-report studies. In this respect they provide a firmer basis for estimating the 'dark' and the 'grey' figures of crime, particularly with regard to statistics about offences. However, such surveys cannot collect data about victimless crimes, or about certain types of crime (for example, some forms of fraud) which victims do not detect. Also, it is likely that they underestimate corporate crime and so-called 'crimes of the powerful' (see Walklate, 1989).

That apart, recent victim surveys have made major contributions to the criminological research agenda. First, the importance of the victim in criminological inquiry has been reinforced, particularly in terms of the recognition that what is measured as the extent of crime depends a good deal on what victims report as crime. Second, survey findings have drawn attention to important questions about the fear of crime and the relationship of such fear to the reality of crime. Third, the way in which crime is experienced by victims has been emphasized. Previous criminological research traditions have sought to 'humanize the deviant' (Muncie and Fitzgerald, 1981). There is an equally strong case for 'humanizing the victim'. Finally, victim surveys permit a consideration of reasons for not reporting crime. With the left realist surveys in particular this has led to a further consideration of the way in which different sections of the community perceive and relate to the police. The relationships between sections of the community and the police need to be examined in terms of social structure and the divisions which exist within it. In this way, the findings of victim surveys and their relationship to official statistics take such statistics beyond an exclusive concern with crimes and the criminal to a consideration of social structure.

Concluding comments

Criminal statistics have held a central position in criminology, first because of their close association with sociological positivism and later because they became the butt of criticism from both micro-sociological and radical theoretical paradigms. This criticism was part of the general onslaught on positivist approaches to the measurement and explanation of crime in society. The crude positivist approach to the use of official data is hardly tenable. There is a belief that there is a pool of crime and criminals in society and that crime statistics represent objective, valid and reliable measures of this pool. There is recognition that there are technical problems with such data, particularly with regard to the 'dark figure' of crime, but it is believed that under-reporting and under-recording is such that the offences and offenders which do appear in the statistics are representative of the total number of offences and of offenders.

Therefore, official data can provide a basis for estimating the true extent of crime and, secondly, can be used to explain crime in terms of the background characteristics of known offenders or the social features of geographical areas.

The problems with this position have been adequately spotlighted by the ways in which alternative theoretical approaches have addressed crime statistics. For example, the micro-sociological theories associated with the institutionalist position have drawn attention to the way in which statistics are socially constructed, and radical theories have indicated the structural dimension of such data. However, such critiques do not amount to a case for the total abandonment of official statistics on crime. In any case, to abandon criminal statistics for an obsessional concern with specific inter-actions in specific contexts at specific times, for the technical delicacies of victim surveys, or for the all-embracing *ex post facto* justifications of vulgar Marxism is just as sterile. It is dangerous to use crime statistics by themselves to make assertions about crime in society or about the operation of the criminal justice system. But it is equally dangerous to ignore them. The value of criminal statistics lies not in the statistics themselves but in the questions which different theoretical positions (positions which cluster around realist, institutionalist and radical approaches) ask of such statistics. Such questions can form the basis for research agendas which extend beyond a sole concern with the extent of crime and beyond the sole reliance on official forms of data. Central to this is the assumption that there is not just one question to be asked of crime and official statistics but several. Such agendas should have at their centre questions concerning the way in which decisions are taken in relation to those who do, and do not, appear on crime statistics; the significance of interpretative procedures in such decisions; the influence of organizational policies and practices on such pro-cedures; and the way in which such policies and practices reflect and can be understood in terms of wider structural arrangements. What is more, there are ways in which what is not in the statistics can pose fruitful questions about 'crimes of the powerful' or about the experiences and fears of victims. It is in such ways that the connections which have been made between different theoretical approaches and official data can be fruitful in suggesting lines for further empirical investigation. What is more, there is a real sense in which the in-house wrangling, particularly since the 1960s, between different theoretical positions has switched the focus away from a very real but neglected question concerning official data. That is, irrespective of the differing interpretations which can be placed on official data, what interpretations do key decision-makers place upon them and with what outcomes?

Explaining crime: quantitative research

Areal, ecological and epidemiological studies

Crime statistics are not solely used to measure the extent of crime. They can be used also to map geographical distributions of crime and also as the basis for explanations of crime by seeking to relate official crime rates to rates for other social phenomena such as distribution of housing tenure. Typically, this involves a commitment to correlation analysis. The use of crime statistics to map crime owes much to the Chicagoans. The Chicago school of urban sociology comprised a complex interweaving of ideas including functionalism, Darwinism, the notions of survival of the fittest and of the struggle for space, zone growth, interactionism and ecology. Ecological analysis was borrowed from biology where it was concerned with the spatial distribution of plants and animals and with the way in which they are the product of, or influenced by, the immediate environment. It was applied by the Chicagoans in the mapping of 'natural areas' of crime but in a much less deterministic way. This was particularly the case with Shaw and McKay (1929; 1931) in the examination of 'delinquency areas'. The Chicago school has influenced British studies although the latter have tended to focus on specific areas rather than on cities as wholes. What is more, they have moved away from the functionalism implicit in the Chicagoans' work as well as from the influence of biological ecology and the mapping of urban zones and delinquency areas. Instead, emphasis has been placed on the relationship of crime rates to the type of housing (particularly housing tenure) in particular areas and also on the influence of housing policies in creating housing classes.

An early and influential example of these British area studies is Morris's study of Croydon in which he examined the distribution of crime by wards and used correlation analysis to relate crime rates to factors such as population density and overcrowding (Morris, 1957). Other studies include Mays' (1954) work in Liverpool, Spencer's (1964) in Bristol, Wallis and Maliphant's (1967) in London and Baldwin and Bottoms' (1976) in Sheffield. Social geographers have also begun to take an interest in the distribution of crime and have made use of criminological theories in an attempt to get away from geographers' traditional concern with spatial analysis in which environment is seen as the sole determinant of outcomes of social processes. Criminological theories have encouraged geographers to make use of official data but also to look at such social processes (see, for example, Herbert, 1982).

The areal and ecological approaches, then, make use of crime statistics to examine the distribution of crime across areas and to search for correlations between crime rates and rates for other social phenomena, such as type of housing and level of deprivation, in those same areas. Essentially, this is a *cross-sectional* design. The early influence of biology in attempting to examine crime in terms of an ecological adaptation to different areas has been discredited and has disappeared. Instead, ecological studies typically progress by viewing the analysis of correlations as a preliminary but important stage from which more detailed research, less dependent on official statistics, can emerge (see, for example, Baldwin and Bottoms, 1976).

Correlation analysis can also be used to examine relationships between variations in crime rates over time but for one social or geographical unit. This is a *time-series* design. The unit of analysis may be society rather than at the level of the social or ecological area, and although there are differences in nomenclature between writers, we shall call this epidemiological analysis as opposed to areal or ecological analyses which are forms of epidemiological analysis related to specific and small geographical areas or ecologies.

Unemployment and crime

One of the popular everyday propositions of recent years has been that the increase in unemployment has produced an increase in crime. For example, it is often argued that a person who has his or her livelihood taken away but who has to meet fixed overheads will turn to illegitimate means to cover these overheads. There are also criminological theories which might be consistent with this. For instance, strain theory (see, for example, Merton, 1964) suggests that where societal values encourage expectations and aspirations which are blocked to certain groups by structural constraints, those groups will turn to criminal behaviour to meet such expectations and aspirations. One way of examining the general proposition is to seek to relate unemployment rates to crime rates. This can be done in two ways. For example, we can collect, for a given point of time, unemployment rates for a number of areas and correlate them with crime rates for those same areas (*cross-sectional* design). An alternative strategy is to examine unemployment rates and crime rates for the same area but at different points of time (*time-series* design). Time-series analyses of data can be carried out for the country as a whole. We shall consider examples of such analyses, using evidence provided by Tarling (1982) in a critical commentary on studies concerned with the relationship between unemployment and crime. Tarling presents statistics, in graph form, which show the relationship between the number of recorded crimes per 100 of the population and the unemployment rate for the period 1950–80 (see Figure 3.1). No figure is quoted but a visual inspection of the graph shows that the statistical association between the two is strong (although, as Tarling reports, the pattern is not uniform and the relationship during the first half of the time period was weaker

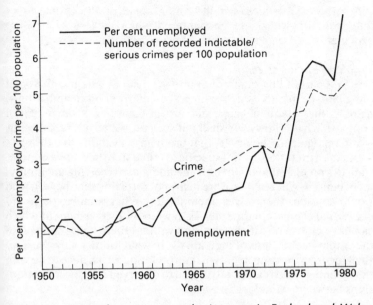

Figure 3.1 *Unemployment rate and crime rate in England and Wales, 1950–80*
Source: Tarling, 1982.

and not statistically significant). In addition, Tarling refers to an analysis for England and Wales which was carried out by Brenner (1976) who used time-series data for the period 1900–70 and found that unemployment was related to recorded crime rates. This relationship persisted even after controlling for other economic variables. Some cross-sectional studies (for example, Carr-Hill and Stern, 1979) provide support for the basic proposition linking crime to unemployment in so far as positive and statistically significant correlations have been discovered, although these are weaker than relationships found in time-series data. (See also Box (1987) for an examination of relationships between economic recession and levels of crime and of prison populations.)

Whether cross-sectional or time-series, such analyses use official data to make assertions about the relationship between indicators of social phenomena, in this case crime and unemployment. Such assertions are founded upon the discovery of statistical associations between these indicators. Although the statistics are the outcomes, on the one hand, of individual criminal actions and, on the other hand, individual employment statuses, the analysis is carried out on *aggregate* data, that is, data aggregated for particular units of analysis. In the remainder of this section this use of aggregate data will serve as a vehicle for indicating some of the problems of interpretation which are encountered when seeking to develop explanations of crime and criminality via quantitative research.

Problems of interpretation
The first part of this chapter has already dealt at length with one of the main problems which can make interpretation ambiguous, namely, the validity of crime statistics as measures of the extent of crime. In what follows, we shall put such problems to one side. It is worth recognizing, however, that problems of validity and disputes about interpretation are not specific to crime statistics. For example, statistics on unemployment only include those receiving unemployment benefit, whereas there are many not receiving such benefit who would consider themselves unemployed. What is more, there are occasional changes in the rules as to who can receive benefit which can have effects on official statistics without there being changes in the employment status of individuals. In what follows, however, we shall focus on those problems of interpretation which have to do with the meaning which can be attributed to observed statistical relationships between variables. These are

(a) the problem of causality
(b) the problem of significance
(c) the problem of the wrong level
(d) the problem of meaning

Correlation and causality
First of all we need to explain what is meant by correlation. Correlation is a statistical measure of association which gives an indication of the extent to which two or more variables co-vary. There are many correlation coefficients but they each share the same basic features. Typically, a coefficient can range from a value of 0, which indicates that two variables do not co-vary, to a value of 1, which indicates that there is perfect co-variation and also that, given the value of one variable (for example, unemployment), the value of another variable (level of crime) can be predicted with absolute certainty. In practice, correlations between these extremes are rarely found, and values lying somewhere between 0 and 1 are more typical. A value of 0.6 or 0.7 is considered to indicate a strong relationship between two variables. It is possible for values of correlation coefficients to vary between 0 and +1 (a positive correlation) or 0 and −1 (a negative correlation). A negative correlation of, say, −0.6, indicates that high scores on one variable tend to be associated with low scores on the other variable. A positive correlation indicates that the variables vary with each other in such a way that high scores

on one tend to be associated with high scores on the other and low scores with low scores. The correlation between unemployment and crime rates is positive in so far as high levels of crime appear to be associated with high levels of unemployment. Correlations carry no assumptions as to causality: they simply indicate that two variables co-vary. For this reason, a correlation indicates no more than that variables are symmetrically related.

The notion of causality is one over which there has been much philosophical debate and disagreement. However, at its centre it has the idea of 'producing', that is, the proposition linking crime to unemployment has some implicit assumption that changes in the crime rate are produced by changes in the level of unemployment. Changes in the crime rate, it is suggested, are *dependent* upon, and *determined* by, changes in the level of unemployment. It is for this reason that the search for causal explanation of crime and criminality are typically associated with psychological and sociological *determinism*. It is also for this reason that causal relations are asymmetrical relations: crime levels are determined by unemployment levels and not vice versa. Causality is not something which can be directly observed. However, quantitative research is often based upon the assumption that it is possible to provide evidence in support of statements about causal relations. One form of evidence is that provided by correlation co-efficients. For instance, evidence that unemployment levels and crime levels co-vary is a good starting point for giving support to the proposition that it is increases in unemployment which cause increases in the level of crime. However, this is not by itself sufficient. Two further pieces of evidence are necessary.

The first of these is connected to what is known as *spuriousness*. A relationship is said to be spurious when there is in fact no direct causal link between two variables even though a quite high correlation may be found. This high coefficient is accounted for by the separate and causal connections between each of the two variables and a third factor. So, for example, it is necessary to satisfy ourselves that the co-variation between unemployment and crime is not due to the possibility that each has a separate causal connection with some third factor, say, level of urbanization. There is always the possibility that urbanization increases crime levels and at the same time also increases unemployment. It is difficult to determine which relationships are, and are not, spurious but there are statistical techniques associated with causal modelling which allow researchers to investigate a suspected spurious relationship between two variables whilst controlling for a third factor (for an elaboration of such techniques and of causal modelling see, for example, Blalock, 1961, 1969, 1971; Heise, 1969, 1975).

That apart, there is still further evidence which is required, namely evidence as to causal direction and time ordering. As indicated earlier, correlations simply indicate a symmetrical relationship in which either changes in unemployment bring about changes in the level of crime or changes in the level of crime bring about changes in the level of unemployment. What we require is evidence that one of these changes occurred after the other. Cross-sectional designs which collect data at particular points of time find it very difficult to provide evidence as to time-ordering. Time-series designs, however, are on much firmer ground in so far as they can observe changes over time and possibly demonstrate, say, that changes in increases in the level of crime only occurred after increases in the level of unemployment. Even here, however, there are ambiguities, particularly where, as with crime rates, there has in any case been a long-term trend of increases. Tarling refers to McClintock and Avison (1968) in noting that, with a few exceptions, recorded crime has continued to rise progressively since the First World War. Where such trends exist it is difficult to attribute any changes in this crime rate to the occurrence of subsequent factors. Tarling agrees with McClintock and Avison's conclusion:

Such a long term trend indicates the need for a cautious approach when considering general explanations based merely on recent social changes or economic conditions and would suggest that a more searching and systematic enquiry into the development of criminality and social structure may be necessary. (McClintock and Avison, 1968, quoted in Tarling, 1982, p. 29)

Statistical and substantive significance
The interpretation of correlations is not confined to examining the value of the co-efficient in order to make some assertion about the strength of relationship between two variables. Typically, researchers will also assess the statistical significance of any correlation. A correlation between two variables is said to be statistically significant if it can be shown that it is highly unlikely to have occurred by chance, and tests of significance are available in order to calculate the odds that this is likely to be the case. In the social sciences it is usual to work to at least a 95 per cent level of probability. This means that for any correlation coefficient which is significant at this level of probability, there is a 5 per cent chance that the result may be a fluke of that particular research. Tarling refers to research findings which indicate that the relationship between unemployment and crime is statistically significant. This means that, in that particular research, unemployment rates and crime rates are related (although not necessarily causally) and the relationship is not likely to be a chance

inding of that particular research. In other words, the connection is ikely to be real. Unfortunately, the use of tests of significance in relation to statistical measures such as correlations is itself given too much significance. Statistical significance only means that the data ndicate the possible existence of a relationship. It gives us some grounds for placing confidence in findings that, say, unemployment and crime are related, but statistical significance by itself does not ell us anything about the *importance* of unemployment rates in explaining changes in crime rates. As Atkins and Jarrett (1979) point out,

> a 'significant' result sounds as if it must be an important result scientifically or socially – such as the clarification of a socially important problem, the development of an explanation for some puzzling phenomenon, or the success of a new programme of action. Not only the general public but social scientists, politicians and statisticians are apt to confuse statistical significance with these other kinds of significance. (Atkins and Jarrett, 1979, p. 89)

One of these other kinds of significance is known as *substantive significance*. In a seminal paper on statistical problems in research design, Kish (1959) emphasized the distinction between statistical and substantive significance and also counselled against the reliance on statistical significance alone. It is obviously important to have some indication of the possibility that a relationship may exist but what is of much more importance is, as Kish points out, the question does the result show a relationship which is of substantive interest because of its nature and its magnitude' (p. 337). Substantive interest permits us to estimate the importance of any variable in explaining, say, variations in the level of crime.

How, then, can we calculate substantive significance. Fortunately, the answer to this is relatively simple. Assume, for example, that research indicates a statistically significant correlation between unemployment rates and levels of crime of $+0.6$ ($r = +0.6$). Also assume at least for theoretical reasons, that, we believe that it is changes in unemployment levels which produce changes in crime rates. On the surface the relationship would appear to be quite strong but is it substantively significant? Substantive significance is given by mathematically squaring the correlation coefficient (i.e. r-squared) and expressing the result in percentage terms. So, for example, the correlation of $+0.6$ tells us that variations in the level of unemployment account for 36 per cent of the variation in the level of crime (that is, $0.6^2 \times 100 = 36\%$). Another way of expressing this is by pointing out that 64 per cent (that is, $100\% - 36\%$) is unexplained by unemployment and can only be accounted for by other factors.

Too heavy reliance on correlation coefficients and their statistical significance would hide important findings and perhaps over-estimate the substantive importance of unemployment.

It is because any single factor is unlikely to account for anything but a small amount of the variation in crime levels that quantitative researchers have made use of forms of multivariate analysis. With multivariate analysis it is possible to consider the relationship between levels of crime and several other variables at one and the same time. The benefits of multivariate analysis include the following; first, it is possible to gain an estimate of the substantive significance of a combined set of explanatory variables; second, weights can be attributed to each explanatory variable which are proportionate to the importance of any variable in explaining variations in crime levels, while holding constant the effects of all other explanatory variables. For example, Baldwin and Bottoms (1976) used multivariate analysis to examine the relationship between crime rates for areas in Sheffield and thirty-one indicators of other features of these areas, of which 'type of housing tenure' emerged as the most substantively significant. (The use of multi-variate analysis in Baldwin and Bottoms' and other criminological research is discussed in detail by Herbert, 1982, pp. 80–9.)

Ecological fallacies

Ecological fallacies relate to what is known as the problem of the wrong level. The research reported by Tarling makes use of aggregate data, that is, data aggregated for units of analysis beyond that of the individual. For example, the data which form the basis of Figure 3.1 relate to England and Wales. A statistically and substantively significant correlation between levels of unemploy-ment and levels of crime can serve as a basis for making *predictions* about the levels of crime which can be expected with certain specified levels of unemployment. What is more, provided we are satisfied as to non-spuriousness and time-ordering the observed co-variation could also serve as a basis for tentative *explanations* of changes in levels of unemployment. However, it is important to recognize that such pre-dictions and explanations will only apply at the aggregate level. A correlation between variables using aggregate data does not automatic-ally carry any predictive or explanatory power with regard to the relation-ship between unemployment and crime *at the level of the individual*.

The incorrectness of jumping from relationships between properties at one level of analysis (for example, unemployment levels and crime levels for England and Wales) to those same properties at another level (for example, unemployment and crime for individuals) is known as the ecological fallacy or the fallacy of the wrong level. This has been described by Galtung as follows:

In general, the 'fallacy of the wrong level' consists not in making *inferences* from one level of analysis to another, but in making direct *translation* of properties *or relations* from one level to another, i.e. making too simple inferences. (Galtung, 1967, p. 45)

It is theoretically possible for correlation at two levels to be identical but this is highly unlikely. (The literature on this, and on the ecological fallacy in general, has become rather technical. Detailed references can be found in Robson, 1969, and in Bulmer, 1986).

As Alker (1969) has pointed out, the fallacy of the wrong level can be committed upwards by projecting incorrectly from properties of individuals to properties of groups or other collectivities of which they are a part. However, more usually it is committed downwards by projecting from aggregates to individuals. This downward fallacy was first spotlighted by Robinson (1950) who, in analysing statistics for region and states in America, found a strong correlation between the percentage of blacks in these areas and the percentage of illiterates. But he also found that the statistical relationship between these properties at the level of the individual was very weak. In terms of the relationship between unemployment and crime the downward ecological fallacy would be committed by using a strong statistically and substantively significant correlation for England and Wales to predict that unemployed individuals commit crimes or to explain individual criminal action in terms of that individual's employment status.

Relationships in aggregate data are valuable in themselves. What is more, while relationships between properties at one level are not transferable to another level they can indicate the value of carrying out research at this other level. For example, correlations between levels of unemployment and levels of crime using aggregate data should provide a spur to research at the level of the individual, perhaps using interview-based surveys. In fact, analyses of data from the Cambridge longitudinal survey of delinquency have found correlations between unemployment and subsequent delinquent behaviour at an individual level (West and Farrington, 1977; West, 1982). These by no means establish whether being unemployed causes crime. More recently, a research paper also from the Cambridge Institute draws on the same survey. It compares the offending rates of sample members while in employment with offending rates while unemployed. The authors estimated that the offending rate while unemployed was significantly higher than when employed. Statistical modelling techniques suggested that the offending rate was 2.41 times greater when a youth was unemployed than when he was employed. However, once again one should exercise caution as to making assertions as to causality. As the authors themselves indicate:

This research is highly suggestive but it does not prove that unemployment causes crime. This could only be demonstrated in a randomised experiment in which employment levels were systematically varied. For ethical reasons, such an experiment would need to consist of an attempt to reduce unemployment levels in an experimental group in comparison with a control group. (Farrington *et al.*, 1986)

Such a research design seems a rather clinical way of studying what can be a very personal concern. However, it does indicate a rather novel way in which social research can improve the life choices of individuals – at least for those chosen to be in the experimental group.

The problem of meaning

Conclusions based upon the analysis of correlations need to be treated with care. As has been pointed out, there are the well known perils of making inferences about causality. There is also the danger of placing too much emphasis upon statistical, as opposed to substantive, significance and there are the risks of committing the fallacy of the wrong level. This does not mean, however, that such quantitative research is without value. What is required is a sensible and realistic stance towards statistical analysis, that is, one that recognizes that there will always be ambiguities of interpretation and that statistical analysis cannot, and will not, provide definitive answers to propositions such as those concerning the relationship between unemployment and crime. Given the inherent ambiguities of interpretation, it is perhaps best to treat the conclusions of correlation analysis as indicative rather than definitive, that is, indicative of certain patterns and connections which are worthy of further and more detailed investigation. This is to agree with Baldwin and Bottoms' viewpoint on ecological analysis that

> if one breaks away from the tradition of regarding epidemiology and ecology as important per se and regards them rather as important *means to an end*, the end being to provide explanation and meanings of the phenomena studied, then such work . . . can be regarded as crucial contributors. This in itself however implies a particular methodology: that one will begin with epidemiological variations as a first stage in research, and then in the second stage go on to investigate more deeply certain relationships discovered (Baldwin and Bottoms, 1976, p. 16)

As has been pointed out there are dangers in using statistical relationships between unemployment levels and crime levels to make assertions about individuals. Nevertheless, such relationships indicate the potential value of research which collects data from and about individuals concerning the effects of unemployment with particular regard to criminal actions. Where such research is survey based it is likely to be geared to the search for statistical associations and sensitivities as to the problems of interpretation must be maintained. But further, particular attention should be paid to *meaning*, that is, to the meaning which unemployment has for the individuals concerned. Correlations between unemployment and crime at whatever level are not in themselves adequate. What is missing is some theoretical explanation of the relationship in terms of the subjective significance which unemployment has for some individuals which leads them to criminal actions. In this way criminal actions are rendered intelligible in terms of unemployment and what it means for the individuals concerned. The problem of meaning is primarily the domain of qualitative research, which is discussed in the following section.

Explaining crime: qualitative research

Nature of qualitative research

In the preceding chapter qualitative data were described as those forms of data collected about the social world which are not set in numerical terms. Qualitative research is research which seeks to collect such data and as such is a very broad and general category which encompasses a wide range of research activities and styles. In this section we are specifically concerned with qualitative research which is in the ethnographic tradition and which gives primacy to descriptions and explanations which are derived from data collected about the actor's point of view of his or her social situation. This research style gives particular emphasis to uncovering social meanings, definitions, stereotypes, typifications and labels, and data are collected by a range of methods which include participant observation and detailed interviews. Discussion of such qualitative research will take place in connection with studies which are concerned with those propositions elaborated earlier which locate crime in the context of schooling, parenting and youth culture.

Early exponents of ethnographic work were the Chicagoans who integrated observational and life-history studies into quantitative ecological research. More recently, qualitative research has been associated with the influence of micro-sociological theories in the study of crime. Such qualitative research flourished in the 1970s as part of the onslaught on positivist explanations of crime and criminality. The micro-sociological framework includes different theoretical strands and influences many of which overlap. Bryman (1988) distinguishes such strands. These are *phenomenology*, which is influenced by the writings of Alfred Schutz and is concerned with the everyday constructs which individuals use to make sense of their world; *ethnomethodology*, which owes much to Harold Garfinkel and which focuses on the methodologies or strategies of practical reasoning used by everyday people; *symbolic interactionism*, derived from the social psychological work of George Herbert Mead, and concerned with social meanings and their generation and modification in processes of interaction; *verstehen*, which is founded upon Weber's edict to seek subjective understanding of actions and to make explanations adequate at the level of meaning; *naturalism*, and the emphasis upon observing and recording actions as they normally occur and in the natural setting and contexts in which they occur; and *ethnogenics*, a mixture of ethology and social psychology associated with writings of Harré, which seeks to observe 'episodes' of social action in order to examine the underlying structure of such episodes in terms of the meanings which actors bring to them.

Although there are differences between such theoretical approaches they coalesce around a number of methodological commitments which typify qualitative research and which directly derive from their main theoretical tenets.

Methodological commitments

First, as already indicated there is a commitment to the actor's point of view. This is closely tied to a fundamental assumption which all micro-sociological theories share, namely, that the social world of any particular group or sub-culture is socially constructed. Therefore, in order to explain, say, crime in that group or sub-culture it is necessary to direct empirical inquiry at social actors and at the way in which they actively engage in the construction of their social world. In turn, this requires that attention should be paid to the sense which individuals make of their own and others' actions and also of events and situations which confront them. They do this, it is argued, by attaching meanings and definitions to such actions, events and situations in order to understand for themselves what is happening, in order to predict what is likely to happen next, and also to prescribe their own future course of action.

Second, such meanings and definitions are not fixed but are generated, 'tested' and refined in social interactions. Therefore, social actions, their meanings, definitions and interpretations should be examined in the context of the normal and everyday exchanges and interactions of the groups and sub-cultures of which they are a part. This not only represents a commitment to naturalism but also to what is termed holism, that is, to the study of specific social actions within their total context. Such a commitment encourages the investigation of, say, crime as part of the fabric of group or sub-cultural life rather than as something which can be extracted from it by answers to a few questions on a questionnaire or an interview schedule. The focus on particular contexts usually means that in contrast with much quantitative work, holistic qualitative research is also small-scale or 'micro' research.

Third, the commitment to the actor's point of view goes hand in hand with the belief that there are many points of view which can be associated with particular individuals or types of individual. The same actions, events or situations can be interpreted differently by different individuals and can result in different prescriptions as to future courses of action. Each interpretation is equally valid and rational for the actors concerned and should be treated as such by the researcher. This commitment to a plurality of meanings and definitions therefore includes a requirement that researchers do not take for granted definitions of, say, crime. So, for instance, there is a requirement to examine different definitions of what is criminal and the ways in which these emerge in specific interactions between, say, individuals and law enforcement officers, and with what effect.

Fourth, qualitative research is typically discovery-based research. Rather than collecting data with which to test some preordained hypothesis, qualitative research seeks to 'discover' hypotheses and generalizations during the process of data collection and analysis. As this process continues hypotheses and generalizations are progressively refined to improve their 'fit' with the data and hence their validity. The systematic and continuous search for negative or falsifying cases, and the subsequent modification of hypotheses and generalization, is known as *analytic induction*, a term first coined by Znaniecki (1934) but which owes much of its prominence to its use by Lindesmith (1968) in his study of opiate addication.

Grounded theory
The discovery-based approach is closely associated with the development of 'grounded theory'. The term grounded theory originated in the writings of Glaser and Strauss (1967) and refers to theory which is generated, tested and refined during fieldwork and by close reference to data. In effect, it is theory which is grounded in data. The notion of grounding theory in data links well with a commitment to collecting data about the actor's point of view in so far as theoretical constructs can be based upon the everyday constructs of actors. What Glaser and Strauss provide is a strategy for handling such data and for formulating theory. The aim is to work outwards from the data to progressively higher levels of theory. In the early stages the researcher uses data to develop important categories such as categories of action or of meaning. Such categories are gradually refined. Later the researcher aims to develop relationships between

categories and to hypothesize about these relationships. Next, the researcher seeks to establish the conditions under which relationships do, or do not, exist and to hypothesize about these. The aim is to generate *substantive* theory, that is, theory developed for a substantive area or empirical context, for example, white-collar crime or youth gangs. The ultimate aim is to subsequently formulate *formal* theory, that is, theory developed for a formal or conceptual area of social science. Ideally, there is a natural progression of movement from data through categorization, to hypothesizing, substantive theory to formal theory.

There are several comments which can be made about the strategy for the development of grounded theory. For example, it assumes that data are lying around waiting to be trawled by researchers and that theory will subsequently emerge from it. It is much more likely that researchers' theoretical presuppositions play an important part in what, in the first place, is selected as data. In turn, such selection will influence what subsequently emerges as theory. Also, the specific strategy as laid down by Glaser and Strauss has rarely, if ever, been religiously followed. Rather, the development of grounded theory represents more of a general commitment for qualitative researchers as opposed to a fixed set of protocols.

The value of grounded theory is that it remains close to the data. However, within this lies one of the difficulties which faces qualitative researchers. The data which are collected are specific to particular individuals, groups and contexts and the desire to remain close to the data has meant that qualitative research has rarely, if ever, moved beyond substantive theory. Indeed, much qualitative research probably gets little further than making empirical generalizations about actions and meanings in the specific context in which they are studied together with some assessment of the applicability to other contexts. Formal theory, on the other hand, has come from pure theorizing. The outcome is that there have been two tendencies, tendencies which are apparent in social science in general as well as within the criminological enterprise. First, there has been a proliferation of empirical studies of particular groups and cultures, for example, youth gangs and police cultures, in particular contexts. These have generated descriptions and explanations of social action in these contexts grounded in the everyday constructs and theories of the actors themselves. Second, there has been sophisticated grand theorizing, typically without reference to first-hand empirical investigation.

Micro–macro relations

The 'tensions' between these two tendencies in the criminological enterprise are most apparent in the connection between participant observation studies and radical theorizing (see cell S in Figure 2.5). It has already been indicated that the first of these tendencies is typified by the micro-sociological investigations of deviant cultures and of police work which developed within criminology as a result of the interactionist challenge to positivism. The second of these tendencies is associated with the detailed and sophisticated debates which have taken place within radical criminology, stimulated particularly by the New Criminology Project (Taylor, Walton and Young, 1973). This project epitomizes these tensions in so far as it was geared to providing a closer integration between, on the one hand, the examination of specific contexts and, on the other, theorizing about social structure. The aim was to produce a full-blown theory of criminology which comprised seven essential components. These included a concern with the immediate background of specific deviant action, say youth gangs, *and* the wider origins of deviance in terms of cultural and structural conflicts, and also concern with the immediate origins of social reaction of, say, police work, *and* with the wider structural contexts of such reaction. In this respect, new criminology sought to integrate interactionist ideas but also to move beyond them by arguing that while individuals choose to act in certain ways they do not do so in conditions of their choosing.

New criminology provided an important stimulus to theoretical discussion and to the development of radical theory. What is more, it provided a potential springboard for an integrated programme of empirical investigation and theorizing about social structure. However, for the most part such research has not materialized (for one recent attempt to relate empirical findings to the propositions of new criminology, see Lowman, 1987). The two tendencies have continued their separate ways with, on the one hand, small-scale qualitative research being accused of naivety in failing to give sufficient weight to the constraints placed on action by structural conflicts and, on the other, macro-theorizing being criticized for taking too many steps backwards along the chain of explanation and thereby failing to explain differential response at the level of the individual and at the level of meaning.

There have, however, been general discussions of the need to integrate naturalistic, participant observational studies with radical structural theory. For example, in a review of naturalistic research into deviant sub-cultures, Roberts (1976), argues for empirical investigation into how the transactions which qualitative research is so adept at uncovering are framed by history and structure. Similarly, Butters (1976) argues for a concern with the 'structural/historical mediations' (p. 270) of participant observational data.

The central problem is, then, to find a way of documenting the ideological practices of youth culture (etc.) which leads to an understanding of the 'structural effectivity' of the complex of contradictions in which they have their determination, while simultaneously opening a road to the identification of the processes of historical movement in which this effectivity is only a conjunctural moment. (Butters, 1976, p. 272)

While obviously addressing the problem it is disappointing that such articulation dulls the enthusiasm to get on with the job of bridging the micro–macro divide.

School and youth culture
Nevertheless, a number of important research-based radical ethnographies have been carried out. For example, with regard to schooling, Sharp and Green's *Education and Social Control* (1975) represents a transition from an interactionist to a Marxist analysis. They summarize their theoretical and methodological position as follows:

The individual can only be understood in terms of his embeddedness in a societal context, giving rise to a level of problem which is emergent from and not reducible to our knowledge of individuals. Indeed, we would go further than this and suggest that the individual may not always be important or even relevant in the course of historical and social change. The task of the social scientist therefore, far from attempting some hermeneutic understanding of the individual acting subject in all his idiosyncracy and uniqueness should be to look behind the level of immediacy in order to try to develop some sociology of situations, their underlying structure and interconnections and the constraints and contingencies they impose. (Sharp and Green, 1975, p. 25)

For Sharp and Green the key aspects of social structure are the modes and forces of material production. These express themselves in the distribution of resources and power not only at a societal level but also within the school. The specific research implications of this were in terms of the collection of data about the unequal distribution of resources and power within the school and how these were expressed in specific relations. For example, they collected data about power implicit in staff relations (particularly headmaster–teacher relations), about teacher–pupil relations and about teacher–parent relations. They also examined power in terms of the ability to impose definitions of reality on others and to constrain the action of others.

Corrigan's (1979) ethnography of two schools in Sunderland is much more centrally concerned with schooling and 'delinquent' youth sub-culture. The natural development of his ethnography reflects the tensions between the micro and the macro. Official statistics on crime have regularly demonstrated that the peak age of delinquent activity corresponds to the last year of compulsory education. When the school-leaving age was raised, the peak offending age increased accordingly. This statistical regularity has acted as a spur to investigations of delinquency and aspects of schooling but these have largely been survey-based and have sought explanations in terms of variables such as 'school performance' or 'scholastic attainment' (for a review of research on schools and delinquency, see Graham, 1986, 1988). Such surveys pay little, if any, attention to social meanings or to the social context of the school. Corrigan's work is very much concerned with such matters. Indeed, initially he was strongly influenced by the theoretical ideas from an interactionist perspective and was keen to capture and describe the experiences of school in the boys' own terms.

The methods he used to collect data were consistent with this. For example, he inevitably turned to participant observation but this had to be rejected on the grounds that the only role available to him was that of teacher and he felt that such a role was likely to place a barrier between himself and the main subjects of his inquiry, the boys. In the end he created a role for himself, that of 'writer':

> The role of writer, of someone writing a book about them, was the truest one: I said I was only interested in them: that *they* were the reason that I was at the school: that I wanted them to say the things the way they wanted, using their language, and I didn't care about spelling or grammar, or talking proper. This had an important effect since I was in their minds Paul Corrigan who was writing a book about them, and also I was actually interested in *their* words and ideas. (Corrigan, 1979, p. 13)

In addition, he used questionnaires to collect background information about the boys and about their experiences of school. The latter was done by administering self-completion sentences such as, 'I come to school because . . .'. He also interviewed boys in one of the schools but was refused permission to conduct interviews by the headmaster of the other. Finally, he spent a considerable amount of time hanging around the school and the streets talking to the boys.

Although Corrigan does not himself describe it as such, his work was discovery-based. The central concepts of interactionism influenced his early collection of data but he gradually developed generalizations which moved away from such interactionism and which, he claims, more closely fit the data.

I went to start my research with one view of education and left with another; the evidence contained in the middle of that process of change in outlook comes mainly from a group of 14–15 year olds. (Corrigan, 1979, p. 2)

The boys consistently referred to their experiences of school, of teachers and of the police in terms of power. This led Corrigan to an explanation of the actions of the kids in terms of the power wielded by the state and its agents (teachers and police), a state which, it is argued, is an expression of the bourgeoisie class in a capitalist society. His analysis uses historical materials from inspectorate reports of the nineteenth century to assert that the history of state education in Britain demonstrates that such education is geared, among other things, to the imposition of bourgeois values and patterns of behaviour on the working class and also to the creation of a disciplined workforce. Education, and policing, are forms of state control and intervention.

The role of the police and the role of the education system are parallel here, because they are both attempting to change the styles of living people who already exist and are seen as threatening by ruling groups in society. (Corrigan, 1979, p. 139)

Truanting, 'mucking about' at school and 'doing nothing' on the streets are attempts to sabotage the attacks which are made upon the boys by the state via schools, teachers and police. Of mucking about at school he enlists the imagery of guerrilla warfare to describe the boys' actions:

The guerrilla forces act within their own ideology of resistance, one which is usually deemed as irrational by the state powers; they use heartlands from which to attack the state power, heartlands which are mainly inaccessible to the agents of the state. (p. 71)

And of getting into trouble on the streets,

The police, like the teachers, are a group of people with power that do some very strange and arbitrary things; their power is massive and has to be coped with, if not obeyed. As in the classroom, the methods of coping with individuals with power are many and varied, like giving wrong names and addresses. (p. 137)

Corrigan's research brings together empirical inquiry of specific meanings and actions in a specific context with theoretical ideas which have to do with social structure. It is 'grounded' in so far as it places reliance on the accounts of the kids themselves, particularly with regard to how they experience schooling and law enforcement. Their actions are viewed as the outcome of what they perceive as the imposition of power by teachers and police officers. However, the difficulty of this analysis is that of demonstrating that actions *are* the result of power relations, particularly those relating to such relations which emanate from the demands of capitalism. The accounts of kids can be justifiably used to sustain an argument that the perceived imposition of power determines actions. However, it is a tall order to expect such accounts to be capable of supporting explanations in terms of differential relations to the modes of production and the role of the state, via education and law enforcement, in maintaining these. In this sense, there is a feeling of macro-theory being used *ex post facto* to provide a total and complete explanation.

Discourse as object of inquiry

Silverman (1985) suggests a research-based strategy which seeks to bridge the micro–macro divide but which also seeks to avoid reductionism (that is, the treatment of all social phenomena, such as youth delinquency, as the product of macro- or, for that matter, micro-processes). He does this by distilling the methodological strengths from some of the writings of Foucault (1977, 1978, 1979, 1980, 1986). In particular, he takes Foucault's focus on *discourse* as a potential object of inquiry which permits the examination of individual action within a macro-setting. For Foucault, discourse is the very essence of communication between individuals; it is not merely a form of interaction, it *is* it. Whilst at a micro-level discourse is the substance of interaction it also originates largely out of our control and therefore has some macro-quality. However, society is viewed as not a concrete objective reality but as comprising an array of discourses. Power is inherent in discourse such that within interactions between, say, youths and law enforcement officers there are notions of what is good and bad, right and wrong, criminal and not criminal and solutions in terms of theoretical explanations of these, as well as techniques of regulation and control. However, such power is not viewed as emanating from one source, but as being much more diffuse. It is not the exclusive property of one class or of the state but is dispersed throughout institutions and relations. So whilst there are similarities with radical Marxist-based theory in terms of an insistence on the importance of power, it is treated differently and it is not seen as having its source in class relations.

The implication of Foucault's position as expressed by Silverman is that a research agenda can be developed which seeks integration of the micro and macro in terms of the analysis of discourse. It does this at the same time as analysing crime and crime control in terms of the network of relations between institutions, and the diffusion of power and the strategies and techniques by which power is exercised within discourse and throughout society. Foucault's research is largely restricted to the analysis of texts, as in *Pierre Riviere* (Foucault, 1978), but inquiry can equally centre on other forms of communication and interaction. What is more, it can examine specific and small-scale interactions between individuals and law enforcement officers and, at a societal level, the publication of official discourses such as reports of Royal Commissions or of judicial inquiries into disorders. There is the possibility of different objects of inquiry examining in different contexts using different methods of research.

Conclusion

The distinction between quantitative and qualitative research is often drawn too sharply. What is more, the connections between quantitative research and positivism and qualitative research and non-positivist paradigms are often presented as necessary connections. As suggested in the preceding chapter, such distinctions and connections can be made. However, as Bryman (1988) persuasively argues, the distinctions between types of research and also the connections which are made between types of research and theoretical paradigms portray too simple a picture. The danger of this is that of too readily assuming that quantitative and qualitative research represent competing approaches and also that they present 'either–or' alternatives as to strategies of research. This is too rigid a formulation for a criminological enterprise which exhibits plurality in terms of the questions which can be asked of crime and the criminal justice system and in terms of the plurality of theoretical perspectives which promote such questions. In some instances quantitative and qualitative methods do represent alternatives but in others they can work hand in hand in such a way that distinctions are blurred. In either case, what is required is a sensitivity to the potentials and the limits of the contributions of different forms of data and different methods of data collection and analysis to the criminological problems under examination and to the theoretical questions being asked of them.

4

Studying the criminal justice system

Introduction

Criminological research is concerned with a wide range of problems and issues. These have been outlined in Chapter 1 and encompass questions such as 'what is the extent of crime?', 'what is the social and ecological distribution of crime?', 'can criminal behaviour be explained in terms of the characteristics of individuals?', 'what are the social determinants of crime?', 'how is crime experienced by victims?', 'what are the systems for the control and prevention of crime and for the punishment and treatment of offenders?'. Research about these questions focuses on particular 'objects' of inquiry. These are the basic units of analyses about which data are collected. They can include specific individuals such as a professional fence (see, for example, Klockars (1974), *The Professional Fence*), social groups such as gangs of soccer hooligans (see, for example, Williams, Dunning and Murphy (1984), *Hooligans Abroad*) and institutions such as the British Police (see, for example, Holdaway (1983) *Inside the British Police*). Here we ground ourselves in case studies about different 'objects' of inquiry with particular reference to those individuals, social groups and institutions which comprise the criminal justice system. This is done as a vehicle by which a number of problems and issues about criminological investigation can be considered. These include problems of getting approval to conduct research in corners of the criminal justice system which, for one reason or another, are closed to outsiders; the ethical dimensions of the collection of data by covert means from individuals who have a vested interest in protecting themselves from the prying eyes of criminological researchers; the problems of getting research findings and conclusions into the public domain, particularly where these appear to compromise powerful groups and individuals; and the use, or non-use, of research findings by politicians and other decision makers.

Such issues are not exclusive to research about the criminal justice system. Indeed, they can be just as pertinent in research we discussed in the preceding section about the extent of crime and about explanations of criminal behaviour. However, there are certain features of the criminal justice system which ensure that such issues are brought into sharp relief. For example, some areas of the criminal justice system, particularly prisons, are formally closed, and any visitor – researcher or otherwise – needs permission to enter. Even where permission is granted, activities are severely curtailed. Where access does not need to be formally negotiated, for example in the courtroom, many of the day-to-day activities are 'backstage' and there are individuals and groups that have interests in ensuring they remain hidden from view. What is more, the criminal justice system as a whole is concerned with practices and policies about the detection, control and punishment of crime, each of which has important security aspects and the interests of security, however they may be defined, invariably run contrary to the goals and aims of researchers. More fundamentally, these practices and policies are inevitably underpinned by important political viewpoints about which there is often considerable dispute. It is not surprising, therefore, that those who formulate such policies and those who activate them are sensitive to and often hostile towards those who appear to be questioning or undermining such policies and practices.

Throughout the case studies we shall consider, two important themes reoccur. First, the need to treat 'objects' of inquiry as subjects; second, the need to examine the respective interests of four broad groups of people – subjects, gatekeepers, sponsors and researchers – and the power relations which exist between them.

'Objects' as subjects

Although we may refer to individuals and groups within the criminal justice system as the 'objects' of our inquiry, they should not be treated as would a chemist treat a chemical substance or a geologist would treat a rock. The objects of criminological inquiry are not inanimate. Rather they are individuals or collectivities of individuals who have feelings and emotions, personal and group values, private and group interests. What is more, they are capable of endowing their own and others' actions with social meanings and definitions. Even where ostensibly we are concerned with a particular institution – say, the prison system – it is inevitable that we must collect data from and about the individuals who fill roles within it.

Recognizing objects as subjects is important to us for two reasons. The first of these we may describe as broadly theoretical. We may seek to conceptualize and theorize in as objective a way as possible about systems of criminal justice but we should not lose sight of the fact that, in large part, such systems are the outcomes of the actions of individuals and groups of individuals. This means that the criminological research agenda often requires us to collect data from and about individuals and to pay attention to their actions and to the subjective processes which influence them. This is very much the thrust of those theoretical approaches discussed in preceding chapters which play down positivist determinist explanations but which seek instead to examine the ways in which reality is socially constructed. The recognition of the importance of social construction is also the recognition of the importance of treating individuals as subjects.

Second, viewing objects as subjects has important political implications for the way in which criminological research can and should be carried out. For those who are the focus of this research, the reality of being part of the criminal justice system cannot easily be separated from the reality of being the object of academic inquiry. The social meanings and definitions, interests and values which have a vital part to play in the way in which participants relate to one another and the way in which the system 'works' also have an important part to play in the way in which these same participants relate to the researcher and to the act of being researched. The objects' of inquiry have a strong stake in what is being researched, about whom and for what reason. They see themselves as having interests which need protection or which deserve promotion and they seek to exert influence – formally and informally – on the research process in order to fulfil these aims. This influence can be exerted in a number of ways. For example, they can seek to ensure that their interests are portrayed in the best light. Alternatively, they can seek to ensure that information that is detrimental to the successful portrayal of such interests is withheld. This can be done either at the stage of data collection where the nature of the information given or not given to the researcher may be formally or informally 'managed', or it can be achieved by ensuring that, by whatever mechanism is available, the findings are not published. More forthrightly, vested interestes may be able to prevent the execution of the research in the first place.

In this chapter we shall put to one side the theoretical reasons for treating objects as subjects and focus instead on the political aspects of criminoligical research. Such political considerations invariably translate into ethical dilemmas for the researcher in so far as he or she has to consider the means by which data can, and should, be collected and also the lengths to which he or she can, and should, go to uncover participants' interests. Whereas the politics of criminological inquiry are concerned with whether subjects are threatened by research, and why, the ethics of such inquiry are concerned with whether subjects are likely to be damaged by research and with whether such damage is justified. The criminological researcher has a commitment to validity, that is, to ensuring that conclusions derived from any investigation are true to what is being described and explained. The protection of interests by subjects is one of the barriers to the maintenance of such validity. The ethical dilemma which faces the researcher is the extent to which particular methods of social investigation should be used to invade such interests in the pursuit of knowledge.

Politics of criminological inquiry

The second main theme is that the subjects of research should not be viewed in isolation from others who also have interests to promote and to protect and therefore also have an interest in the conduct of research into aspects of criminal justice. Therefore it is important to examine the politics of criminological inquiry beyond the research relationship between researcher and subject to encompass an analysis of a wider circle of political interests. To do this we can draw upon Barnes's (1979) typology of groups of individuals who have some interest in the research process. Although this typology is used by Barnes to refer to social science research in general it provides a useful means of uncovering the key vested interests to criminological research.

Subjects of inquiry

First, Barnes refers to 'citizens' which can be treated here as being synonymous with what we have termed *subjects*. (Barnes uses the term 'citizens' out of recognition of the fact that the subjects of social inquiry have rights and duties as members of society. Whilst not wanting to deny the usefulness of this point, the term 'subjects' is preferred here to emphasize the earlier distinction which was made between objects of inquiry and subjects.) In terms of the case studies which will be considered in subsequent sections, subjects include prisoners, police officers, court officials, barristers and defendants, and young offenders. Although each may have rights and duties as citizens in terms of their membership of society, such rights and duties can be restricted or enhanced by the fact of their position in the criminal justice system. For example, the rights of prisoners are severely limited if only because of their incarceration. This can severely inhibit their positive freedom to do whatever they want but also their negative freedom to prevent having things done to them. The latter may, of course, include being the subject of some officially sponsored or officially recognized prison research.

The duties of police officers, on the other hand, are greater, at least in practice, than those of everyday citizens. With regard to the legal position of the police, the constable is said to have an 'original' and 'independent' status. The 1962 Royal Commission on the Police, whose report was followed by the Police Act 1964, summarized the position as follows:

> The present status of the office of constable has been defined by the Courts as that of an officer whose authority is original, not delegated, and is exercised at his own discretion by virtue of his office; he is neither a crown servant nor a servant of the police authority. We do not recommend any alteration in the legal status of police officers of any rank. (Royal Commission on the Police, 1962)

This does not mean, however, that the constable's actions are unbounded. There exists, at least in theory, a number of checks on police actions. In the first place, the general law of the land enforced by the courts does not permit police constables to do anything unlawful. Second, the direction of police duties is in the hands of the chief constable, and constables have a duty to obey the lawful instructions of senior police officers providing this does not clash with their 'original' and 'independent' overriding duty to the law. Nevertheless, the constable's position in law gives him or her rights, duties and obligations over and above those of everyday citizens. What is more, the way in which these can be activated can be the subject of considerable discretion as a result of the constable's position in police organization. The police officer works in a system similar to what has been called 'front line organization' (Smith, 1965) in which individuals working at the front line have considerable scope for action, even though they are formally under command from the centre. In front-line organization, the initiative is often in the hands of front line units (individuals or groups). The front-line unit can perform its tasks independently of other units, and, according to the nature of the job, there are often barriers to the direct supervision of the activities of some units. As Jones points out:

> Uniformed patrol officers are difficult to supervise because constant observation of their activities is not possible, nor is subsequent inspection of their actions easily achieved. Patrol officers usually work alone on beats outside police stations where the usual organizational controls of hierarchical and peer group supervision are largely ineffective . . . Difficulty in providing supervision is one of the sources of the patrol man's autonomy and discretion and, therefore, why from a control point of view he must be of most important concern to the police organization. (Jones, 1979, p. 8)

The special position of the constable in law together with the scope for discretionary action place an onus on the officer to be open about the conduct of his or her actions. But in reality this can result in the clouding of what is done in any particular situation. All citizens can claim a right to be free from the gaze of social researchers. However, as will be argued later, the enhanced rights and duties of police officers under the law provides a reciprocal reduced right of such officers to be free from the investigations of criminological researches.

Researchers

We can now turn to the 'scientists'. The scientists are those who carry out empirical investigations and who analyse the data derived from such investigations with a view to reaching certain conclusions. For our purposes they are researchers who populate what we have termed the criminological enterprise. They are interested in the range of issues and problems we discussed in Chapter 1, and they come from different discriplinary backgrounds, usually psychology and sociology; they have differing theoretical commitments, such as commitments to personality theories, socialization theories, labelling approaches or Marxism; and they work in different institutional contexts, such as in academia, or in official state-sponsored research institutes. Here we shall use the term *researcher* rather than scientist so as not to present an impression of a commitment to the 'criminologist-as-scientist' viewpoint.

Gatekeepers

Next, there are *gatekeepers*. Gatekeepers are people who can control the access which the researchers are permitted to have to the subjects of research or to secondary sources such as organizational records and statistics. They can be individuals from whom official permission is required in order to enter a particular research context or individuals who have to be manoeuvred in so far as they have informal means of withholding access to subjects or to other sources of data. In some investigations researchers will have to manoeuvre layers of gatekeepers, some formal and others informal. Gate keepers can exercise a formidable influence on the research process. They can prevent the start of any project, and even if they do not they can steer the research in particular directions for their own benefit. For example, they can direct the researcher to certain kinds of subjects and to certain types of data and they can fail to direct the researcher to other kinds of subjects and other types of data. Because of its 'closed' nature, the criminal justice system is littered with gate keepers, formal and informal. As we shall see in the next section the Home Office has the formal right and the formal means to contro

research in prisons. In a further section we will discuss Punch's study
of Amsterdam police which demonstrates that even where formal
access is granted there are numerous, often informal, gates to be
manoeuvred. In certain instances the researcher is often not even
aware that such gates exist. This can result in research being aborted.

Sponsors of research

Finally, there are *sponsors*. Not all social research requires funding
and indeed many researchers deliberately do not seek funding so as
to avoid the risk of constraints which may be placed upon their work
by sponsors. Nevertheless, a great deal of criminological research is
funded, and because of its cale, could not be completed without such
funding. Two major suppliers of finance for criminological research
are the Economic and Social Research Council (ESRC) and also the
Home Office via the work of the Home Office Research and Planning
Unit (HORPU). Both initiate major programmes of research but
also respond to requests from individual researchers for support for
their investigations. In certain instances ESRC and HORPU work
together in the development of prospectuses for proposed criminological research, and invite tenders, which can have a major influence
on current and future research agendas. In addition to ESRC and
HORPU, there are other independent grant-giving bodies which
support research in the social sciences, for example, the Nuffield
Foundation, or in specific aspects of research in the criminal justice
system, for example, the Police Foundation.

Interests, alliances and power

Distinctions between subjects, researchers, gatekeepers and sponsors form the basis of a typology to assist in the examination of the
politics of criminological research. In the subsequent discussion of
case studies of research this basic model will be further elaborated
in a number of ways. For example, each of the categories of
individuals can be viewed as having goals and aims and, above all,
interests which they seek to promote and protect. Some individuals
have an investment in the protection of personal interests. Punch's
study of Amsterdam police shows the way in which individual
officers' fears of having their corrupt practices exposed had a major
bearing on the course of his research. Others may be concerned with
the protection and even the promotion of group interests. For
example, the consideration of Cohen and Taylor's research in E
Wing will illustrate the way in which the prisoners wanted to use the
research process to further the goals and aims of the prisoner group.
Alternatively, individuals or groups of individuals may have an
investment in the protection of interests of the 'system' of which they
see themselves as being a part or the protection of what they perceive

as being the 'public interest'. For example, as we shall discover, leading members of the Law Society sought to prevent the publication of Baldwin and McConville's research on magistrates' courts on the grounds that it was contrary to the public interest.

We can go further. It is not simply that there are four categories of individuals – subjects, researchers, sponsors, gatekeepers – with interests to protect. Alliances of interest can form (as in the alliance between the political interests of the prisoner group in Durham's E Wing and the political and academic interests of Cohen and Taylor) and conflicts of interest can develop and escalate (as in the conflict between on the one hand the prisoner group and Cohen and Taylor and on the other the Home Office's prison department). There is also the possibility of overlaps between categories of individuals, for example, where sponsors of research are also important gate-keepers. Much of the research in British prisons which has been successfully completed has been sponsored by the Home Office and access to prison facilities and to prisons has been facilitated by the Home Office's prison department (see, for example, Banister *et al.* (1973) and Emery (1970)). The ability of particular groups, or alliances of groups, to protect and promote their goals, aims and interests is dependent upon the *power* each holds *vis-à-vis* the others and the power can either be officially endowed and legitimated, say by the law, or unofficially and informally accumulated by the control and manipulation of everyday social relations. The research process then, is a dynamic interplay between different types of individuals, their interests, goals and aims, the alliances they strike, and the differential power relations which exist between them. The effects of this interplay are felt at different levels. For example, they can influence the everyday practice of research – whether access is successfully negotiated, whether data can be collected and from whom – but perhaps more fundamentally, the interplay influences the ultimate composition of the criminological research agenda – what gets researched, by whom and with what effect.

The analysis can be extended even further. Just as the research act needs to be located within the interplay between subjects, researchers, gatekeepers and sponsors, the interplay itself needs to be placed within the context of the political climate at any given time. Indeed, the relations which represent this interplay are very much influenced by this climate, particularly in terms of the relative power each of the groups derives from it. This political climate is both reflected in, and framed by, the government of the day and it can affect both ends of the research process in terms of what in the first place gets placed on the research agenda and what ultimately gets used in decision-making.

Two aspects of the political climate of the 1980s are worthy of note

First, the 1980s witnessed what Hall (1980) described as a 'drift towards a law and order society'. This found expression in government policies involving greater and more effective policing, stronger emphasis upon crime prevention, greater concern for victims and tougher sentences for offenders. These policy concerns percolated into the official Home Office research agenda via the work of the Research and Planning Unit. The link between such policy concerns and research in relation to them was very much influenced by the government's determination that the HORPU should concentrate on policy related research via its customer-researcher principle (see Chapter 1). Indeed, this was mirrored in the government's belief that social science in general should play greater emphasis on policy-related research. Although the direct influence of the political climate is less easy to demonstrate, research taking place outside official institutions in the 1980s also showed a greater concern with matters of policing, crime prevention, victims and sentencing and a greater concern with the evaluation of policy. The 1980s was not just an era of law-and-order policies. It was also one during which the social sciences were treated with much scepticism by government. The social sciences were viewed either as attacking the 'system' and its policies or, where projects were specifically geared to policy-making, they were considered as not producing sufficiently precise results to provide firm bases for decision-making. Either way, in contrast to the 1960s when the social sciences had an important influence on government decision-making (for example, in the formulation of education policy), the 1980s saw social science findings being pushed down what Becker (1967) called the 'hierarchies of credibility' in terms of being influential on political decision-making. Later in this chapter we shall consider a government-sponsored research project concerned with the effects of tougher detention regimes on young offenders' subsequent behaviour. Although the research showed that such regimes did not have the effect of reducing recidivism these regimes were introduced in all detention centres. The political push for tougher sentences was much more influential that social science research findings in the subsequent decision-making about the introduction of such sentencing policies.

We can summarize the argument so far. It is important to treat the objects of criminological inquiry as 'subjects' for a number of reasons. The way in which individuals are actively involved in the social construction of their world is of fundamental theoretical and methodological interest to the criminological researcher. What is more, the way in which subjects define and react to the research act is of further importance in terms of the kind of data that can be collected or indeed whether subjects will participate in the research at all. These invoke the political and ethical dimensions of the research relationship with subjects. Further, the subjects of criminological research should not be viewed in isolation from researchers, gatekeepers and sponsors. Each of these groups of individuals has particular aims and interests to protect and may seek alliances with others in these endeavours. The ability of groups or alliances of groups to further these aims and interests is dependent upon the extent of power they hold *vis-à-vis* each other. The extent of power is, in part, influenced by the wider political context and the way in which the activities of groups are legitimated by this context. The interplay between subjects, researchers, gatekeepers and sponsors can influence the everyday practice of research – how data are collected and from whom – and wider issues about what research enters the public domain and with what effect.

In the following we look at ways in which research into aspects of the criminal justice system have been influenced by relationships between groups, the interests they represent and the degree of power they hold. We shall consider a number of case studies. In many respects these case studies are *causes célèbres* in so far as they have received considerable publicity and were the focus of much public discussion. Most criminological research faces operational difficulties but only a few projects cause more than a few ripples. Those that do, do so because they have produced some threat to the interests of other parties and particularly to those who have power to influence the course or outcome of research. It is when this happens that the key issues about the ethics and the politics of criminological research are thrown into sharp relief.

Gaining access: research in prisons

All social research involves gaining access to data. Access involves being able to obtain data which is considered relevant or appropriate to the research aims of the investigation. The individuals who are most closely associated with problems of gaining access to data are usually known as gatekeepers. The 'gate' can be exercised in a number of ways. For example, the gatekeeper may have formal powers to exclude researchers from the research situation or he or she may be able to exercise informal management of social situations such that researchers are unwittingly, but effectively, denied access to particular informants and particular forms of data. Often there are layers of gatekeepers to be negotiated, with hierarchies of authority and power between them. For example, in police research the superintendent of a police sub-division can prevent access to officers. However, whatever his wishes or desires, his decisions as to access are worthless if overruled by a chief constable.

The difficulties of obtaining formal access have been most graphically highlighted in relation to some research in prisons. In England and Wales prisons are the responsibility of the prison department within the Home Office. This is headed by the Director General of the Prison Service who is a senior civil servant and who is responsible for the formulation of overall policy, subject to the ratification of the Home Secretary and ultimately Parliament. Individual prisons are administered by a governor. The prison system in Scotland is the responsibility of the Secretary of State for Scotland and civil servants within the Scottish Home and Health Department of the Scottish Office. Within this department there is the equivalent of the prison department in England and Wales, headed by a director. The day-to-day running of Scottish prisons is in the hands of prison governors.

Over the past two decades research in prisons has been decreasing, partly because of cutbacks in the research activities of the HORPU but also because of the suspiciousness of the Home Office towards social science research following the publication of writings about Durham's E Wing by Cohen and Taylor (1972). Such suspiciousness has led to problems of gaining access for researchers. Nevertheless, some research has taken place. For example, King and Elliott (1977) distinguish four types of research: *independent*, where the social scientist is carrying out his or her own research (see, for example, Morris and Morris, 1962); *officially sponsored* (see, for example, Emery, 1970); research based upon *mutual staff and researcher interests* (see, for example, Bottoms and McClintock, 1973); and research based upon *mutual prisoner and researcher interests* (see, for example, Cohen and Taylor, 1972). It is with the last type of research that the problems of gaining access are most likely to occur.

Long-term imprisonment
A central concern of research in prisons has been the problem of long-term prisoners. In England and Wales long-term male prisoners are those sentenced to over four years and long-term female prisoners are those sentenced to over three years imprisonment. In Scotland long-term refers to a sentence of over eighteen months for both sexes. There have been personal accounts of the effects of long-term imprisonment by prisoners themselves (see, for example, Boyle, 1977; McVicar, 1979; and Probyn, 1977). In the late 1960s two social scientists, Stanley Cohen and Laurie Taylor, started research work which was also concerned with the effect of long-term imprisonment and which also sought to describe it from the point of view of prisoners. Their work developed out of classes about sociology with long-term prisoners in the maximum security E-Wing of Durham prison. The classes soon developed into exchanges and

conversations about a whole range of issues of mutual concern. Cohen and Taylor refer to these exchanges and conversations as 'talk' (Cohen and Taylor, 1977, p. 68). This 'talk' was to become an essential component of research which Cohen and Taylor subsequently published in their book *Psychological Survival: the Experience of Long Term Imprisonment* (1972).

Psychological survival in Durham's E Wing

The use of 'talk' as a central pillar of the early researchers was in complete contrast to the more formal research protocols of a group of Home Office researchers, who, coincidentally, had arrived at the prison to carry out psychological research – using structured questionnaires and personality and other psychometric tests – to examine the effects of long-term imprisonment. Their research design was cross-sectional and involved formal interviews with prisoners serving different lengths of imprisonment with a view to testing hypotheses that the effect of imprisonment was to damage intellectual and other faculties. Findings of this research were published in a series of articles in the 1970s. One of these reports that length of imprisonment was not correlated with a reduction in intellectual faculties as measured by intelligence tests (Banister *et al.*, 1973). Further papers gave results derived from the administration of a large battery of standard personality inventories and showed that length of imprisonment was associated with a decrease in extraversion and an increase in hostility particularly as directed against the self. There did not, however, appear to be any effect on neuroticism, emotional stability or spontaneity (Heskin *et al.*, 1973, 1974). A retesting of prisoners and comparisons with an outside control group confirmed the changes in extraversion and in self-directed hostility (Bolton *et al.*, 1976). Overall, the research was highly statistical and within that tradition which emphasizes measurement, hypothesis-testing and explanations in psychological terms.

Theoretical and methodological commitments

To act as a balance to what they saw as an overly psychological approach, Cohen and Taylor suggested embarking on a collaborative research project on exactly the same topic as the Home Office researchers but with different theoretical and methodological thrusts. For example, Cohen and Taylor's aim was to focus on the way in which inmates subjectively interpreted and experienced long-term imprisonment with particular reference to the passage and marking of time, the significance of inmate subculture and the nature of inmate solidarity. Their work was to be discovery-based, being concerned with the description and formulation of ideas about these aspects rather than with the formal testing of hypotheses which is a feature of much of the psychological research which characterized the Home Office project. What is more, they were concerned with prisoners' deterioration in a much wider sense than could be measured by formal tests of cognitive ability. Cohen and Taylor's research was intended as inherently naturalistic, that is, concerned with uncovering the subjective experiences of the inmates in their natural surroundings and as they typically experienced them. As they point out:

> Our research did not look at a specifically constituted experimental environment – like the McGill coffin or the Ames room – but looked rather at a natural one which had been assembled in the real social and political world for a set of specific purposes over a long period of time. The environment, unlike its standard experimental counterpart, was already rich in symbolism, it had a known history and a forseeable future. In all these respects and others, it was unique. (Cohen and Taylor, 1977, p. 71)

Although 'talk' was central to the research, the data Cohen and Taylor collected gradually became more structured. For example, they asked the inmates to respond to specific questions and encouraged them to produce stories, essays and poems on particular topics. Such structured forms of data became the basis for further 'talk' and exchange of mutual interpretations. They also entered into a form of collaborative research in which subjects and researchers are viewed as equal partners and have some equal contribution to make to the final product. The rationale for such collaboration is that if subjects recognize themselves in research accounts this provides one way of establishing the validity of such accounts.

The recognition that the research act is a form of social interaction which all participants endow with meanings and definitions is of fundamental methodological significance since it is relevant to the debate about whether social scientists can, or should, be viewed as objective observers. In this case, however, it was also of critical political significance in terms of whether or not Cohen and Taylor would subsequently be allowed to continue with their research. The unstructured and informal methods of data collection and the recognition of, and use of, the subjects in the research were vital to the theoretical and methodological commitments of Cohen and Taylor. But is was perceived by Home Office officials as the antithesis of what they viewed as the correct protocols of more formal research methods such as experiments and surveys, and was used to justify the claim that Cohen and Taylor were not engaging in legitimate research. There was another way in which a concentration on informal methods, and on 'talk' in particular, contributed to the downfall of the project. Not only was 'talk' open to accusations of being 'unscientific' by prison authorities but it was also an activity over which these authorities have formal control. They have the power to prevent prisoners from talking to researchers and sought to do so partly under the cloak of arguing that the methodological justifications for such talk were not legitimate.

History of the project
So much for the theoretical and methodological underpinnings of Cohen and Taylor's work and the important part they played in its subsequent abortion. The following is a brief history of the research project (the description of events is largely drawn from the only comprehensive accounts available, those by Cohen and Taylor (1975, 1977)). As indicated earlier, Cohen and Taylor began their work with the inmates in the late 1960s and in 1969 formally outlined to the governor of the prison the way in which they hoped to develop their research and announced their intention to publish an article in the journal *New Society*. Cohen and Taylor believed that he was happy with these developments. The Prison Department of the Home Office were not. The department wrote to Cohen and Taylor outlining objections to the research largely on the grounds that their work was too concerned with particular aspects of long-term imprisonment and that its methodological approach was journalistic. Nevertheless, they continued with their classes and with collecting their material. The *New Society* article, entitled 'The experience of time in long term imprisonment', was published in 1970. It emphasized the ways in which prisoners experience and structure time and the way in which inmates seek to mark time in order to combat what for them is a major fear of deterioration during their imprisonment. The Home Office objected to the article because the authors had failed to get official clearance before publication, because of their belief that the research was too subjective and based on too small a number of inmates, and because of the failure, as they saw it, of the researchers to recognize that prison conditions were improving.

In 1971 E Wing was closed and the men were transferred to other prisons. The classes were obviously at an end. Cohen and Taylor had hopes of maintaining contact with the inmates. However, permission to visit them was refused and letters sent to inmates were returned on the grounds that such communications should not be used for research. Cohen and Taylor tried to retrieve their research programme by addressing one of the complaints that had been levelled at their work, namely, that it was based upon a small and unrepresentative sample. They proposed a follow-up project which would include two sub-samples, the original E-Wing inmates and another group of long-termers, but the Home Office rejected the idea of continuing with the original sample. The response of Cohen and Taylor was to publish their work to date in *Psychological Survival: The Experience of Long Term Imprisonment* (1972). The book re-emphasized the inmates' fear of deterioration and further elaborated their earlier analysis of the way in which prisoners handle time and seek to maintain their self-identity. It also contained a detailed rebuff of the accusation that they were referring to conditions which were no longer relevant and a critique of the methodological approach adopted by the Home Office sponsored researchers coupled to a justification of the methods of research they had themselves adopted. The publication of the book led to a further cooling of relations between the Home Office and the researchers. All was not lost, however, and negotiations were renewed at a later date. One positive development was a research proposal submitted by Cohen and Taylor which involved following the original Durham group and another group and included the use of more conventional questionnaire and interview methods. At one point Cohen and Taylor believed that their proposal had been accepted in principle and they even obtained a grant from the (then) Social Science Research Council to cover research costs. However, the Home Office subsequently insisted upon a number of controls upon the way in which the research was to be carried out, including restricted access and proposed censorship of the interview material by the Prison Department's officials. At this point, and in the face of these constraints, Cohen and Taylor abandoned their work.

No doubt the precise story of what did or did not happen in relation to this project can be the subject of differing interpretations and differing claims and counter-claims. This is not the place to enter into some adjudication of these. Rather, we can use the story, as told by Cohen and Taylor, to exemplify and further elaborate the dynamics and the interplay between subjects, researchers, gatekeepers and sponsors. There can be overlaps between the different categories of individuals who have an interest in the research, and in certain instances they can be one and the same. For example, where the Home Office commissions research into, say, the psychological effects of long term imprisonment, there is a considerable overlap between sponsor and gatekeeper and no doubt the researchers' problems of gaining formal access to subjects can be considerably eased. There is no reference, for instance, in the writings of Banister *et al.* (1973) to the problems of gaining access to prisoners at Durham nor in commissioned research carried out at other prisons at the same time (see, for example, Emery, 1970).

In some cases, alliances between different individuals or groups can emerge because such alliances are to the benefit of these individuals or groups, even where the respective interests are not necessarily the same. For example, the inmates of E Wing were concerned to tell their own story on their own terms and in the way in which they wanted, no doubt to alleviate the conditions in which they were imprisoned. In part, this complemented the aims and interests of the researchers who for theoretical reasons (to capture the subjective experiences) and methodological reasons (to do so as naturalistically as possible) were also interested in encouraging the men to tell their story in the way in which they wanted. The researchers also had an interest in alleviating the conditions for long-term prisoners but differed from the inmates in so far as they were concerned with following the well-established means of developing academic careers, that is, by making contributions to the existing stock of knowledge by the publication of books and papers. These differences apart, the subjects and the researchers formed an alliance of interests – albeit a relatively powerless alliance – in terms of wanting to continue with the project and see its conclusions published.

This is in contrast to the relationship between the inmates and the Home Office sponsored researchers where there is some evidence of conflicts of interest. The prisoners were interested in publishing the conditions which prevailed in E Wing and their effects upon those who endured them. They did not feel that these aims could be facilitated by the kind and style of research which was envisaged, and no doubt antagonisms were fuelled by the official sponsorship of the research. Cohen and Taylor described the reactions of the men as follows:

> In their many years of experience of the penal system, the men had built up a cynical attitude towards research in general and psychological research in particular. Psychologists 'come in and use you for other things they are doing outside', as one of them remarked. It was not therefore surprising to us that these researchers were met by a partial boycott; one member of the class was apparently delegated to inform them as politely as possible that the approach they were adopting did not meet with the approval of most of the men and would they therefore find some other subject. (Cohen and Taylor, 1977, p. 72)

Much more fundamental, however, was the clash of interests between Cohen and Taylor and the Prison Department of the Home Office. This highlights the importance of the role of gatekeepers in the pursuit of social research. In our preceding discussion we referred to 'gatekeeper' as if it were some single unitary position to be negotiated. In fact, there are often layers of gatekeepers to be negotiated and the gatekeepers are themselves in some hierarchical relationship with differentials of power between them. For example, what this case study reveals is two main gatekeepers – the prison governor and the Prison Department of the Home Office in London. Cohen and Taylor refer to keeping the governor fully informed of their work at all times and of their intentions to publish. The picture that is portrayed is of a local gatekeeper who had the power to prevent access but who was reasonably happy with the progress of the project, at least in its early stages. Of governors and other local officials Cohen and Taylor write:

> Throughout these years we had had many sympathetic contacts with Governors, Assistant Governors and prison psychologists. But this local support has counted for little. Such individuals are unable to give any public indication of their approval or disapproval; they may not even enter the public debate about prison life. This blanket of silence (justified by reference to the all-embracing Official Secrets Act) immunizes the system from criticism and positively encourages the type of 'sensation revelation – official denial' sequence which characterizes public information on our penal institutions. (Cohen and Taylor, 1977, p. 85)

More crucial gatekeepers in prison research are officials within the Prison Department of the Home Office in London who are able to exercise power over local governors because of their position in the organizational hierarchy. The clash of interests between Cohen and Taylor and the Prison Department was fundamental to the eventual outcome of the project. The researchers wanted to carry out and publish research which was predominantly discovery-based, naturalistic and grounded in unstructured forms of data collection. They also wanted to be free of the constraints which surround official controls on data collection, analysis and publication. The Prison Department objected to the subject matter on several grounds. They felt that the research was focusing on what they perceived as the lurid aspects of long-term imprisonment; that Cohen and Taylor were not giving sufficient recognition to the viewpoint that conditions were improving; and that they were distorting official policy on long-term imprisonment. What is more, the very theoretical and methodological commitments at the centre of the research served to justify the claim by the Home Office that it was unscientific and therefore could not be relied upon to provide a valid picture and assessment of these aspects. The Prison Department held the power *vis-à-vis* the researchers who had little scope for bargining. Cohen and Taylor summarize the sources of this power, and the means by which it was exercised, as follows:

(1) *Centralisation of power:* power centralised in the prison department with few discretionary powers given to local governors

(2) *Legalisation of secrecy:* the use of the Official Secrets Act to prohibit the publication of anything discovered in the course of prison talk or observation

(3) *Standardisation of research:* either carrying out its own research – through such bodies as the Home Office Research Unit – or using its definition of 'proper' research to exclude outsiders

(4) *Mystifying the decision structure:* the inpenetrability of civil service decision making

(5) *Appealing to the public interest:* applying moral pressure by presenting a viewpoint of representing public interests.

Commentary: rights of subjects and researchers

The claims and counter-claims which surrounded the research at Durham prison, and its eventual outcome, illuminate aspects of the politics of social research. These relate to problems of gaining access to subjects who are in closed situations and where there are gatekeepers who have interests to protect – interests which are not the same as the subjects of the research – and who have the formal power to deny such access. In this instance, the gatekeepers had powers over the activities of both the subjects and the researchers. In addition to these formal powers they were able to mobilize informal mechanisms to abort the research (or at least to make it, in the eyes of the researchers, difficult to complete). In providing an illustration of the different parties at work – subjects, researchers, sponsors and gatekeepers – and the way in which they are able to protect their interests, the case study gives an insight into 'what is' or 'what can be'. However, it also raises issues about 'what should be', that is, about how power *should* be exercised in relation to research, with particular reference to the rights of different individuals and groups who are either central to the research or who are in some way affected by it. Here we restrict ourselves to brief comments about issues raised by the case study with particular reference to subjects and researchers.

The rights of the subjects of research are often discussed with reference to the doctrine of informed consent, a doctrine which asserts that subjects should be aware of any research and should give their consent to the part they play within it. The information which is given to subjects can vary. For example, they may simply be aware that the research is taking place; they may be told that they are the subjects within the research; they may be given details of the research procedures to be used; and they may be forwarned of the potential consequences, say, on publication. There is considerable discussion as to how far and over how many of these aspects the doctrine should extend. Let us take the basic right, that is, the right to know that one is participating in research and to have the option as to whether or not to participate in it. It has been argued by some (see, for example, Berreman, 1972) that deceit is a part of everyday life and therefore the social researcher who is interested in studying aspects of this life should not feel bound by ethical principles which dictate that subjects should know of their participation in such research. A fundamental assumption which is made here is that, whether or not such deceit is a part of everyday life, the researcher should grant to all citizens the right of letting them know that they are to become the subjects of research and thereby facilitate the opportunity to opt out of this role. This basic tenet becomes complicated when one is talking about inmates in a prison for they are not everyday citizens who have basic human rights. Some human rights have been removed from them because they have been convicted of criminal offences. However, there is no reason why suspension of such rights should extend to rights which are given to everyday citizens to know about their participation in social research and thereby choose whether or not to participate. The removal of the rights to freedom of liberty are very much part of the prisoner's role. Once that right is taken away prisoners should have the rights of everyday citizens and these should include rights in relation to the principle of informed consent. They have given up the positive freedom of liberty because of criminal actions but that does not mean that they should surrender the negative freedom to be free from the interference of others and particularly in this context the interference of social researchers. (For a discussion of the distinction between positive and negative freedom see Sir Isaiah Berlin's *Two Concepts of Liberty* (1958).)

The inmates in Durham's E Wing were told of the officially-sponsored research carried out by Banister *et al.* and had their own means of non-participation. A much more difficult question, however, is raised by the Cohen and Taylor project. This is whether inmates should have the positive rights to be involved in research which they see as being in their interests, say, in permitting them to express their feelings about the effects of long-term imprisonment, even where the authorities feel that it is not in the interests of the 'system' or of security and where authorities take decisions about participation in research on behalf of the inmates and without consulting them. Prisoners who have committed serious crimes quite rightly lose the most fundamental right of all, the right to freedom. Provided their inclusion in properly conducted research does not threaten the curtailment of this freedom, prisoners should not be denied the right to participate in such research. Taking away an individual's freedom by incarceration should not take away that individual's freedom to know about research and to opt out of it. Equally, it should not take away that individual's positive right to know about research and to take part in it if he or she so wishes. Where authorities believe that there is a real danger that research may threaten prison or state security then they have an obligation to the researchers to make quite explicit the way in which such security is likely to be threatened. Hiding behind a cloak of secrecy is not sufficient. Equally, there is an obligation on the researcher not to undertake any work which is likely to result in the reduction of such security.

Reference to 'properly conducted research' raises the question of what is, and is not, legitimate methodology, and it touches upon the rights of researchers to carry out their trade in the way in which they feel most appropriate according to the theoretical and methodological commitments of the disciplines they represent. A fundamental tenet of this book is that criminological research is pluralistic and that it benefits from such pluralism because of the range of problems it addresses and the range of theoretical paradigms it uses to address them. The researcher should have the right to choose methods appropriate to what he or she is examining and to the theoretical ideas upon which he or she wishes to draw. There should be no constraint in terms of what gatekeepers or sponsors perceive as legitimate or properly conducted research. The value of contributions of any project, and any methodological approach adopted within such a project, can be assessed on publication of findings and should not be used at the point of entry into the research field to deny access to willing subjects.

Collecting data: researching the police

Subjects as gatekeepers

It would be wrong to think of research activity as a straightforward process within which data collection can be accomplished with ease once formal gatekeepers have been successfully negotiated. Indeed, as we have already pointed out, there can be layers of gatekeepers – not necessarily sharing the same interests – and gaining access can be a continuous process. Two points can be further developed. First, negotiating and gaining access should be considered as part of the process of collecting data. The individuals and groups to be confronted, the interests they represent, and the blocks or constraints they seek to impose upon research activity provide, in their own right, important forms of data about the criminal justice system and the way in which it works. So, for example, the reactions of the Prison Department to Cohen and Taylor's research plans provide us with some insight into the way in which this department jealously guards information about prison activities and also about the means by which it is able to accomplish this. Second, this continuous process of negotiating access does not end when one has successfully bypassed all those who have some formal power to prevent the research taking place. Arrival at the sources of data provides no guarantee that research work can begin.

We have previously emphasized that the objects of criminological research should be treated as 'subjects', not least because they also have interests they want to protect and aims and goals they wish to promote. But further, like gatekeepers, they have their own means of blocking such research or of ensuring that it is conducted in certain ways and with certain kinds of outcomes. The reaction of subjects is likely to depend on whether their interests are in tune, or at variance with, the interests of formal gatekeepers. For example, prisoners who are asked to participate in officially sponsored research are not likely to have a strong investment in facilitating its successful completion. Such research is likely to be perceived as being against the interests of individual prisoners or of the prison group as a whole and perhaps as another official activity which treats inmates as objects rather than as individuals. How such perceptions – accurate or otherwise – are likely to affect the outcome of research is often difficult to gauge. Where subjects refuse to participate the outcome is clear cut but where subjects deliberately withhold information or provide a 'false' story it is often difficult to detect and estimate the extent to which ultimate conclusions are invalid. In short, the objects of criminological inquiry should not only be treated as 'subjects' but also as gatekeepers. They have their own means of influencing the direction of research and indeed can often prevent it from taking place in the first place.

Research on the police
In this section we switch from research in prisons to research on the police. Research on the police has flourished in the United Kingdom over the past two decades, if only because of the increasing public concern with questions of law and order, inner-city disturbances and debates about the way in which such disorders have been policed. Some of this research focuses upon the role of policemen in their organizational and cultural contexts (see, for example, Cain, 1973; Chatterton, 1983; Holdaway, 1983). An important aspect of the police officer's role is the exercise of discretion in terms of the application of the law to offenders or potential offenders, and much research has looked at this, for example, in terms of discriminatory practices in 'stop and search' (see, for example, Willis, 1983) and the referral of young offenders to juvenile bureaux (see, for example, Landau, 1981, 1983). Concern with the relationships between police

officers and ethnic groups in society has generated considerable research which has proliferated into further concerns with police work in relation to a whole range of social groups and social divisions within society (for a summary of work in this area, see Brogden, Jefferson and Walklate, 1988). The effectiveness of particular aspects of police work, for example, patrol work (Ericson, 1983) and detection of criminal offences (Bottomley and Coleman, 1981) has also been researched, as have the benefits to be derived from innovative policing strategies, such as beat patrol schemes and community policing (Weatheritt, 1986).

Police officers are inevitably very sensitive about opening up their world to social researchers. On the one hand their decision-making is expected to be open and beyond reproach and yet what they see as the success of their activities is often dependent upon what has been variously defined as 'police theory' (Rock, 1973) and 'cop culture' (Reiner, 1985). It is the informal actions which are the outcome of everyday police theories and which are part of cop culture that police officers often seek to hide from view. They can do this by erecting barriers to insulate themselves from social researchers and others or by seeking to present a favourable image of their actions by mystifying and even falsifying the nature of police work (Manning, 1974).

This desire to 'hide from view' is, of course, not specific to those working within the criminal justice system. It also applies to other subjects of criminological research such as those who are engaged in criminal acts and who are the clients or potential clients of police officers. However, where those involved in crime are also police officers, and where criminal activity is also a part of cop culture, the imperative to hide from view becomes even stronger. Police corruption (using one's office for personal gain) and police deviance (a wider concept than corruption, including all kinds of dishonest and illegal practices such as brutality, intimidation and harrassment) represent fusions of aspcts of cop culture and criminal activity. Such corruption and deviance are not endemic in the police force but over the past few decades their incidence has been very much in the public eye. For example, during the late 1970s there were a number of corruption scandals in the Metropolitan Police. There were frequent accusations that members of the drug squad used unorthodox methods in going about their work, including planting drugs and granting immunity to drug dealers in return for information, and also that members of the obscene publication squad – the so-called porn squad – had very close personal relationships with individuals who ran the pornography business in London's Soho (Cox, Shirley and Short, 1977). In 1978 a gang held up a delivery of money to the *Daily Mirror* newspaper and a security guard was shot dead. There were continuous accusations that police officers had been involved in the planning of the raid which subsequently led to the setting up of Operation Countryman to investigate wide-ranging corrupt practices in the Metropolitan Police. After four years of investigation there were only two arrests and there were accusations by the senior officer in charge that his investigations had been obstructed. In the mid-1980s a conspiracy of a different kind rocked the Metropolitan Police when police officers prevented the detection of colleagues who seriously assaulted a group of youths in north London until an anonymous call from one officer named the culprits. In both cases senior police officers found it difficult to penetrate the wall of silence. So what hope for a social researcher who is interested in investigating corrupt practices?

Studying corruption in Amsterdam

The work of Maurice Punch illustrates some of the ways in which subjects can influence the course of research on policing and particularly research which strays into police corruption and police deviance. Punch began his initial work on the Amsterdam City Police in the mid-1970s. His research conclusions were eventually published in 1979 as *Policing the Inner City* (Punch, 1979). This was an ethnographic, observational study of police officers in the central areas of Amsterdam. Observational methods were used because they were viewed as appropriate to the interactionist and interpretative theoretical perspectives favoured by Punch (giving a focus on inter-actions and facilitating some access to social meanings, definitions and labels) but also because of the closed nature of policing and the belief that observational methods can bypass some of the barriers which are erected. Punch was assigned to a shift of fifteen men and spent most of his time going on foot and in car patrols with them, observing inter-actions between police officers as well as encounters with the population of central Amsterdam. The practical and the methodological strengths of participant observation are described by Punch as follows:

> Participant observation enables one to go behind the public front of a conspicuous public bureaucracy to witness 'backstage' behaviour when the actors are off-stage, not performing to a public, and not pedalling stereotyped scripts for the benefit of bystanders. In essence the appeal of field work is that it is concerned with real people and that confrontation with people in all their baffling complexity, is a fruitful antidote to a positivist methodology and a natural science model for the social sciences. (Punch, 1979, p. 18)

Despite the value of participant observation in getting 'backstage', Punch's initial research experiences and writings are testaments to the way in which researchers can be seduced by subjects into accepting a particular representation of police work. The overriding impression presented by *Policing the Inner City* is that of a group of officers dealing with difficult situations and individuals under difficult circumstances. Central Amsterdam is portrayed as soaked with deviance but police organization is not. Punch explicitly notes the absence of corruption and deviant practices:

> In six months graft and corruption were scarcely mentioned, not even jokingly or on informal occasions out of duty, and revelations of such practices in the papers were non-existent. (Punch, 1979, p. 12)

However, on closing fieldwork it became apparent that his informants had been engaging in impression management and that the deviant sub-culture of police work had largely escaped him (it was only revealed towards the end at a party and even then only because some of the officers had had too much to drink). In subsequent writings Punch reflects on his early experiences:

> Most of my time was spent with patrolmen and I was struck by the *absence* of deviance. In fact it was going on around me, almost literally under my nose, but I did not see it. (Punch, 1985, p. 210)

It was after finishing his first project that a corruption scandal surfaced in the press. This scandal largely concerned activities at the police station where Punch had carried out most of his research work. He therefore asked for, and received, permission to return to that station to carry out further work on police corruption by interviewing police officers and by looking at documentary evidence. He also initiated a third project which was concerned with the management of aspects of policing which not only brought him into contact with senior officers but also with detectives. In time the second and third projects merged in so far as he was able to examine aspects of the corruption scandal from the point of view of both junior and senior officers. In doing this he could look at individual and organizational responses to corruption within a context where those who were supposed to be the controllers of corruption may also have been the corrupt. His analysis revealed a divided organization which, in seeking to keep itself from being labelled as corrupt, sought to scapegoat and point the finger of guilt at those officers at the bottom of the organizational hierarchy. However, in turn these officers sought to resist the scapegoating by developing counter-strategies which would force the label back up the hierarchy and at those who were in charge of the organization.

In contrast with other researches on the police, Punch faced no difficulties in gaining formal access to sources of data for each of his projects. This was true for his research on corruption which one might expect to be the most sensitive with formal gatekeepers. He obtained the approval and support of the chief constable, although this was assisted by management of impressions ('I couched my investigation in palatable terms of analysing "dilemmas of law enforcement in the city centre" in order not to frighten off people by blazening the word "corruption" all over the proposal' (p. 211)), and by unspoken research bargains ('the department was petrified of an external commission of inquiry. I could be passed off, if necessary, as an outside academic who was already investigating the issue' (p. 211)).

The data Punch collected were derived from observation, interviews, police and other documents, use of informants and journalistic accounts of others who were trying to uncover corruption. Such data were *about* corruption but the variety of methods of collecting data failed to uncover and observe corruption at first hand. This was partly because, although formal access had been granted at the top of the organizational hierarchy, gates were being closed lower down. He found that he was being excluded from certain situations and conversations, that he was not welcome at certain meetings and that he was refused documents which, officially, he had been promised. As Punch commented 'some people were already running for cover', and 'some people were simply keeping quiet, having doubtless sound reasons for saying as little as possible' (p. 216). Even where access to data sources was not denied, Punch reports that interviews were generating different stories from different parts of the organization and that documents were incomplete and only included what the writers of them wished to include. In short, although Punch had successfully negotiated formal access, he failed at a number of levels and in different ways to obtain informal or secondary access.

To sum up, corruption and other deviance were ingrained in the routine police-work practices on the streets of Amsterdam. However, they were also part of the hierarchy of police organization, from district to headquarters, and it was when Punch came close to threatening the interests of powerful groups and individuals within that hierarchy that the research was eventually aborted. He was keen to continue with the project,

> but I just could not see how I would ever get to the level of information needed. It was clearly in no-one's interest to give it to me. Perhaps we have to recognize that, as we move up the hierarchy of organization and as we begin to encounter powerful, entrenched groups and individuals who are identifiable, jealous of

their reputations, prepared to fight for their survival, and powerful enough to deflect attention, that we may be attempting to research areas of institutional life which are to all intents and purposes unresearchable, such as unmasking the relationship between police and Free Masonry in Britain. For me, at any rate, the 'breakthrough' had proved to be a dead-end. (Punch, 1985, p. 219)

Commentary: ethics and observation
A number of points emerge from the research we have just considered. First, there were no sponsors of the research. Punch was very much the lone investigator carrying out his own work and pursuing his own academic interests. In contrast with large-scale surveys and evaluation experiments, the most valuable resource in investigations which are ethnographic and 'discovery-based' is the researcher's own time and not large research budgets. Indeed, such budgets may well detract from creativity and originality in the research process. Second, unlike Cohen and Taylor, Punch reports that he had no difficulty with formal gatekeepers. In respect of all three projects he received the approval, and indeed the support, of the chief constable although there is recognition that he actively created favourable impressions of his research intentions. The reason for the difference is that Cohen and Taylor were keen to represent the interests of the subjects (interests with which they had some sympathy) and such representation was perceived by the Prison Department as being a threat to security and not in the public interest. In Punch's case, the researcher was not crystallizing and accentuating the conflicts of interest between gatekeepers and subjects. Third, as the case study illustrates, formal permission as to access does not guarantee that fieldwork can be accomplished successfully. As with Cohen and Taylor's relationships with inmates in Durham's E Wing, Punch enjoyed the trust of his subjects, shared their interests, and comments in *Policing the Inner City* that 'to a large extent I accepted police work as an enterprise and "morally" approved of its activities' and that 'I reservedly accepted the side I was on' (p. 17). However, it was when he began his investigation of corruption at the Warmoesstraat police station where he had previously been accepted, and also its percolation throughout the Amsterdam police organization, that relationships with subjects became difficult and secondary access was prevented. Subjects, like formal gatekeepers, have interests to promote and to protect and when these interests are perceived as being threatened by social research it is not surprising that subjects seek to mobilize mechanisms to steer research in particular directions or even to ensure that it is aborted.

This highlights a central dilemma for the social researcher *vis-à-vis* the subjects of inquiry, particularly in connection with the nature of the research role to be adopted. Ethnographic, investigative and discovery-based research of the kind conducted by Punch has a strong commitment to naturalism, that is, to studying social actions in their natural contexts and as they normally occur. However, such a commitment is often at odds with an overt research situation where the subjects are aware that they are being researched and may also be aware of why they are being researched. Subjects can seek to hide behind 'masks' (Berreman, 1972) and to engage in impression management. It is, of course, difficult to estimate the extent to which this takes place, but it is likely that the degree to which false fronts can be sustained over long periods of time can be overestimated. This is particularly the case with regard to activities such as police work where there is often a need to respond quickly to unforeseen events and little time to be concerned with the presence of a researcher or with presenting a favourable image. However, where the activities of the researcher are a threat to the interests of the subjects, as with police corruption, blocking mechanisms are likely to be activated and sustained. The alternative is for the researcher to engage in some form of deception (an alternative, incidentally, which was not actively pursued by Punch). This can take a number of forms. For example, the subjects may be aware that some form of research is under way but may have been deliberately misinformed as to its true purpose or aim. Such deception is, of course, quite common in social research. For example, in Chapter 2 we have noted the importance of 'cover stories', and therefore deception, in research involving laboratory-type experiments.

In ethnographic research deception as to purpose can be accompanied by deception by concealment. Where a covert role is adopted the researcher seeks to participate as fully as possible in the group he is studying and yet hide his true role and also the research purposes of that role. Such concealment and deception raise fundamental ethical issues which are expressed in a slightly different way in ethnographic, as opposed to experimental, research. These concern the extent to which a researcher should conceal his true role and true purpose and thereby deceive subjects who relate to the researcher on an everyday basis and who, at least in part, do so on some basis of trust. One resolution to this dilemma lies in the argument that deception is such an essential part of everyday interaction, in terms of the way in which the 'self' is presented, that researchers should not seek to set themselves apart from such deception and covert research practices are thereby justified (see, for example, Berreman, 1972). The viewpoint presented here is that justifications cast in such terms are not totally satisfactory. The belief that deception is an essential element of everyday life is based upon a particular model of interactions, albeit a fairly persuasive model, and is not something which has been demonstrated beyond doubt. Even if this were the case, it would not totally justify the deliberate and deceptive incursions of researchers into the lives of everyday citizens who have certain moral, if not legal, rights to be free from such incursions. However, where the subjects of inquiry have general rights, duties and obligations *over and above* those of everyday citizens, as is the case with the police, then the moral right to be free from social investigation (or indeed any kind of investigation) is correspondingly reduced. What is more, where groups with such enhanced rights, duties and obligations have an important commitment to decision-making based upon the principles of openness and impartiality – as is the case with professional groups, including police, in the criminal justice system – the power of this argument is increased. (This is also the case, incidentally, in relation to justifications for a vigorous and independent system for investigating complaints against the police.) It is often the case, as illustrated by Punch's research experiences, that those enhanced rights and duties, and commitments to openness and impartiality, go hand in hand with the development of practices of mystification, and even blocking, to protect individual and group interests from the prying eyes of researchers and other investigators. In this respect, one cannot help but be attracted by the view expressed by Holdaway that:

> the case for covert research is strengthened by the central and powerful situation of the police within out social structure. The police are said to be accountable to the rule of law, a constitutional constraint which restricts their right to privacy but which they can neutralize by maintaining a protective occupational culture. When such an institution is over-protective, its members restrict the right to privacy that they possess. It is important that they be researched. (Holdaway, 1983, p. 5)

The researcher may feel that there is a right, indeed duty, to pierce the protective shield of powerful institutions, but what of the obligations? The researcher has a commitment to the investigation of the central problems of the criminological enterprise. This includes a commitment to drawing upon the central theoretical ideas and methodological approaches which abound in that enterprise. What is more, there is an obligation to publish findings and conclusions so that they enter the public domain, not simply in search of personal gratification or to satisfy academic peers but, more fundamentally, because the issues of criminology are of great social and political concern. In doing this there is a responsibility to the subjects of inquiry, particularly where promises of confidentiality and anonymity have been made. This is especially the case where subjects are not in a sufficiently powerful position to protect themselves against any of the threats to interests which arise from a breach of such promises. However, where such promises have not been made there is no obligation to protect the interests of those who hold a powerful or privileged position in society or who have a commitment to open decision-making. Having said that, however, this obligation should be in terms of a commitment to the investigation of the central research problems of criminology and to addressing such problems in publication rather than to the public vilification of particular individuals.

Publishing results: plea-bargaining in courts

Publication and protection of interests

All parties are likely to have some interest in the publication of results and conclusions about a research topic or a research context in which they have some stake. Researchers, for example, have an interest in ensuring that their work receives due attention by its entry into the public domain. They are also interested in publication because this is a major indicator of professional prowess and a means by which academic careers can be furthered. The subjects of research are likely to be concerned with the way in which they are portrayed, either as individuals or as a group, and with whether their individual or group interests are likely to be endangered by publication. The collection of data from, and about, individuals raises for the researcher ethical aspects of whether to abide by promises of confidentiality and of ensuring anonymity in publications. Most researchers give guarantees of confidentiality. But the extent to which they can ensure anonymity varies according to the nature of the research design. For example, individual responses to question-naires in large-scale surveys get lost in the aggregate data which are generated from such surveys. What is more, experiments are typically concerned with looking for differences between groups caused by the introduction of an experimental treatment. Individual responses and reactions are buried in the statistical measures which are used to examine such differences. However, with ethnographic research in small-scale, naturalistic contexts, qualitative descrip-tions of the social actions of specific individuals are often easily recognizable. Pseudonyms can be used and there are ways of disguising contexts, but to go too far in this direction is to risk the production of a rounded description which deviates so far from reality as to be no longer valid. There is a professional and academic commitment to validity and also to publication as well as an ethical commitment to subjects. As a general rule, provided the researcher has taken whatever steps as are reasonable to ensure anonymity there is no reason to refrain from publication.

The interests of sponsors are likely to vary according to their connection with the problem being researched and the context in which research is taking place. Where sponsors have directly commissioned research about themselves or about institutions for which they are responsible, they will be concerned with the way in which they are portrayed, with the way in which their management and control of the institutions is portrayed and also with the way in which conclusions might be used by others – say, in criticizing or undermining their management and control. In some instances researchers grant a right of veto to publication to sponsors. Unless this is done, researchers have a right to publish irrespective of the pressures which may be showered upon them not to do so.

Gatekeepers also have interests to safeguard. For example, low-level gatekeepers, such as prison governors or controllers of police sub-divisions, are likely to be interested in the outcomes of any approval for access they may have given. What is more, they will be concerned with the consequences this outcome may have for their relations with other, more powerful, gatekeepers higher up the organizational hierarchy. Where gatekeepers view themselves as keepers of institutional interests they will be concerned to ensure that these interests have not been undermined by publication.

The serious threats to publication of research are most likely to come from those individuals or groups – whether subjects, sponsors or gatekeepers – who have power to protect their interests. The nature of the threats can vary but typically include attempts to prevent publication and the issuing of writs claiming defamation. It is rare that criminological research is discussed in Parliament or becomes the subject of a question to a Minister of State during question time in the House of Commons. However, the impending publication of John Baldwin and Michael McConville's research on plea-bargaining in courts provoked one such question in 1977, particularly after the Senate of the Inns of Court and the Bar made representations to the Home Secretary that publication should be stopped (the Home Office had commissioned the research). The conclusions of the research, particularly those relating to the incidence of plea-bargaining, also became the subject of letters to *The Times* by representatives of the of the legal profession and provoked much heated debate among politicians and furore within the legal profession.

Research on courts
Leaving on one side the main Courts of Appeal, two courts are responsible for adjudication in relation to criminal charges and for

the sentencing of individuals found guilty of such charges. The magistrates' courts try the less serious criminal cases, but they also serve as preliminary examining courts in so far as they pass on to the Crown Court the more serious cases where magistrates believe that there is a case to answer. In carrying out this latter function the magistrates' courts are dealing with 'committal' procedures. Cases are heard by magistrates who in the main are lay and unpaid members of the public. Crown Courts deal with the more serious criminal cases which have been passed on to them by magistrates' courts where a committal hearing will have taken place. In Crown Courts decisions as to the guilt or innocence of defendants are taken by juries comprising members of the public and decisions as to points of law and sentencing are taken by a judge.

Research has taken place on a number of aspects of the court system. For example, there has been work on the social background of the magistracy and the judiciary with particular respect to the way in which it does not reflect all sections of the community (see, for example, Baldwin, 1976; Bartlett and Walker, 1978; Griffith, 1977). Also, there has been concern with regional variations in the outcomes of court proceedings, for example, sentencing and bail. Research has shown wide variations in sentences given for the same offences (Tarling, 1979) and also wide variations in the numbers of people granted bail in relation to the same offences (see, for example, King, 1981). Most defendants before both types of court plead guilty and there is evidence to suggest that a minority of those who plead guilty are innocent (Bottoms and McClean, 1976; Dell, 1971). Pleading guilty when innocent is very closely related to the practice of plea-bargaining whereby the defendant makes a prior agreement, usually via his representative, to plead guilty to at least one charge in return for some concession from the prosecution or the judge or both. The concessions can include the dropping of serious charges in favour of lesser charges and the imposition of a lighter sentence than would otherwise be the case. Plea-bargaining has certain advantages to the court system in so far as guilty pleas save considerable amounts of time in what is usually a very congested court timetable and there is also a saving of police time in so far as police are not required to attend the court and can continue with their everyday police activity. Also, there can be benefits to the defendant in so far as he or she may receive lighter sentences than they would normally have expected. Nevertheless, the practice is not without its disadvantages. It is contrary to the principle of openness within the court system and against the principle that justice should be seen to be done. Also there have been suspicions that plea-bargaining can often work to the disadvantage of certain defendants. Plea-bargaining is a well recognized practice in American courts and has been the subject of a considerable amount of research (see, for example, Sudnow, 1968), but prior to the 1970s very little was known about it in the United Kingdom and there was very little empirical evidence to support assertions about its incidence and about the extent to which it may operate to the disadvantage of defendants.

Plea-bargaining in Crown Courts

In 1974 the Home Office funded a study of the outcomes of jury cases in Birmingham's Crown Court. John Baldwin and Michael McConville – the researchers asked to carry out the work – decided that as part of their project they would focus upon the practice of plea-bargaining. This involved examining the cases of those who decided to change their plea to guilty, often to a lesser charge and often just prior to the beginning of the trial, after originally pleading not guilty. Over a fifteen-month period the cases of 150 defendants appeared to the researchers to involve some element of plea-bargaining. They interviewed 121 of the defendants from these cases, the sample being deemed by them to be representative on most significant characteristics of the total. There was no systematic interviewing of police officers or solicitors involved with these cases but in certain instances corroborative evidence was provided by them. Informal and unstructured interviews were used to collect data. The informal interview strategy was consistent with a methodological commitment on the part of the researchers to capturing experiences, particularly subjective experiences, in the words of the interviewees themselves:

> It is important to note that, as far as possible, all respondents were asked to tell their own story in response to a series of simple and neutral questions. All interviewees played very much a passive role though it was frequently to tackle a respondent about apparent inconsistencies in his account of what took place or to probe for clarification on some point. There was, for instance, no mention whatever in the interview schedule, used by all the interviewers, of terms such as bargain or negotiation and, where these were mentioned in the course of an interview, they arose invariably from the defendants' spontaneous accounts of their experiences. (Baldwin and McConville, 1977, p. 6)

The interview data drew attention to the amount of pressure which was applied to defendants by their counsel to plead guilty and also to the inducements that they were offered such as promises of light sentences. The data suggested that pressure was applied to a degree that was greater than expressed in the so-called Turner rules (as laid down in the case of *Turner* (1970, 54, 32, Cr. App. R. 136) which indicated the limits to which counsel should go in advising clients. These rules suggest that counsel should not advise any client to plead guilty unless he has committed the offences with which he is charged and also that the defendant should have complete freedom as to how he or she wishes to plead. Baldwin and McConville's research suggested that it was likely that a small number of people who pleaded guilty were innocent and that there were others, whether innocent or not, who pleaded guilty but who were likely to be acquitted. On these grounds they questioned the so-called advantages of the system of plea-bargaining. There was no suggestion that there was a highly organized system of plea-bargaining as in the United States nor that it affected the majority of cases. Nevertheless, their researches showed that a minority of defendants were involved in some form of negotiation via their counsel in relation to the way in which they should plead which had subsequent consequences for the outcome of their case.

Twenty-two of the defendants claimed they had been explicitly involved in plea-bargaining. In most cases they had been offered a reduction in sentence and in most cases this promise had been honoured. Half of these defendants had been told in advance of a specific sentence they would receive on pleading guilty. The biggest influence on defendants in suddenly changing plea was defence counsel, particularly their persuasive arguments which were based upon putting forward the sentencing alternatives of pleading guilty and of pleading not guilty (but subsequently being found guilty). More than half of the defendants involved in plea-bargaining felt the decision about what they should do and how they should plead was taken out of their hands by counsel. They also felt that they were unable to decide whose side counsel was on, largely because he appeared to be so closely involved in the network of relations within the court between prosecution, judiciary and other counsel. Overall, defendants expressed a feeling of alienation from preliminary

Table 4.1   *Reasons given by Defendants for Pleading Guilty*

	No.	%
No deal or pressure – defendant guilty as pleaded	35	28.9
Plea-bargain – an offer made and accepted by defendant and benefit accrues to him	22	18.2
No explicit bargain but defendant thinks or assumes that a bargain struck on his behalf	16	13.2
Pressure from barrister but no specific offer made to defendant	48	39.7
Total	121	100

Source: Baldwin and McConville, 1977, p. 28.

pre-trial negotiations and court proceedings. The following are typical of the case-study materials presented by Baldwin and McConville. The first is used to illustrate the variety of bargain described by defendants and the second is used to present defendants' feelings of being bypassed by the machinery of justice and of having little say in what should happen to them:

Case 13 (specific offer to a defendant): the barrister wanted to get it over with. He went to see the judge with the other barrister and told me that if I pleaded guilty, I would get a suspended sentence but if I fought the case, I'd be done for wasting the court's time and would get three years imprisonment or, if I was lucky, a suspended sentence. He left it up to me – so I pleaded guilty and got a suspended sentence. (p. 29)

Case 148: I never made any decisions, they were all taken for me. I felt like I wasn't controlling things with the solicitor and barrister; I was just being dragged along. I just had no say in what was happening, I was just carried along on the tide of what they said. I had to follow a set route all the way through. I couldn't say 'no, I don't want to go that way', the way it was put there was only one route to follow. It's just like a blind-folded man being guided through a maze; I had to go but I wasn't sure where I was going. (p. 85)

The impending publication of such materials caused great furore within the legal profession. The Home Secretary and representatives of the legal profession were shown a draft manuscript. The viewpoint of the Home Secretary, Merlyn Rees, was that although he had received representatives from the Senate of the Inns of Court and the Bar, and despite agreeing with them that the research did not provide sufficient evidence to justify the conclusions reached by Baldwin and McConville, he had no desire – or indeed, power – to stop publication of the book. Equally, the legal profession had no power to prevent publication but, as well as exerting direct pressure on the Home Secretary, it sought to apply indirect influence via the columns of serious newspapers. For example, the president of the Law Society wrote a letter to the *Daily Telegraph* stating that it is 'wholly improper to present a document of this nature as if it were a piece of reliable research' and the chairman of the Bar wrote to *The Times* that the report 'cannot possibly be described as "research" ' (quoted in an Introductory Note to Baldwin and McConville's *Negotiated Justice* by C. M. Campbell and Paul Wiles). The two authors came under considerable pressure, particularly in the face of serious attacks, upon their academic and professional credibility.

In the event, the book, *Negotiated Justice*, was eventually published after the vice-chancellor of the university at which Baldwin and McConville were employed commissioned an independent assessment from three distinguished academics. These concluded:

> We consider the present work to be academically respectable. The conclusions are reasonably drawn from evidence, so far as one can judge from the manuscript alone. Other people might have carried out a different study, used different methods and perhaps reached different conclusions; but this does not invalidate the present work. The authors have shown that there is a problem needing further investigation. They would not have claimed to have written the last word. (Quoted in the Forward by Sir Robert Hunter, Vice-Chancellor, University of Birmingham, in Baldwin and McConville, 1977)

Commentary: definitions of 'proper' research

It is worth looking in a little more detail at the criticisms that were levelled at Baldwin and McConville's work by the senior members of the legal profession. Many of these revolved around what is, or is not, reliable and appropriate methodology. Baldwin and McConville chose to use detailed in-depth interviews for theoretical and also for practical reasons. For example, at the heart of their research was the notion that formal legal structures should not be taken for granted. They wanted to look behind the procedures as they are formally presented and to look at those social processes which produce the outcomes from Crown Court proceedings. Official statistics which show the number of convictions and the length of sentences would not reveal the kinds of practices and procedures which Baldwin and McConville eventually uncovered; nor would highly structured formal questionnaires. Informal interviews were most appropriate to the task at hand. What is more, the researchers were not simply interested in the outcomes of particular cases but also in the way in which these were experienced by defendants. Informal, ethnographic-type interviews are most appropriate to the uncovering of defendants' subjective experiences and perceptions. It may or may not have been the case that defendants were shut out from negotiations with regard to their destiny, but what is important, particularly from the methodological commitment of Baldwin and McConville, is the viewpoint that if defendants feel that they have been shut out from such negotiations that is just as significant. As the authors point out:

> Whether or not these statements by defendants are accepted as valid . . . the more important point, in our view, is that they reflect

the defendants' experiences as *they* understood and perceived them. For instance, where defendants say they have been 'forced' to plead guilty by their barrister, this interpretation of the encounter is more significant than whether the conduct of the barrister in question was in fact outside the strict ethical rules governing the advice that can be given in this regard. (Baldwin and McConville, 1977, p. 11)

The methodological approach of Baldwin and McConville did not approximate to the formal research strategies associated with positivist methodology. In this respect it was bound to be open to criticism by those who assume that such positivist methodology is *the* way in which the social world can be investigated. However, an important aspect of criminological investigation is concerned with the social meanings and definitions, labels, stereotypes of participants within the criminal justice system and informal interviews of the kind adopted by Baldwin and McConville are appropriate to this task. What is more, such interviews provide one of the few means by which the practices of plea-bargaining could be uncovered, observed and reported.

A second but related criticism of their work concerned the validity of findings which rely upon reports from defendants, some of whom were experienced criminals, and all of whom were subsequently found guilty of offences. In essence, this is a question mark against the internal validity of Baldwin and McConville's findings. That is, to what extent does their research report accurately portray the social process in the Crown Court in Birmingham and also the way in which they were perceived and experienced by the informants they interviewed? Baldwin and McConville built appropriate mechanisms into their research procedures to safeguard the validity of their findings. In the first place, they approached the Bar with a view to getting detailed interviews from barristers about the particular cases of the defendants they had interviewed but co-operation was refused because it would breach the obligation of confidentiality to clients. Therefore, they were forced to rely on the accounts of the defendants who were subsequently to become convicted criminals. The researchers gave very little warning to their informants that they were hoping to interview them and a short introductory letter gave scant indication of the subject matter which they wished to broach. Therefore, there was very little time for informants to fabricate an elaborate story about their experiences in the Crown Court. Further, Baldwin and McConville were able, in certain instances, to gain corroboration from co-defendants in the same case who had been interviewed separately and who had not spoken to one another since sentence had been passed. In other instances there was supporting evidence from solicitors and police officers. What is more, as Baldwin and McConville argue, the subjects may well have had reason to lie about their involvement in crime but there was little reason to lie about the events prior to their trial. To do so would certainly be of no advantage to them. Also, a very close and detailed consideration of the interviews showed that the subjects were able to discriminate between all of the professionals they had come across from the time they were arrested until they were sentenced, and not all received the degree of criticism levelled at barristers and others involved in the pre-trial negotiations. It would be unreasonable, therefore, to suggest that the subjects were attempting to get their own back at the system which had resulted in their being sentenced. All in all, consideration of the procedures used by the researchers and of the evidence they provide indicates that there is little reason to suspect the internal validity of their findings. At the very most they did whatever they could to maintain the validity of such findings.

A third criticism which was levelled at the research findings was that they releated to a few isolated cases held in a particular Crown court at a particular time. In essence, this is the problem of external validity – that is, to what extent findings can be generalized from a small sample interviewed at a particular point in time in a particular context to wider samples in other contexts and at other points of time. To criticize the work simply on the grounds that it represented a sample of people, of time and of context is unreasonable in so far as all research is of this nature. What is important is that the researchers are able to demonstrate the extent to which the samples they choose are representative of some wider whole. Baldwin and McConville took appropriate precautions in order to demonstrate such representativeness where it was deemed appropriate. But in any case this criticism about the external validity of the sample of individuals partially misses the point. The argument of the researchers related not to particular individuals but to institutional structures. Their fundamental conclusion was that plea-bargaining is an essential and almost necessary part of the Crown Court system. What is more, they were simply raising questions and issues about the received wisdom that such plea-bargaining was to the advantage of all concerned. As their findings demonstrated, it was not to the advantage of certain individuals and it was not perceived by those individuals as being to their advantage. The value of Baldwin and McConville's work, therefore, lies not in its ability to demonstrate beyond doubt the external validity of the findings but in its raising of questions and issues about the operation of the Crown Court system which up to that point had not been considered and which clearly needed to be the subject of further investigation and research. To fail to recognize this questioning function of criminological research is to fail to understand the nature of criminological research. It is to raise and address issues and problems and to formulate generalizations in relation to these rather than to provide precise answers.

By way of conclusion one or two general points should be made about Baldwin and McConville's *Negotiated Justice*. First of all it is a testament to the notion that small-scale research can make an important contribution within criminology. It is not necessary to conduct large-scale surveys and generate reams of statistical tables for research to be of value. The response of the legal profession to the prospective publication of *Negotiated Justice* is one indication of the extent to which interviews with just 121 individuals had succeeded in uncovering practices and procedures which were, and still are, such an important part of the systems of adjudication and sentencing. Second, their research shows the value of informal, qualitative methods of research within the criminological enterprise. Such methods are not only appropriate to the subject matter which they wanted to investigate – subject matter which was hardly lying around waiting to be observed – but also to one of the central methodological commitments of their work, that is, a commitment to capturing the subjective experiences of subjects. Provided appropriate precautions are taken to establish the internal validity and external validity of research findings such informal, qualitative methods are as valid as any other and should not become the butt of criticisms from those who, for whatever reason, wish to prevent research from taking place or from its findings being subsequently published. The only way in which to judge the validity of research findings and their contribution to an understanding of crime or to the workings of the criminal justice system is by ensuring that they enter the public domain and not by attempting to inhibit such entry. Criminological research has a duty to address central issues about crime and criminal justice, particularly where, as in this case, it is concerned with institutions which place a high value on openness of justice but which give legitimacy to informal and backstage institutional practices which can work to the disadvantage of those with whom the institution deals and particularly those who are relatively powerless in relation to the institution.

Getting research used: the short, sharp shock

The use of social research

Radical or critical criminology is unlikely, by its very nature, to have any immediate and direct effect on official policies. Theoretical ideas which challenge, and sometimes encourage the replacement of, existing institutional structures are unlikely to find favour with those who control and manage such structures. Research founded upon more conventional criminological approaches is much more likely to be viewed as 'useful' and to be employed to assess official policies and to aid decision-making. In many instances such research is carried out by the state's own agencies (such as the HORPU) or is commissioned from academics by government departments or by institutions within the criminal justice system. (For a discussion of ways in which social research has influenced policy, see Bulmer, 1982, 1986.) There is no universal law which asserts that, even when officially commissioned, social research will contribute to decision-making. There are many other powerful and significant inputs to contend with. What is more, one has to take account of the credibility with which social research findings are endowed by decision-makers. Even where the contributions of social research are enlisted, its findings and conclusions are overlaid by the ideologies of those wishing to make use of them. In this section we consider one example of officially commissioned research into the punishment of juvenile offenders and the use of this research in subsequent decision-making.

Juvenile offenders: care versus control

The disposal of juvenile offenders has been surrounded by one central debate, that concerning the degree of emphasis which should be given to 'care' as opposed to 'control' in dealing with young offenders. In general terms, this distinction is the same as that between a 'treatment' approach to offenders as opposed to a 'punishment' approach. This central debate, and the uneasy tension between these approaches, has found expression in the enactment and implementation of legislation concerned with juvenile justice. The Children and Young Persons Act, 1969, for instance, formally represented a swing towards a social welfare approach but the old system which emphasized punishment and control was not replaced. For example, one intention of the Act was to abolish detention centres, which symbolize systems of punishment, and yet they were never phased out.

The tension is also represented in the range of 'orders' (equivalent to sentences for adults) which are available for dealing with young offenders. At the welfare end of the spectrum are supervision and care orders which usually involve probation officers whereas at the punishment end are detention centre orders. Detention centres represent one of the most controversial features of the juvenile justice system. They were established by the Criminal Justice Act, 1948, and were first opened in 1952. It was intended that they would be experimental although they still remain in existence. There are two types: junior for 14 to 17 year olds and senior for those aged 17 and under 21. Even though they symbolize the punishment and retributive elements of criminal justice, a tension between the constructive aspects and the deterrent aspects of detention centre provision has existed. In the 1970s there was a swing towards the former with greater emphasis given to education and training, to fostering positive relations between staff and offenders, and to the introduction of social workers. However, by the end of the decade the pendulum had swung back towards punishment and deterrence. As part of its general law-and-order policy and its specific belief that it was time to 'get tough' with young offenders the government of the day announced its tougher regimes project.

The tougher regimes project

The tougher regimes project began in the early 1980s in two detention centres for young offenders. One of these, Send in Surrey, is a junior centre for youths aged 14 years and under 17 years. The other, New Hall in West Yorkshire, is a senior centre for youths aged 17 years and under 21 years. The project became known as the 'short, sharp shock experiment' following a statement of intent in the Conservative Party manifesto of 1979 which promised that 'in certain detention centres we will experiment with a tougher regime as a short sharp shock for young criminals'.

The proposed regime was subsequently outlined by the Home Secretary of the day, William Whitelaw, to the Conservative Party Conference:

> life will be conducted at a brisk tempo. Much greater emphasis will be put on hard and constructive activities, on discipline and tidiness, on self respect and respect for those in authority. We will introduce on a regular basis drill, parades and inspections. Offenders will have to earn their limited privileges by good behaviour . . . these will be no holiday camps and I sincerely hope that those who attend them will not ever want to go back there. (Quoted in Home Office, 1984, p. 1)

At Send, for example, these broad principles were expressed in specific changes in practices. Staff dressed in prison uniform rather than in civilian clothes as previously; formal drill sessions were introduced and the number of parades and inspections was increased; physical education was increased and the emphasis was placed upon activities such as weight and circuit training rather than upon the teaching of physical skills; the time available for education was reduced by one-third; and 'inappropriate' activities such as pottery and soft-toy making were replaced by woodwork and metalwork.

The effects of the introduction of the new regimes at Send and New

Hall were evaluated by the Prison Department's Young Offender Psychology Unit (located within the Home Office) in conjunction with the Home Office Statistical Department. Central to this evaluation was a research hypothesis which involved assessing 'whether spending a period of weeks in a detention centre with a more rigorous and demanding regime could effectively deter young offenders from committing further offences' (Home Office, 1984, p. 2).

The research design was experimental. The 'experimental' group comprised the Send and the New Hall detention centres. A 'control' group was constructed to facilitate comparison, and comprised four centres (Eastwood Park, Campsfield House, Buckley Hall and Werrington House) where the new regime was not to be introduced. Data were collected at two points of time. At Period I the new regimes had not been introduced and therefore all centres were operating 'ordinary' regimes, whereas at Period II the tough regimes had been introduced at New Hall and Send but not at the four centres which comprised the 'control' group.

Data were collected in a number of ways and about different aspects of the detention centres and the effects of their regimes on staff and inmates. For example, two researchers visited all six centres to observe the day-to-day activities and they focused particularly upon the two experimental centres and the way in which the principles of the tougher regime (as formally expressed in the Home Office's circular *Tougher Regimes Pilot Project in Two Detention Centres: Note of Guidance to Staff*) were implemented in practice. The researchers visited New Hall and Send for extensive periods between 1980 and 1982. The observers described the procedures by which offenders were received, the daily pattern of inmates, the facilities in which they carried out their sentence, and they particularly focused upon the introduction of drill and the extension of physical training. They noted the way in which in comparison with ordinary regimes such as activities displaced routine work. A major conclusion was that drill and physical training were viewed by the observers as being much more strenuous at New Hall and Send after the introduction of the new regime, although these activities appeared to be enjoyed by the inmates. The findings of the observers were intended as background to the evaluation project and were not directly geared to the central hypothesis. The latter was assessed by reference to data collected about the characteristics of offenders, the experiences and viewpoints of the staff, the reactions of inmates to the introduction of the regime and, more importantly, by the collection of statistics about reconviction rates.

Four sources of data were used to examine the characteristics of offenders sent to all six detention centres. The Home Office's

Offender's Index provided information about the previous convictions of all of the inmates: questionnaires were administered to groups of trainees to collect data about personality and other characteristics; interviews were used to collect data about the trainees' backgrounds (such as their family, their education and their experience of local authority residential care); and detention centre records were used to generate details about the medical and disciplinary records of offenders during detention. The analysis of such data was of intrinsic interest in its own right in so far as it provided some insight into the characteristics of young offenders at all six of the detention centres. For example,

> the majority of trainees came from families of intermediate occupational status. They were probably not different in intelligence from similar age groups outside. Perhaps 10% were illiterate. For the senior trainees, the vast majority of whom had left school, nearly a half were unemployed prior to detention centre. (Home Office, 1984, p. 239)

However, the analysis was also important as a mechanism of 'control' in relation to the main research hypothesis. That is, by statistically controlling or holding constant the effects of such background and personality variables on subsequent reconviction for all offenders at the six centres, the researchers were able to assess the effects of the introduction of the tough regime at New Hall and Send upon such reconviction.

The trainees' experiences of and reactions to the detention centre were examined by the use of formal interviews using card-sort techniques and also scaling techniques. Data were collected from trainees at all six centres at Periods I and II. (It had been hoped to survey trainees from New Hall and Send after discharge but while still under supervision, to see if being part of the experiment had any lasting effects on attitudes after release. However, this required the support of probation officers. The National Association of Probation Officers advised members not to co-operate. This part of the project was aborted.) In general, the results supported the conclusion that after the introduction of the new regime inmates at New Hall and Send looked upon staff more positively. The regime did not, however, result in an improvement in trainees' conduct and disciplinary record.

The central pillar of the project was the analysis of reconviction rates of the young offenders in so far as it provided the main mechanism for examining the hypothesis that the introduction of a more rigorous and demanding regime would deter offenders from committing further offences. If this hypothesis was to be supported then it would be necessary to find evidence that reconviction rates for the 'experimental' centres would drop significantly after the introduction of the tough regime in comparison with the equivalent rates for the 'control' centres for the same time scale. The Offenders' Index had been used to generate information about previous and current convictions. It also provided reconviction data which enabled the researchers to discover whether or not each trainee had been reconvicted during the twelve months following release. The percentage of individuals reconvicted was calculated for each centre, and for Periods I and II the results are presented in Table 4.2.

For both the junior (Send) and the senior (New Hall) centres there is a small estimated effect of the introduction of the tougher regimes. These effects are not, however, in the same direction and they are not sufficiently large to be statistically significant. The researchers conclude:

> To sum up then, our results suggest that the pilot regimes do not have a distinctive effect on overall reconviction rates. We have identified four factors which might potentially have distorted these results but none of them seems likely to have caused more than a trivial degree of distortion. It seems reasonable, therefore, to conclude that the pilot project regimes had about the same effect on overall reconviction rates as ordinary detention centre regimes. (Home Office, 1984, p. 221)

The evaluation project was primarily concerned with the potential effects of the tougher regimes upon the individuals who were subjected to them. However, a smaller aspect of the project was concerned with whether the announcement of the tougher regimes by the Home Secretary would have a general deterrent effect on all potential offenders, particularly in the catchment areas of Send and New Hall. This was examined by an analysis of crime rates before and after the introduction of the new regimes. The authors conclude:

> It is clear from the statistical examination of these data that if there had been a general effect on the levels of crime at or soon after the stage when the tougher regime project was being announced and implemented, then it has not been possible to distinguish this effect from the general movement in levels of recorded crime. (p.231)

There are theoretical and methodological comments which could be made about this research. For example, it relies heavily on official statistics on crime in order to assess the effect of the 'short, sharp shock' regime on subsequent criminal behaviour and yet, as was

Table 4.2 *Comparison of Reconviction Rates for Experimental and Control Detention Centres*

Junior centres

Detention centre	Send		Eastwood Park		Campsfield House		Estimated effect of regime change	Statistical significance
Period Type of regime	I Ord.	II Pilot	I Ord.	II Pilot	I Ord.	II Pilot		
% Reconvicted in 12 months follow-up	57	57	50	51	50	51	−1.3	Not significant

Senior centres

Detention centre	New Hall		Buckley Hall		Werrington House		Estimated effect of regime change	Statistical significance
Period Type of regime	I Ord.	II Pilot	I Ord.	II Pilot	I Ord.	II Pilot		
% Reconvicted in 12 months follow-up	46	48	48	52	47	43	+1.6	Not significant

Source: Home Office, 1984.

pointed out in the preceding chapter, the validity of such data is almost universally questioned. What is more, in focusing on the potential effect of systems of punishment on subsequent criminal behaviour the research operates from a very narrow theoretical base which precludes a consideration of other factors, particularly those social structural factors which operate outside the bounds of detention centres. However, we shall put such matters to one side and restrict ourselves to a consideration of the four main parties to the research, their relationships to one another and their inputs to the conduct of the research and its subsequent use.

In comparison with Cohen and Taylor's writings, little is reported about the interests of the subjects or of how these might have influenced their reactions to the research. We do not know whether they were willing participants or whether they were aware that they were the subjects of inquiry. The research was officially sponsored by the Home Office and conducted by its researchers. This does not guarantee that fieldwork can be completed (see, for example, Clarke and Cornish, 1972) but there was clearly no need to convince Home Office officials about the need for access and local gatekeepers gave whatever help they could. For example:

No part of the regime was closed to the observers, who were given their own set of keys and who had entry to the institution at all hours of the day or night. Thus, they were able to attend all staff meetings, the night watch, the reception and discharge as well as the more ordinary points of the working day. The Board of Visitors also allowed them to attend their meetings. (Home Office, 1984, p. 66)

The main interest of the case study lies in the use which was made of the research conclusions. The project is typical of what Bulmer (1982) described as *programme evaluation* in which researchers address policy issues formulated by sponsors. In such situations, researchers have no power, or indeed rights, in relation to the use that should be made of findings and conclusions. (There is no indication that in this specific instance researchers wanted to have such rights.) The power lies with those who sponsor research and who are in formal positions to take decisions about the use to which it is to be put. The basic conclusion of the 'short, sharp shock' project was that tougher regimes had no discernible effect on trainees' reconviction rates. Nor were crime trends among young people apparently affected. Despite such findings, the then Home Secretary, Leon Brittan, formally announced in a written reply to a question in the House of Commons that the tougher regimes would be extended to all detention centres:

The evaluation report finds that the experimental regime had no statistically significant effect on the rate at which trainees were reconvicted; while it was right to test whether any such effect would be produced this conclusion is not surprising against the general background of research findings on the identifiable deterrent effect of particular sentences. Nor does it alter in any way the need to establish a positive and well defined detention centre regime. (*Hansard*, 24 July 1984)

This does not mean that all the research report's findings were ignored. For example, the research highlighted the dramatic impact on inmates of the first few days of sentence. The Home Secretary commented:

We shall build on this finding . . . to make a brisk and structured initial two week programme a key feature of the new regime. This will highlight basic and unpopular work such as scrubbing floors, increased emphasis on parades and inspection: and minimal privileges and association. (*Hansard*, 24 July 1984)

The report also found that, in comparison with many of the activities, formal drill and extra physical education were positively atractive to inmates. The Home Secretary's response was as follows:

Formal drill sessions and extra physical education will not be continued: many trainees came to find them undemanding and their inclusion would leave less time for other features – notably work – which the new regime will emphasize. (*Hansard*, 24 July 1984)

Commentary: the importance of political decision-making
Here we have been concerned with the relations between sponsors of research and those who carry it out. Some research is commissioned by institutions, such as government departments, from independent researchers, often academics working in higher education. With the tougher regimes project the researchers were part of the Home Office's own research establishment. Whether independent or otherwise, the researchers have few, if any, rights *vis-à-vis* those who commission the research.

A number of models of the relationship between research and policy have been propounded. One of these is *programme evaluation* (Bulmer, 1982), in which experimental or quasi-experimental methods are used to evaluate the introduction of some new policy initiative. The programme evaluation model partially fits the tougher regimes project. In the main, models such as this are cast in terms of the contributions which social science can make to decision-making and as such are prescriptive models. Where they fall down as descriptive models is in failing to take account of the wider political climate and particularly the role and influence of political ideologies in decision-making. It is not simply a matter of social research feeding back findings which are then implemented by decision-makers. As is seen with those aspects of tougher regimes projects which were ignored and those which were emphasized, political ideas and beliefs can overlay findings in such a way that some conclusions are spotlighted as reinforcing certain decision-making choices and others are played down, rationalized or buried.

Conclusion

Criminological inquiry is not simply a matter of researchers setting about the task of collecting data from and about the objects of their inquiry with a view to analysing and presenting data about these objects. In the first place, the objects of inquiry are individuals and groups of individuals which have interests to promote and to protect in relation to that research. What is more, there is often a complex and dynamic set of relations between subjects, researchers, gate-keepers and sponsors, each of which is endowed with differential degrees of power in relation to the others. The balance of power between the different parties, and the way in which it is exercised, determines what gets studied, by whom, and with what outcome.

An examination of such issues is important at a practical level in so far as it may alert researchers to the pitfalls to be avoided in the planning of future research. However, the issues also have funda-mental theoretical significance. Throughout this book the import-ance of theory has been emphasized in terms of the connections which are made with methods of data collection and analysis in the pursuit of explanations of crime. Yet theory is also important in opening up questions about problems of gaining access, data collection, publication and about the use to which research findings are, or are not, put. This is particularly the contribution of critical sociological theory which encourages a focus which is wider than a concern with crime and criminals in favour of one which seeks an examination of the role of the institutions of criminal justice in relation to such crime and crime control. One important way of uncovering institutional policies and practices is via an examination of the institutional reactions to criminological research in terms of what is and is not constrained; what is and is not facilitated; and what is and is not favoured. This is suggestive of a criminological enterprise which is not solely concerned with criminals as objects of inquiry but which also embraces an examination of the research process itself in terms of what it can tell us about the interests of different groups, the relations of power which exist between them and the way in which they seek to promote and protect such interests by the mobilization of relations of power.

5

Conclusion

Research strategies and designs are geared to the collection and analysis of data in relation to the key problems of the criminological enterprise. A basic assumption has been made here that this enterprise is characterized by plurality. There is plurality in terms of the range of questions which can be asked of crime. These include questions about the nature of crime, the extent of crime, the explanations of crime but they go much further than this to encompass questions about the way in which crime is experienced by victims, about the systems for the control, prevention and treatment of crime, and about the relationship between these systems and wider social structure. There is also plurality in terms of the institutional contexts within which research takes place, especially the institutional contexts of subjects, researchers, gate-keepers and sponsors. These locations, and the interests and powers which go with them, are important for the process of research and also for its outcome.

More fundamentally, there is plurality in terms of the range of theoretical perspectives which contribute to the criminological enterprise. It has been emphasized throughout that a consideration of methods of criminological research should not be divorced from a consideration of theory. There are typical, but not necessary, connections which can be made between types of theory and types of method, and the plurality of theory in the criminological enterprise is mirrored by a plurality of method. The contributions of theory lie in the multiplicity of aspects of crime which are opened up for examination by methods of research. In emphasizing the values of a plurality of theories there is a danger of suggesting that a theoretical synthesis is possible, a synthesis which is likely to be so diluted as to say very little. In any case, different theoretical approaches hold core assumptions which are simply not capable of reconciliation. For example, sociological functionalism and radical criminology have diametrically opposed views on the nature and role of conflict in society as to be incapable of integration. However, they do have certain things in common such as a concern with analysis at the level of social structure and they do encourage research at this level. Despite fundamental differences, theoretical approaches can be treated as suggesting a range of ideas, concepts and questions about crime for inclusion on a criminological research agenda. The validity of such ideas, concepts and questions can be assessed by criminological inquiry. This represents a viewpoint of theoretical positions as means of constructing such agenda and as guides to the pursuit of such inquiry rather than of theoretical positions as warring and intransigent fortresses. What is more, such a viewpoint is one which is suggestive of a closer integration between theory and methods of criminological research.

References

Abrams, P. (1968), *The Origins of British Sociology 1834–1914* (Chicago: University of Chicago Press).

Alker, H. R. (1969), 'A typology of ecological fallacies', in M. Dogan and S. Rokkan (eds), *Quantitative Ecological Analysis in the Social Sciences* (Cambridge, Mass.: MIT Press), pp. 69–86.

Anderson, N. (1923), *The Hobo* (Chicago: University of Chicago Press).

Antilla, I. and Jaakola, R. (1966), *Unrecorded Criminality in Finland* (Helsinki: Kriminologinen Tutkimuslaitos).

Atkins, L. and Jarrett, D. (1979), 'The significance of significance tests', in Irvine, Miles and Evans, op. cit., pp. 87–109.

Baldwin, J. (1976), 'The social composition of the judiciary', *British Journal of Criminology*, 16.

Baldwin, J. and Bottoms, A. E. (1976), *The Urban Criminal* (London: Tavistock).

Baldwin, J. and McConville, S. (1977), *Negotiated Justice* (Oxford: Martin Robertson).

Banister, P. A., Smith, F. V., Heskin, K. J. and Bolton, N. (1973), 'Psychological correlates of long-term imprisonment I: cognitive variables', *British Journal of Criminology*, vol. 13, no. 4, pp. 312–23.

Barnes, J. (1979), *Who Should Know What?* (Harmondsworth: Penguin).

Bartlett, D. and Walker, J. (1978), 'Inner circle', in J. Baldwin and A. K. Bottomley (eds), *Criminal Justice: Selected Readings* (Oxford: Martin Robertson), pp. 56–72.

Becker, H. (1963), *Outsiders: Studies in the Sociology of Deviance* (New York: Free Press).

Becker, H. (1967), 'Whose side are we on?', *Social Problems*, vol. 14, no. 3, pp. 239–47.

Becker, H. (1974), 'Labelling theory reconsidered', in P. Rock and M. McIntosh (eds), *Deviance and Social Control* (London: Tavistock), pp. 121–32.

Belson, W. A. (1969), *The Extent of Stealing by London Boys and Some of Its Origins* (London: Survey Research Centre, London School of Economics).

Belson, W. A. (1975), *Juvenile Theft: The Causal Factors* (London: Harper & Row).

Bennett, T. and Wright, R. (1984), *Burglars on Burglary* (Aldershot: Gower).

Berlin, Sir I. (1958), *Two Concepts of Liberty* (Oxford: Clarendon).

Berreman, G. D. (1972), *Hindus of the Himalays: Ethnography and Change* (Berkeley, Calif.: University of California Press).

Biderman, A. D. and Reiss, A. J. (1967), 'On explaining the "dark figure" of crime', *Annals of the American Academy of Political and Social Science*, vol. 374, pp. 1–15.

Blalock, H. M. (1961), *Causal Inferences in Non-Experimental Research* (Chapel Hill, NC: University of North Carolina).

Blalock, H. M. (1969), *Theory Construction* (Englewood Cliffs, NJ: Prentice Hall).

Blalock, H. M. (ed.) (1971), *Causal Models in the Social Sciences* (London: Macmillan).

Bolton, N., Smith, F. V., Heskin, K. J. and Banister, P. A. (1976), 'Psychological correlates of long-term imprisonment IV: a longitudinal analysis', *British Journal of Criminology*, vol. 16, no. 1, pp. 38–47.

Bottomley, A. K. (1979), *Criminology in Focus* (Oxford: Martin Robertson).

Bottomley, A. K. and Coleman, C. A. (1981), *Understanding Crime Rates: Police and Public Roles in the Production of Official Statistics* (Aldershot: Gower).

Bottomley, A. K. and Pease, K. (1986), *Crime and Punishment: Interpreting the Data* (Milton Keynes: Open University Press).

Bottoms, A. E. and McClean, J. D. (1976), *Defendants in the Criminal Process* (London: Routledge & Kegan Paul).

Bottoms, A. E. and McClintock, F. H. (1973), *Criminals Coming of Age* (London: Heinemann).

Bowles, G. and Duelli Klein, R. (eds) (1983), *Theories of Women's Studies* (London: Routledge & Kegan Paul).

Box, S. (1981), *Deviance, Reality and Society*, 2nd edn (London: Holt Rinehart & Winston).

Box, S. (1987), *Recession, Crime and Punishment* (London: Macmillan).

Boyle, J. (1977), *A Sense of Freedom* (London: Pan).

Bracht, G. H. and Glass, G. V. (1968), 'The external validity of experiments', *American Educational Research Journal*, vol. 5, no. 1, pp. 437–74.

Brenner, M. H. (1976), 'Effects of the economy on criminal behaviour and the administration of criminal justice in the United States, Canada, England and Wales and Scotland', in *Economic Crisis and Crime* (Rome: UNSDRI).

Brogden, M., Jefferson, T. and Walklate, S. (1988), *Introducing Policework* (London: Unwin Hyman).

Bryman, A. (1988), *Quantity and Quality in Social Research* (London: Unwin Hyman).

Bulmer, M. (1982), *The Uses of Social Research* (London: Allen & Unwin).

Bulmer, M. (ed.) (1986), *Social Science and Social Policy* (London: Allen & Unwin).

Bulmer, M. (1986a), 'The ecological fallacy: its implications for social policy analysis', in Bulmer, op. cit., pp. 223–46.

Bulmer, M. (1986b), 'Evaluation, research and experimentation', in Bulmer, op. cit., pp. 155–79.

Bulmer, M. (1986c), 'The value of qualitative methods', in Bulmer, op. cit., pp. 180–203.

Burgess, R. (1984), *In the Field* (London: Allen & Unwin).

Burrows, J. and Tarling, R. (1982), *Clearing Up Crime*, Home Office Research Study No. 73 (London: HMSO).

Butters, S. (1976), 'The logic of enquiry of participant observation', in S. Hall and T. Jefferson, *Resistance Through Rituals: Youth Sub-Cultures in Post-War Britain* (London: Hutchinson), pp. 253–74.

Cain, M. E. (1973), *Society and the Policeman's Role* (London: Routledge & Kegan Paul).

Campbell, A. (1981), *Girl Delinquents* (Oxford: Blackwell).

Campbell, D. T. (1969), 'Reforms as experiments', *American Psychologist*, vol. 24, pp. 409–29.

Campbell, D. T. and Stanley, J. C. (1963), 'Experimental and quasi-experimental designs for research as teaching', in N. L. Gage (ed.), *Handbook of Research on Teaching* (Chicago: Rand McNally), pp. 171–246.

Canadian Crime Statistics (annual) (Ottowa: Statistics Canada).

Carlen, P. (1980), 'Radical criminology, penal politics and the rule of law', in P. Carlen and M. Collison, *Radical Issues in Criminology* (Oxford: Martin Robertson), pp. 7–24.

Carlen, P. (ed.) (1985), *Criminal Women: Some Autobiographical Accounts* (Oxford: Polity Press).

Carr-Hill, R. A. and Stern, N. H. (1979), *Crime, the Police and Criminal Statistics* (New York: Academic Press).

Chambers, G. and Tombs, J. (1984), *The British Crime Survey Scotland* (Edinburgh: HMSO).

Chatterton, M. (1983), 'Police work and assault charges', in M. Punch (ed.), *Control in Police Organisation* (Cambridge, Mass.: MIT Press).

Cicourel, A. V. (1976), *The Social Organisation of Juvenile Justice*, 2nd edn (London: Heinemann).

Clarke, R. V. G. and Cornish, D. B. (1972), *The Controlled Trial in Institutional Research – Paradigm or Pitfall?*, Home Office Research Study No. 15 (London: HMSO).

Clarke, R. V. G. and Cornish, D. B. (eds) (1983), *Crime Control in Britain* (New York: State University of New York Press).

Clarke, R. V. G. and Hough, M. (1984), *Crime and Police Effectiveness*, Home Office Research Study No. 79 (London: HMSO).

Clarke, R. V. G. and Mayhew, P. (eds) (1980), *Designing Out Crime* (London: HMSO).

Clarke, J. P. and Tifft, L. L. (1966), 'Polygraph and the interview validation of self-reported deviant behaviour', *American Sociological Review*, vol. 31, no. 1, pp. 516–23.

Cloward, R. and Ohlin, L. (1961), *Delinquency and Opportunity: a Theory of Delinquent Gangs* (London: Routledge & Kegan Paul).

Cohen, A. (1955), *Delinquent Boys: the Culture of the Gang* (Chicago: Free Press).

Cohen, S. (1981), 'Criminology and the sociology of deviance', in M. Fitzgerald, G. McLennan and J. Pawson, *Crime and Society: Readings in History and Theory* (London: Routledge & Kegan Paul), pp. 220–47.

Cohen, S. and Taylor, L. (1970), 'The experience of time in long-term imprisonment', *New Society*, vol. 16, 31 December, pp. 1156–9.

Cohen, S. and Taylor, L. (1972), *Psychological Survival: The Experience of Long-Term Imprisonment* (Harmondsworth: Penguin).

Cohen, S. and Taylor, L. (1975), 'Prison research: a cautionary tale', *New Society*, vol. 31, no. 643, pp. 253–5.

Cohen, S. and Taylor, L. (1977), 'Talking about prison blues', in C. Bell and H. Newby (eds), *Doing Sociological Research* (London: Allen & Unwin), pp. 67–86.

Corrigan, P. (1979), *Schooling the Smash Street Kids* (London: Macmillan).

Cox, B., Shirley, J. and Short, M. (1977), *The Fall of Scotland Yard* (Harmondsworth: Penguin).

Cressey, P. G. (1932), *The Taxi-Dance Hall: a Sociological Study in Commercialised Recreation and City Life* (Chicago: University of Chicago Press).

Dallos, R. J. and Sapsford, R. J. (1981), 'The person and group reality', in M. Fitzgerald, G. McLennan and J. Pawson (eds), *Crime and Society: Readings in History and Theory* (London: Routledge & Kegan Paul), pp. 429–60.

Dell, S. (1971), *Silent in Court* (London: Bell).

Denzin, N. (1970), *The Research Act* (Chicago: Aldine).

Douglas, J. W. B. (1964), *The Home and the School* (London: MacGibbon & Kee).

Douglas, J. W. B. (1976), 'The use and abuse of national cohorts', in M. Shipman (ed.), *The Limitations of Social Research* (London: Longman).

Douglas, J. W. B., Ross, J. M. and Simpson, H. R. (1968), *All Our Future* (London: Peter Davies).

Downes, D. and Rock, P. (1982), *Understanding Deviance* (Oxford: Oxford University Press).

Durkheim, E. (1952), *Suicide: a Study in Sociology* (London: Routledge & Kegan Paul).

Durkheim, E. (1964a), *The Division of Labour in Society* (Glencoe: Free Press).

Durkheim, E. (1964b), *The Rules of Sociological Method* (Glencoe: Free Press).

Eglin, P. (1987), 'The dispute over the meaning and use of official statistics in the explanation of deviance (suicide and crime)', in J. Hughes, J. Anderson and W. Sharrock, *Classic Disputes in Sociology* (London: Allen & Unwin), pp. 108–36.

Elmhorn, K. (1965), ' A study in self-reported delinquency among school children in Stockholm', in K. O. Christiansen (ed.), *Scandinavian Studies in Criminology* (London: Tavistock), vol. 1, pp. 86–116.

Emery, F. E. (1970), *Freedom and Justice Within These Walls: The Bristol Prison Experiment* (London: Tavistock).

Empey, L. T. and Eriksen, M. L. (1966), 'Hidden delinquency and social status', *Social Forces*, vol. 44, pp. 546–54.

Ennis, P. (1967), *Criminal Victimisation in the United States: A Report of a National Survey* (Washington, DC: President's Commission on Law Enforcement and Administration of Justice).

Ericson, R. (1981), *Making Crime: A Study of Detective Work* (Toronto: Butterworth).

Ericson, R. (1983), *Reproducing Order: A Study of Police Work* (Toronto: University of Toronto Press).

Eysenck, H. J. (1960), *The Structure of Human Personality* (London: Methuen).

Eysenck, H. J. (1964), *Crime and Personality* (London: Routledge & Kegan Paul).

Farrington, D. P., Gallagher, B., Morley, L., St Ledger, R. J. and West, D. P. (1986), 'Unemployment, school leaving and crime', *British Journal of Criminology*, vol. 26, no. 4, pp. 335–56.

Feldman, C. (1976), *Criminal Behaviour: a Psychological Analysis* (Chichester: Wiley).

Fitzgerald, M., McLennan, G. and Sim, J. (1987), 'Intervention, regulation and surveillance', in *Crime, Justice and Society*, D310 (Milton Keynes: Open University Press).

Foucault, M. (1977), *Discipline and Punish* (London: Allen Lane).

Foucault, M. (1978), *I, Pierre Riviere, Having Slaughtered My Mother, My Sister and My Brother . . .* (Harmondsworth: Penguin).

Foucault, M. (1979), *History of Sexuality*, vol. 1: *An Introduction* (Harmondsworth: Allen Lane).

Foucault, M. (1980), *Herculine Barbine: Being the Recently Discovered Memoirs of a Nineteenth Century French Hermaphrodite* (New York: Pantheon).

Foucault, M. (1986), *History of Sexuality*, vol. 2: *The Use of Pleasure* (London: Viking).

Galtung, J. (1967), *Theory and Methods of Social Research* (London: Allen & Unwin).

Glaser, B. and Strauss, A. L. (1967), *The Discovery of Grounded Theory* (Chicago: Aldine).

Glueck, S. and Glueck, E. T. (1950), *Unravelling Juvenile Delinquency* (London: Routledge & Kegan Paul).

Glueck, S. and Glueck, E. T. (1962), *Family Environment and Delinquency* (London: Routledge & Kegan Paul).

Graham, J. (1986), 'Schools and delinquency', *Home Office Research Bulletin*, no. 21 (London: HMSO), pp. 21–6.

Graham, J. (1988), *Schools, Disruptive Behaviour and Delinquency: A Review of Research*, Home Office Research Study No. 96 (London: HMSO).

Griffith, J. (1977), *The Politics of the Judiciary* (London: Fontana).

Hakim, C. (1982), *Secondary Analyses in Social Research* (London: Allen & Unwin).

Halfpenny, P. (1982), *Positivism and Sociology: Explaining Social Life* (London: Allen & Unwin).

Hall, S. (1980), *Drifting into a Law and Order Society* (London: Cobden Trust).

Hall, S., Critcher, C., Jefferson, T., Clarke, J. and Roberts, B. (1978), *Policing the Crisis: Mugging, the State and Law and Order* (London: Macmillan).

Hall, S. and McLennan, G. (1987), 'Custom and law: law and crime as historical processes', in *Crime, Justice and Society*, D310 (Milton Keynes: Open University Press), pp. 13–58.

Hall, S. and Scraton, P. (1981), 'Law, class and control', in M. Fitzgerald G. McLennan and J. Pawson (eds), *Crime and Society: Readings in History and Theory* (London: Routledge & Kegan Paul), pp. 460–94.

Haney, C., Banks, C. and Zimbardo, P. (1973), 'Interpersonal dynamics in a simulated prison', *International Journal of Criminology and Penology* vol. 1, no. 2, pp. 69–97.

Heal, K. and Laycock, G. (eds) (1986), *Situational Crime Prevention: From Theory into Practice* (London: HMSO).

Heise, D. R. (1969), 'Problems in path analysis and causal inference', in E. F. Borgatta and G. N. Bohrnstedt (eds), *Sociological Methodology* (San Francisco: Jossey Bass).

Heise, D. R. (1975), *Causal Analysis* (New York: Wiley).

Herbert, D. T. (1982), *The Geography of Urban Crime* (London Longman).

Heskin, K. J., Bolton, N., Smith, F. V. and Banister, P. A. (1974) 'Psychological correlates of long-term imprisonment III: attitudina variables', *British Journal of Criminology*, vol. 14, no. 3, pp. 421–30.

Heskin, K. J., Smith, F. V., Banister, P. A. and Bolton, N. (1973) 'Psychological correlates of long-term imprisonment II: personality variables', *British Journal of Criminology*, vol. 13, pp. 323–30.

Hindess, B. (1973), *The Use of Official Statistics in Sociology: A Critique o Positivism and Ethnomethodology* (London: Macmillan).

Hirschi, T. (1969), *Causes of Delinquency* (Berkeley, Calif.: University o California Press).

Holdaway, S. (1983), *Inside the British Police* (Oxford: Blackwell).

Home Office (1974), *IMPACT: Intensive Matched Probation and After Care Treatment*, Vol. 1, *The Design of the Probation Experiment and an Interim Evaluation*, Research Study No. 24 (London: HMSO).

Home Office (1976), *IMPACT: Intensive Matched Probation and After Care Treatment*, Vol. II, *The Results of the Experiment*, Research Study No. 36 (London: HMSO).

Home Office (1984), *Tougher Regimes in Detention Centres, Report of an Evaluation by the Young Offender Psychology Unit* (London: HMSO).

Home Office (1985), *Crowd Safety and Control at Sports Grounds*, Cmnc 9710 (London: HMSO).

Home Office Research and Planning Unit (1987), *Research Programme 1987–1988* (London: HMSO).

Home Office (annual), *Criminal Statistics England and Wales* (London HMSO).

Hope, T. and Shaw, M, (1988), *Communities and Crime Reduction* (London: HMSO).

Hough, M., and Mayhew, P. (1983), *The British Crime Survey: First Report* Home Office Research Study No. 76 (London: HMSO).

Hough, M. and Mayhew, P. (1985), *Taking Account of Crime: Key Finding from the Second British Crime Survey*, Home Office Research Study No 85 (London: HMSO).

Irvine, J., Miles, I. and Evans, J. (eds) (1979), *Demystifying Social Statistic* (London: Pluto Press).

Johnson, R. E. (1979), *Delinquency and its Origins* (Cambridge: Cambridge University Press).

Jones, J. M. (1979), *Organisational Aspects of Police Behaviour* (Aldershot: Gower).

Jones, T., MacLean, B. and Young, J. (1986), *The Islington Crime Survey: Crime Victimisation and Policing in Inner City London* (Aldershot: Gower).

Kelly, G. (1955), *The Psychology of Personal Constructs* (New York: Norton).

King, M. (1981), *The Framework of Criminal Justice* (London: Croom Helm).

King, R. D. and Elliott, K. W. (1977), *Albany: Birth of a Prison – End of an Era* (London: Routledge & Kegan Paul).

Kinsey, R. (1984), *Merseyside Crime Survey: First Report* (Liverpool: Merseyside County Council).

Kinsey, R. (1985), *Merseyside Crime and Police Surveys: Final Report* (Liverpool: Merseyside County Council).

Kinsey, R. (1986), 'Crime in the city', *Marxism Today*, May, pp. 6–10.

Kinsey, R., Lea, J. and Young, J. (1986), *Losing the Fight Against Crime* (Oxford: Blackwell).

Kish, L. (1959), 'Some statistical problems in research design', *American Sociological Review*, vol. 24, no. 2, pp. 328–38.

Kitsuse, J. and Cicourel, A. V. (1963), 'A note on the use of official statistics', *Social Problems*, vol. II, no 2 (Fall), pp. 131–9.

Klockars, C. B. (1974), *The Professional Fence* (London: Tavistock).

Kohlberg, L. (1969), 'State and sequence: the cognitive developmental approach to socialisation', in D. A. Goslin (ed.), *Handbook of Socialisation Theory and Research* (New York: Rand McNally), pp. 169–94.

Kohlberg, L. (1975), *Just Community Approach to Corrections* (Cambridge, Mass.: Harvard University Press).

Lambert, J. R. (1970), *Crime, Police and Race Relations* (London: Oxford University Press).

Landau, S. (1981), 'Juveniles and the police', *British Journal of Criminology*, vol. 21, no. 1 (January), pp. 27–46.

Landau, S. (1983), 'Selecting delinquents for cautioning in the London Metropolitan area', *British Journal of Criminology*, vol. 28, no. 2 (April), pp. 128–49.

Lea, J. and Young, J. (1984), *What is to be Done about Law and Order?* (Harmondsworth: Penguin).

Lemert, E. (1967), *Human Deviance, Social Problems and Social Control* (Englewood Cliffs, NJ: Prentice Hall).

Lindesmith, A. (1968), *Addiction and Opiates* (Chicago: Aldine).

Lombroso, C. (1911), *Crime: Its Causes and Remedies*, first published in 1876 as *L'Uomo Delinquente* (Boston: Little, Brown & Co.).

Lombroso, C., and Ferrero, W. (1895), *The Female Offender* (London: T. F. Unwin).

Lowman, J. (1987), 'Taking young prostitutes seriously', *Canadian Review of Sociology and Anthropology*, vol. 24, no. 1, pp. 99–116.

McCabe, S. and Sutcliffe, F. *Defining Crime* (Oxford: Blackwell).

McClintock, F. H. and Avison, N. H. (1968), *Crime in England and Wales* (London: Heinemann).

McDonald, L. (1969), *Social Class and Delinquency* (London: Faber).

McGuire, M. and Pointing, J. (1988), *Victims of Crime – A New Deal* (Milton Keynes: Open University Press).

McVicar, J. (1979), *McVicar by Himself* (London: Arrow).

Manning, P. K. (1974), 'Police lying', *Urban Life and Culture*, vol. 3, pp. 283–305.

Marsh, P., Rosser, E. and Harré (1978), *The Rules of Disorder* (London: Routledge & Kegan Paul).

Matza, D. (1961), *Becoming Deviant* (Englewood Cliffs, NJ: Prentice Hall).

Matza, D. (1964), *Delinquency and Drift* (New York: Wiley).

Mays, J. B. (1954), *Growing up in the City* (Liverpool: Liverpool University Press).

Merton, R. (1938), 'Social structure and anomie', *American Sociological Review*, vol. 3, no. 1, pp. 672–82.

Merton, R. K. (1956), 'The social-cultural environment and anomie', in H. Witmer and R. Kotinsky (eds), *New Perspectives for Research on Juvenile Delinquency* (Washington, DC: US Government Printing Office), pp. 72–109.

Merton, R. (1957), *Social Theory and Social Structure* (New York: Free Press).

Merton, R. K. (1964), 'Anomie, anomia and social interaction', in M. Clinard (ed.), *Anomie and Deviant Behaviour* (New York: Free Press).

Mies, M. (1983), 'Towards a methodology for feminist research', in Bowles and Duelli Klein, op. cit., pp. 91–106.

Miles, I. and Irvine, J. (1979), 'The critique of official statistics', in Irvine, Miles and Evans, op. cit., pp. 113–29.

Milgram, S. (1973), 'Behavioural study of obedience', in L. S. Wrightsman and J. C. Bingham (eds), *Contemporary Issues in Social Psychology* (Belmont, Calif.: Brooks/Cole).

Milgram, S. (1974), *Obedience to Authority: An Experimental View* (London: Tavistock).

Mills, C. Wright (1970), *The Sociological Imagination* (Harmondsworth: Penguin).

Morris, T. P. (1957), *The Criminal Area: A Study in Social Ecology* (London: Routledge & Kegan Paul).

Morris, T. and Morris, P. (1962), *Pentonville: A Sociological Study of an English Prison* (London: Routledge & Kegan Paul).

Muncie, J. and Fitzgerald, M. (1981), 'Humanising the deviant', in M. Fitzgerald, G. McLennan and J. Pawson (eds), *Crime and Society: Readings in History and Theory* (London: Routledge & Kegan Paul).

Nye, F. I., Short, J. and Olson, V. J. (1958), 'Socio-economic status and delinquent behaviour', *American Journal of Sociology*, vol. 63, pp. 318–39.

Oakley, A. (1981), 'Interviewing women: a contradiction in terms', in Roberts, op. cit., pp. 30–61.

Parker, H. (1974), *View From the Boys* (Newton Abbot: David & Charles).
Parker, T. (1963), *The Unknown Citizen* (London: Hutchinson).
Parker, T. (1965), *Five Women* (London: Hutchinson).
Parker, T. (1967), *A Man of Good Abilities* (London: Hutchinson).
Parker, T. (1969), *The Twisting Lane* (London: Hutchinson).
Patrick, J. (1973), *A Glasgow Gang Observed* (London: Eyre Methuen).
Pearce, F. (1976), *Crimes of the Powerful* (London: Pluto Press).
Pearson, G. (1983), *Hooligan: A History of Respectable Fears* (London: Macmillan).
Plummer, K. (1983), *Documents of Life* (London: Allen & Unwin).
Probyn, W. (1977), *Angel Face: the Making of a Criminal* (London: Allen & Unwin).
Punch, M. (1979), *Policing the Inner City* (London: Macmillan).
Punch, M. (1985), *Conduct Unbecoming* (London: Tavistock).

Reiner, R. (1985), *The Politics of the Police* (London: Wheatsheaf).
Rettig, R., Torres, M. and Garrett, G. (1977), *Manny: A Criminal Addict's Story* (Boston: Houghton-Mifflin).
Roberts, B. (1976), 'Naturalistic research into sub-cultures and deviance: an account of a sociological tendency', in S. Hall and T. Jefferson, *Resistance Through Rituals: Youth Sub-Cultures in Post-War Britain* (London: Hutchinson), pp. 243–52.
Roberts, H. (1981), *Doing Feminist Research* (London: Routledge & Kegan Paul).
Robinson, W. S. (1950), 'Ecological correlation and the behaviour of individuals', *American Sociological Review*, vol. 15, pp. 351–7.
Robson, B. T. (1969), *Urban Analysis: A Study of City Centre Structure* (Cambridge: Cambridge University Press).
Rock, P. (1973), *Deviant Behaviour* (London: Hutchinson).

Samuel, R. (1981), *East End Underworld: Chapters in the Life of Arthur Harding* (London: Routledge & Kegan Paul).
Scarman, Lord Justice (1981), *The Brixton Disorders 10–12 April, 1981*, Cmnd 8427 (London: HMSO).
Schwartz, H. and Jacobs, J. (1979), *Qualitative Sociology* (New York: Free Press).
Scraton, P. (1985), *The State of the Police* (London: Pluto Press).
Scraton, P. (1987), 'Policing society, policing crime', in *Crime, Justice and Society*, D310 (Milton Keynes: Open University Press), pp. 31–78.
Shapland, J. (1978), 'Self reported delinquency in boys aged 11 to 14', *British Journal of Criminology*, vol. 18, no. 3, pp. 255–66.
Sharp, R. and Green, A. (1975), *Education and Social Control: A Study in Progressive Primary Education* (London: Routledge & Kegan Paul).
Shaw, C. R. (1930), *The Jack Roller* (Chicago: University of Chicago Press).
Shaw, C. R. and McKay, H. D. (1929), *Delinquency Areas* (Chicago: University of Chicago Press).

Shaw, C. R. and McKay, M. D. (1931), *Social Factors in Juvenile Delinquency* (Washington, DC: US Government Printing Office).

Short, J. and Nye, F. I. (1958), 'Extent of unrecorded juvenile delinquency: tentative conclusions', *Journal of Criminal Law, Criminology and Police Science*, vol. 49, pp. 226–33.

Silverman, D. (1985), *Qualitative Methodology and Sociology* (Aldershot: Gower).

Smith, D. (1965), 'Front line organisation of the state mental hospital', *Administrative Science Quarterly*, vol. 10, no. 3, pp. 441–56.

Smith, D. J. and Gray, J. (1983), *Police and People in London*, vols 1–4 (London: Policy Studies Institute).

Sparks, R. F., Genn, H. G. and Dodd, D. J. (1977), *Surveying Victims: A Study of the Measurement of Criminal Victimisation* (New York: Wiley).

Spencer, J. (1964), *Stress and Release in an Urban Estate* (London: Tavistock).

Sudnow, D. (1968), 'Normal crimes: sociological features of the penal code in a public defender office', in E. Rubington and M. Weinberg (eds), *Deviance: the Interactionist Perspective* (New York: Macmillan).

Sutherland, E. H. (1937), *The Professional Thief by a Professional Thief* (Chicago: University of Chicago Press).

Sutherland, E. H. and Cressey, D. (1947), *Principles of Criminology* (Philadelphia: Lippincott).

Tarling, R. (1979), *Sentencing Prisoners in Magistrates' Courts*, Home Office Research Study No. 56 (London: HMSO).

Tarling, R. (1982), 'Unemployment and crime', Home Office Research Study No. 14 (London: HMSO), pp. 28–33.

Taylor, I. (1982), 'On the sports violence question: soccer hooliganism revisited', in J. Hargreaves (ed.), *Sport Culture and Ideology* (London: Routledge & Kegan Paul), pp. 72–90.

Taylor, I., Walton, P. and Young, J. (1973), *The New Criminology* (London: Routledge & Kegan Paul).

Taylor, I., Walton, P. and Young, J. (eds) (1975), *Critical Criminology* (London: Routledge & Kegan Paul).

Thrasher, F. (1928), *The Gang: A Study of 1,313 Gangs in Chicago* (Chicago: University of Chicago Press).

Tutt, N. (1981), 'A decade of policy', *British Journal of Criminology*, vol. 21, no. 3, pp. 246–56.

Uniform Crime Reports (annual) (Washington, DC: Federal Bureau of Investigation).

Von Hentig, H. (1948), *The Criminal and his Victim: Studies in the Sociobiology of Crime* (New Haven, Conn.: Yale University Press).

Walklate, S. (1989), *Victimology: The Victim and the Criminal Justice System* (London: Unwin Hyman).

Wallis, C. P. and Malliphant, R. (1967), 'Delinquent areas in the County of London: ecological factors', *British Journal of Criminology*, vol. 7, pp. 250–84.

Weatheritt, M. (1986), *Innovations in Policing* (London: Croom Helm).

Webb, E. J., Campbell, D. T., Swartz, R. D. and Sechrest, L. (1966), *Unobtrusive Measures: Nonreactive Research in the Social Sciences* (Chicago: Rand McNally).

West, D. J. (1967), *The Young Offender* (Harmondsworth: Penguin).

West, D. J. (1969), *Present Conduct and Future Delinquency* (London: Heinemann).

West, D. J. (1982), *Delinquency: Its Roots, Careers and Prospects* (London: Heinemann).

West, D. J. and Farrington, D. P. (1973), *Who Becomes Delinquents?* (London: Heinemann).

West, D. J. and Farrington, D. P. (1977), *The Delinquent Way of Life* (London: Heinemann).

Whyte, W. F. (1943), *Street Corner Society*, 2nd edn 1955 (Chicago: University of Chicago Press).

Wiles, P. (1971), 'Criminal statistics and sociological explanations of crime', in W. G. Carson and P. Wiles (eds), *Crime and Delinquency in Britain* (Oxford: Martin Robertson), pp. 174–92.

Williams, J., Dunning, E. and Murphy, P. J. (1984), *Hooligans Abroad* (London: Routledge & Kegan Paul).

Williams, J., Dunning, E. and Murphy, P. J. (1987), *The Social Roots of Football Hooliganism* (London: Routledge & Kegan Paul).

Willis, C. (1983), *The Use, Effectiveness and Impact of Police Stop and Search Powers* (London: Home Office Research Unit).

Wilson, E. O. (1975), *Sociobiology: the New Synthesis* (Cambridge, Mass.: Harvard University Press).

Young, J. (1971), *The Drug Takers* (London: Paladin).

Young, J. (1986), 'The failure of criminology', in R. Matthews, and J. Young (eds), *Confronting Crime* (London: Sage), pp. 4–30.

Young, J. (1987), *Realist Criminology* (Aldershot: Gower).

Young, J. (1988), 'Risk of crime and fear of crime: a realist critique of survey based assumptions', in M. McGuire and J. Pointing (eds), *Victims of Crime – A New Deal* (Milton Keynes: Open University Press), pp. 66–72.

Znaniecki, F. (1934), *The Method of Sociology* (New York: Farrar & Rinehart).

Index